CREATIVE HOMEOWNER® **ULTIMATE GUIDE**

DECKS

— PLAN / DESIGN / BUILD —

ULTIMATE GUIDE

DECKS

PLAN / DESIGN / BUILD

UPDATED 5TH EDITION

30 PROJECTS TO PLAN, DESIGN, AND BUILD

CRE**A**TIVE
HOMEOWNER®
CreativeHomeowner.com

CRE🏠TIVE
HOMEOWNER®

Creative Homeowner® is a registered trademark of New Design Originals Corporation.

All Decked Out® is a trademark of Gary Marsh.

Ultimate Guide: Decks, Updated 5th Edition
Vice President-Content: Christopher Reggio
Editor: Anthony Regolino
Cover Designer: Justin Speers
Page Designer: Justin Speers and David Fisk
Technical Editor: David Schiff
Technical Consultant: Ken Kroog
Indexer: Jay Kreider

Printed in Malaysia

Current Printing (last digit)
10 9 8 7 6 5 4 3 2

ISBN 978-1-58011-796-8

Library of Congress Cataloging-in-Publication Data

Names: Fox Chapel Publishing, issuing body.
Title: Ultimate guide : decks.
Description: Updated 5th edition. | Mount Joy, PA : Fox Chapel Publishing,
   2018. | Includes index.
Identifiers: LCCN 2017053837 | ISBN 9781580117968 (softcover)
Subjects: LCSH: Decks (Architecture, Domestic)--Design and
   construction--Amateurs' manuals.
Classification: LCC TH4970 .U485 2018 | DDC 690/.893--dc23
LC record available at https://lccn.loc.gov/2017053837

We are always looking for talented authors. To submit an idea, please send a brief inquiry to
acquisitions@foxchapelpublishing.com.

Creative Homeowner®, *www.creativehomeowner.com*, is an imprint of New Design Originals Corporation and distributed exclusively in North America by Fox Chapel Publishing Company, Inc., 800-457-9112, 903 Square Street, Mount Joy, PA 17552, and in the United Kingdom by Grantham Book Service, Trent Road, Grantham, Lincolnshire, NG31 7XQ.

SAFETY

Although the methods in this book have been reviewed for safety, it is not possible to overstate the importance of using the safest methods you can. What follows are reminders—some do's and don'ts of work safety—to use along with your common sense.

· Always use caution, care, and good judgment when following the procedures described in this book.
· Always be sure that the electrical setup is safe, that no circuit is overloaded, and that all power tools and outlets are properly grounded. Do not use power tools in wet locations.
· Always read container labels on paints, solvents, and other products; provide ventilation; and observe all other warnings.
· Always read the manufacturer's instructions for using a tool, especially the warnings.
· Use hold-downs and push sticks whenever possible when working on a table saw. Avoid working short pieces if you can.
· Always remove the key from any drill chuck (portable or press) before starting the drill.
· Always pay deliberate attention to how a tool works so that you can avoid being injured.
· Always know the limitations of your tools. Do not try to force them to do what they were not designed to do.
· Always make sure that any adjustment is locked before proceeding. For example, always check the rip fence on a table saw or the bevel adjustment on a portable saw before starting to work.
· Always clamp small pieces to a bench or other work surface when using a power tool.
· Always wear the appropriate rubber gloves or work gloves when handling chemicals, moving or stacking lumber, working with concrete, or doing heavy construction.
· Always wear a disposable face mask when you create dust by sawing or sanding. Use a special filtering respirator when working with toxic substances and solvents.
· Always wear eye protection, especially when using power tools or striking metal on metal or concrete; a chip can fly off, for example, when chiseling concrete.
· Never work while wearing loose clothing, open cuffs, or jewelry; tie back long hair.
· Always be aware that there is seldom enough time for your body's reflexes to save you from injury from a power tool in a dangerous situation; everything happens too fast. Be alert!
· Always keep your hands away from the business ends of blades, cutters, and bits.
· Always hold a circular saw firmly, usually with both hands.
· Always use a drill with an auxiliary handle to control the torque when using large-size bits.
· Always check your local building codes when planning new construction. The codes are intended to protect public safety and should be observed to the letter.
· Never work with power tools when you are tired or under the influence of alcohol or drugs.
· Never cut tiny pieces of wood or pipe using a power saw. When you need a small piece, saw it from a securely clamped longer piece.
· Never change a saw blade or a drill or router bit unless the power cord is unplugged. Do not depend on the switch being off. You might accidentally hit it.
· Never work in insufficient lighting.
· Never work with dull tools. Have them sharpened, or learn how to sharpen them yourself.
· Never use a power tool on a workpiece—large or small—that is not firmly supported.
· Never saw a workpiece that spans a large distance between horses without close support on each side of the cut; the piece can bend, closing on and jamming the blade, causing saw kickback.
· When sawing, never support a workpiece from underneath with your leg or other part of your body.
· Never carry sharp or pointed tools, such as utility knives, awls, or chisels, in your pocket. If you want to carry any of these tools, use a special-purpose tool belt that has leather pockets and holders.

CONTENTS

INTRODUCTION

Adding a new deck is one of the most popular ways to enhance the outdoor living area of your home. Decks make entertaining easy, providing a pleasant spot where you can enjoy the company of your family and friends. Or use your deck as a private getaway—a spot to enjoy a good book or take a nap in the warm afternoon sun.

Ultimate Guide: Decks provides both building knowledge and design inspiration. You'll learn how to build a deck, including information on framing, decking, and stairs. Use the appendices to brush up on tools, materials, and construction techniques. The second section contains 30 unique deck designs to help you create the deck of your dreams.

GUIDE TO SKILL LEVEL

🐦🐦🐦 **Easy.** Made for beginners.

🐦🐦🐦 **Challenging.** Can be done by beginners who have the patience and willingness to learn.

🐦🐦🐦 **Difficult.** Can be handled by most experienced do-it-yourselfers who have mastered basic construction skills. Consider consulting a specialist.

Adding curves, left, to a deck makes the design more appealing and distinctive.

Built-in benches, opposite, add to a deck's usefulness. The wide railing cap is used for serving food.

Introduction

"Making a Square Deck Livelier," page 286

Slotted Benches

Deck design depends on how you want to use the deck, the shape of the house, and the size and terrain in your yard, among other things. The deck designs that begin on page 214 include an overall drawing, such as the one show above, a framing detail, materials list, and construction details, such as the bench shown at left. The designs are from six deck designers who each represent a different area of the country. Use them as inspiration to create the deck you want.

Separate activity areas, opposite, make a deck more useful. Note how the deck "walkways" connect the different areas.

Benches, right, add seating and can provide a sense of enclosure. Note how the planters support the benches on this deck.

DECK DESIGN AND CONSTRUCTION

For some people, the hardest part of building a deck, or having one built for you, may be coming up with a design that meets all of your requirements and suits the terrain of your yard. How will you use the deck? What's the best place in your yard to place the deck? Will it be on one level or do you want a multilevel design with separate activity areas? These are only a few of the questions you need to consider during the design process. This chapter will guide you through that process so that you can create an original design. Or you can select from one of the dozens of decks from six of the country's top deck designers. (See pages 216 to 385.) To actually build the deck, you will need only basic carpentry tools and techniques.

BEGINNING THE PROCESS

We all have different reasons for adding a new deck to our home. Most people find they want a new deck for a variety of practical and financial reasons. With a deck, you expand your living space and increase your home's value for a fraction of what it would cost to build an addition. You enhance your living style as well, gaining a new space for entertaining and socializing. But for a deck to do all these things, you need to start out with a good plan.

A well-planned deck will harmonize with the house in both size and shape and provide a smooth transition down to the yard. It can offer more exposure or more privacy, and either take advantage of a cool breeze or protect you from a stiff ocean wind.

What to Expect. Building a deck is a straightforward job, and anyone with some basic carpentry skills and the time to work carefully can handle the task. The project won't totally disrupt your home life, either, as kitchen remodeling would. All the mess is kept outdoors, and as long as you have a good place to store materials, the job can stretch from weekend to weekend with no major problem.

During your initial planning, include the whole family and develop a wish list of features. Gradually, you will pare away the excesses and zero in on a design that works for your situation. Then you'll work through the project step-by-step, from drawing plans, getting permits, choosing a framing style, and selecting materials and patterns for your decking, railings, and stairs, to applying finishes and maintaining your deck.

In some cases, a deck is the only way to gain outdoor living space, above.

A small pond adds an unusual feature to this deck, left.

The proportions of a well-designed deck fit with the house, top right.

This deck, right, includes a graceful transition to the yard.

CHOOSING A DESIGN

While deck materials, shapes, sizes, and costs can vary widely, there are several design decisions common to almost every deck project. Although most decks are simply platforms raised above the yard, they are really an extension of the house—more like living space than yard space—even though they are outside. Because a deck connects to and expands the adjacent indoor space, deck additions are likely to be most appropriate and useful added onto living/family room areas and kitchen/dining room areas. For example, replacing a solid wall with sliding glass doors leading to an expansive deck is a quick and relatively inexpensive way to make a cramped living room seem a lot larger.

Draw a series of rough sketches as you proceed. Expect to fill a wastebasket or two with these. Don't think of them as actual designs so much as focal points for conversations—it's usually easier to point to a place on your drawing than to walk around the house.

Feel free to steal ideas from books, magazines, and other decks in your neighborhood. When you see a deck that particularly pleases you and seems appropriate for your situation, talk to the owners about how their deck works for them. Jot down some notes, and ask permission to take a few photos. Most people will be flattered that you like their deck and will be more than happy to tell you all about it. And don't forget about the designs that begin on page 216.

You will probably discover lots of terrific deck ideas that you end up not using, either because you no longer like the way they look, you discover that they just won't work with your design, or the extra expense for exotic materials will blow the budget. Don't be discouraged. In fact, expect it to happen—and happen several times—before you come up with a design.

How You Will Use Your Deck

Everyone in the family probably has different visions of the ideal deck. Gather all their opinions, and figure out an overall design that will work for everybody. Consider the following items.

Entertaining and Barbecuing. Plan a convenient cooking area, probably somewhere near the kitchen. Figure out where you'll put tables for sit-down dinners as well as a good place to set up a buffet table. If you'll have a grill on the deck and plan to do a lot of barbecuing, you might want to add a small sink near the cooking area.

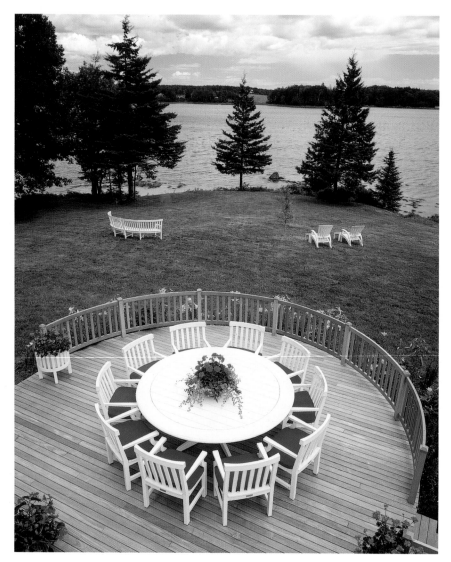

Begin the design process by settling on how you plan on using your new deck, left. Sharing meals was a prime consideration for this deck.

Decks are great places to entertain during pleasant weather, opposite top.

Built-in benches, opposite bottom, provide seating and design interest. A circular design helps promote conversation among people on the deck.

💡 SMART TIP

START AN IDEA SCRAPBOOK

Keep your ideas and your wish list in order by starting a design scrap book. Buy a notebook that contains flaps on the covers. That way you'll have a place to keep photos you take of decks you like and pages from magazines and catalogs, as well as ample space to jot down your ideas and plans

Lounging and Sunning. Pencil in space for a hammock or a swinging chair—a shady spot is often best. Sun worshippers will congregate on an expanse of deck that gets full sun.

Balancing Privacy and Openness. Think about whether you want the deck to feel airy and open to the world or cozy and secluded. A small deck will generally feel cozier than a large deck. Low benches and railings designed with large, open sections give a feeling of openness. A narrow deck that hugs the house will have a more sequestered feel than one that juts into the yard.

Decks are usually raised off the ground, which might mean that you and your family will be on display for all the neighborhood to see. Existing fences may be too low to shield you from view. Sometimes the problem can be solved by stepping the deck down in stages or by planting trees and shrubs.

If you feel overexposed, a well-placed trellis or pergola added to the deck can give you some nice climbing plants to look at as well as provide a pleasant enclosure and screen.

Enjoying the View. Plan your landscape along with your deck to get the best view. Orient the deck so that you will be looking at the best features of your yard and to take advantage of a nice view beyond your property line.

Planning for Children's Play. A jungle gym will probably look better in the yard, but your deck design should provide an inviting place where kids can play. Build the stairway extra wide or have a series of descending platforms, and children will spend hours playing with dolls and trucks and letting their imaginations run wild. Plan a spot for a comfortable chair where you can relax while keeping an unobstructed eye on the kids in your yard.

Lighting for Nighttime Use. Plan some appropriate lighting if you want to use the deck after dark. Whether you choose standard 120-volt wiring or a low-voltage Light Emitting Diode (LED) option, plan to run the wires somewhere out of sight, maybe even underground.

Including a Pool or Whirlpool. Built with a surface of rot-resistant wood or composite material, a deck makes an ideal surface next to a pool or spa. Both materials are softer than tile or concrete and wood, making the deck a pleasant place to sit or lounge when you get out of the water. An inexpensive aboveground pool gains a lot of class when you surround it with a deck. If your design includes a spa or hot tub, position it for privacy as well as an unobstructed view of the stars.

Container Gardening. It is almost impossible to put too much foliage on or near a deck. Find planters that will

go well with your deck and your house, or plan to build some from the same material as the decking. With enough sun, tomatoes, peppers, and all sorts of vegetables do well. An herb garden flourishes without a lot of work and still looks great after a bit of harvesting. If you're an avid gardener, you might even consider putting a greenhouse on the deck. Just be sure that water from planting containers doesn't get trapped on the deck—standing water invites rot.

Plan a lighting scheme if you plan on using your deck after dark, below.

Closed designs tend to make a deck feel cozier than one that is open, opposite. This design also provides a certain amount of privacy.

Be sure to plan on connecting your deck to the indoors with passages to the most frequently used rooms in the house. Don't forget stairs that lead down to the yard.

Traffic Patterns

Make the deck easy to reach by installing French doors or sliders—the more entrances, the better. Large windows that look onto the deck will entice people outside. If you plan to eat a lot of meals out on the deck, make sure it's close to the kitchen.

Also take the time to plan the approaches to the deck. Plan a clear, unobstructed path to the deck from indoor entertainment areas and from areas where your family spends a lot of time. A door out to the deck near the kitchen and another near the living room help avoid bottlenecks during parties. A small patio or concrete pad at the bottom of the stairs down to the yard reduces wear and tear on the grass and is usually required by code.

Weather Considerations

Think about how the weather and the seasons will affect the ways you use the deck, and plan accordingly. For example, a deck with a greenhouse on a southern exposure will help extend

TRAFFIC PATTERNS

TRAFFIC OBSTRUCTED

Deck

Kitchen

Single Door

TRAFFIC FLOWS FREELY

Deck

Double Door

Window

SEASONAL CONDITIONS

MIDDAY SUMMER SUN stands high in the sky: buildings and trees cast little shadow.

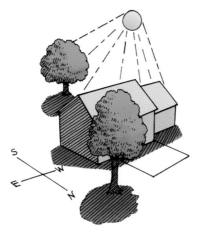

LATE AFTERNOON SUMMER SUN casts a small amount of shade on the north and east of buildings.

MIDDAY SPRING AND AUTUMN SUN is lower: buildings and full-leafed trees cast considerable shadows.

LATE AFTERNOON SPRING AND AUTUMN SUN is low in the sky; long shadows to the north and east.

MIDDAY WINTER SUN is at its lowest point; buildings cast deep shadows; leafless trees cast little shadow.

AFTERNOON WINTER SUN stands low and to the south; buildings cast deep shadows to the north and east.

the growing season in a cold climate. The three main weather variables with which you need to concern yourself are sun, wind, and rain.

Sun. Decide how much sun and how much shade you want, and take this into account when siting the deck. A deck on the north side of a house will be in shade most of the day. This can be an advantage if you live in a very hot climate and a disadvantage for most everyone else. An eastern exposure gives the deck morning sun and afternoon shade; this is often the best choice in warm climates. In cold climates, a southwest exposure provides full late afternoon sun, making the deck warmer on cool days in the spring and fall.

Also consider the angle of the sun above the horizon. The sun is highest in the summer and lowest in the winter. This means that in the winter a south-oriented deck will receive less direct sunlight than during the summer. A fence or tree that does not block out the high summer sun may block out sunlight during other times of the year when the sun is lower.

You may want continuous shade for a hammock, afternoon shade only for an eating area, and as much sun as possible for potted plants and a sunning area. You may need to change your foliage, pruning branches or planting more trees and shrubs.

Wind. If heat is a problem and you want to maximize the breeze, plan to prune trees or remove shrubs. If you have more wind than you want, you may need to plant new foliage. A raised deck will be windier than one near the ground.

For extreme conditions, you may need to construct a windbreak of some sort. A louvered or lattice wall covered with climbing plants is much more attractive than a solid fence and does a good job of diffusing a strong wind.

Rain. Most people think of sunny, clear weather as the best time to enjoy life on the deck, but you may live in an area where it rains much of the year, or perhaps you just like to watch the rain. If your house's roof has little or no slope, consider extending it to cover part of the deck. Or install a large set of sliding glass doors between the deck and the living room, so you can open the doors and enjoy the patter of rain as it falls on your deck and potted plants.

Envisioning the Contours

You'll find that areas defined on sketches tend to look larger than they actually are in real life. To avoid disappointment later in the project, transfer the scale drawings to the actual building site. You can drive stakes into the ground and connect them with string to outline the deck.

Arrange lawn furniture inside the deck's planned outline, and try it on for size. Imagine yourselves doing what you hope to do on your new deck, and ask some obvious questions: is there enough room for a planter here? Is this the right-size space for a buffet table if you have a party with 15 guests? Is there room for a table and chairs here, and room for people to get to their seats? Will the hammock fit over there? Where will the barbecue be? Would an L- or T-shape work better? What if you put some hanging planters or large potted plants over there, to give a sense of separate spaces? In this way, you will come up with some fairly specific ideas about the shape and size of your deck.

If it feels cramped, consider extending the deck in logical increments. Using 12-foot-long joists instead of 10-footers, for example, has little effect on labor costs and increases material costs only marginally, but may dramatically increase the deck's usefulness and sense of space.

If you have the space and the money, you may be tempted to build a very large deck. If you've got a large house and plenty of deck furniture, this can work well, but a jumbo deck can sometimes overwhelm a smaller home. Plan deck areas that feel comfortable and are scaled to the size of your house.

💡 SMART TIP

PREVIEW THE DECK CONTOURS

To help you visualize the actual size of a deck plan that's sketched out on a drawing, measure the rough dimensions on several of the potential building sites and stretch out an extension cord or a garden hose to mark the contours.

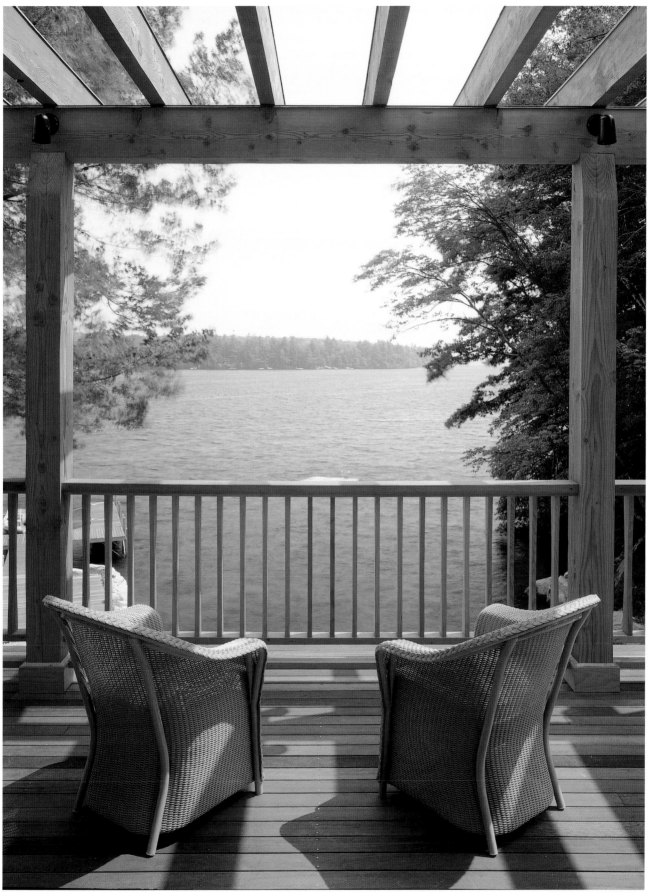

The surrounding area will play an important role in determining how popular the deck becomes. Create designs that enhance the views.

IMPROVING YOUR HOUSE AND YARD

A deck usually does not stand alone; it is attached to your house and sits on top of your yard. So consider not only how the deck itself will look but also how it will fit in with its surroundings. This does not necessarily mean striving to make the deck blend in and disappear, but any contrasts should be pleasing to onlookers rather than jarring.

Although the decking boards are probably the most visible element when you look at the deck from the house, the structural elements may loom large from other perspectives. Railings, stairways, and fascia boards are often the things people see first. If the deck is raised far above the ground, the posts, beam, and even the framing hardware may become the most prominent visual features.

Basic Elements

There are four basic elements to consider when matching your deck design with your house and yard: shape, mass, color, and texture.

Shape. The shape you choose for the deck should harmonize with the lines of your house. The alignment of a deck should in most cases be much more horizontal than vertical. This will give it the light, breezy feeling that you want from an informal space. However, if you are building a raised deck, the posts will define strong vertical lines. If your house is tall and narrow, some of this vertical sense will be welcome, and you may want to repeat these lines. In many cases, you will want to soften the vertical aspect with a series of horizontal lines, using decking and railings.

Think about the deck's overall shape, as well. If your house has a pleasing L-shape, for example, you can repeat that shape with a deck. A house with a confusing shape can be softened with a deck that is simple, and a plain-looking house can be jazzed up with a deck that has a bold shape.

Most people choose to have a deck that is attached to the back of the house and leads to the backyard. You may want to consider other options, such as a wraparound deck, a deck that incorporates a tree, or an island or peninsula deck.

Also examine your house and your yard for existing lines: rectangles, curves, projections, even triangles. Use these as starting points, and think of your deck as providing variations on those themes. If your existing lines are a bit boring, you will want to liven things up a bit with some new angles—octagonal and other rectilinear shapes are good choices, as are curved lines. But if you already have a good variety of lines, adding complex shapes with your deck will only make for a muddled general impression. Usually, simplicity is best: two or three lines artfully repeated are more pleasing than a jumble of shapes.

You probably can't change the shape of your house to suit your deck, but it is often possible to change your landscape in conjunction with building a deck. You can also design garden edgings or patio surfaces to complement the lines of your deck.

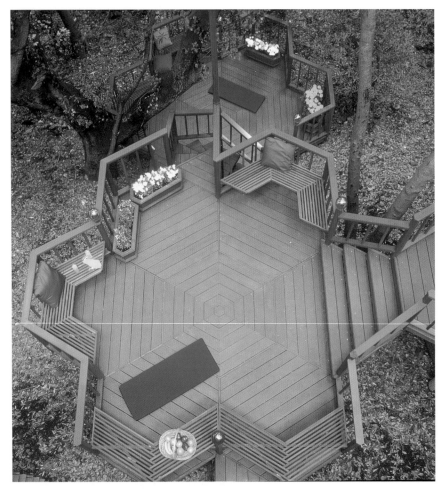

Sharp angles create areas for built-in seating and planting.

A curved deck provides the setting for a graceful railing design.

DECK SHAPES

WRAPAROUND

A wraparound deck allows you to follow the sun or the shade.

OBLIQUE

This deck is accessible from two doorways and incorporates a large tree.

ISLAND

An island deck is unattached to the house, so it can be surrounded with foliage.

PENNINSULA

With this penninsula design, you walk onto a place that feels much different from the house.

Mass. The size of a deck should suit the house. The most common problem is a deck that is too massive and overpowers a small house, making the house appear even smaller than it is. Decide which vantage points are the most important, and think about how your deck will appear from the yard and the house.

Many factors affect the visual mass of a deck. For example, building low to the ground or designing railings that are low or light-looking will help the deck recede and thus appear smaller. Large visible beams, railings that are densely packed with boards, and wide fascia boards all will make a deck seem more massive.

Thick 6x6 posts supporting an elevated deck might be the most obvious feature, but an interesting pattern of cross bracing draws attention to thinner wood. And the longer these posts are, the less thick they appear.

Color. When people think of a deck, they automatically think of exposed wood. The colors of wood and patterns of wood grain project a relaxed, casual mood. Redwood or cedar decking has beautiful color and looks great right away, but some people find the green tint of some pressure-treated decking unpleasant. All of them will gradually fade to gray after a few years of exposure to the sun unless you stain the deck regularly.

Deck stains come in a wide range of colors, so you can easily find a stain that complements the color of your house. Often a combination of natural wood and stain works—one option is to stain the entire deck except for the cap piece that sits on top of the railing. Another option that avoids a lot of maintenance is to use composite decking and railings that are made to look like wood.

Texture. Wood has a fairly rough texture: Knots, minor cracks, and rough spots are usually considered part of the charm of a deck. Such casualness goes well with almost all landscaping, but it may be unsuitable beside your house. If you need to clean up the lines a bit, buy more-expensive wood with fewer knots. Some synthetic decking materials have an embossed surface that imitates clear wood grain. Some of the better synthetic products have color variations that do a very good job of imitating the look, if not the feel, of wood. (See Chapter 3, page 50 for more on these products.) Other options include metal railings, glass windscreens, latticework, and rough-sawn lumber.

Plan the size and shape of your deck so that it works with the design of the house.

This decking, complements the textures of the garden.

💡 **SMART TIP**

PLAN FOR A BETTER VIEW

Avoid one of the common flaws in many deck designs: a railing that blocks your view. Because most railings rise at least 36 inches above the deck surface, it's wise to place them far away from glass doors and windows. Even on a sloping site where you want the main deck area close to the ground, you can add platform steps near the house, and install the railings around the perimeter of the main deck area. Place shade structures close to the house where they won't block the views.

Built-in benches are a popular option.

Consider how the deck will form a transition from the house to the yard or garden beyond.

Bridging House and Yard

Your deck will be a destination for outdoor living, but it will also be a bridge linking your house and your yard. In fact, a well-designed deck will feel something like a bridge, not only because it is suspended over the ground but also because it balances the amenities of the indoors with those of the outdoors. In addition to the basic elements of mass, shape, color, and texture, here are some specific ways to ensure that your deck makes a graceful transition:

Stepping Down. Where possible, avoid long sections of stairway. Use a series of landings on multiple levels to step down in a way that feels more natural and graceful. Often the challenge is to make sure that each level is a usable and visually pleasing space. Solve this by making the levels cascade—falling off each other at different points or even at different angles—rather than just progressing downward in a straight line like huge steps.

Deck stairs look best when they are wider and more gradual than you'd typically find indoors. A standard 36-inch-wide stairway starts to look like a ladder if it is more than six steps long. An accurately scaled drawing can help you visualize the best design.

Patio Transition. The stairway from your deck might lead down to a lawn, but a patio or path at the bottom of your steps might work better. Materials that echo your house—bricks, concrete pavers, or colorful crushed stone—are good choices because they strike a nice balance. Patio materials can be rustic or formal, ranging from rough landscaping timbers to mortar-set tiles. Natural stone and brick, which are midway between formal and rustic, often work well. Plan the lines of your patio carefully—they are a continuation of the lines in your deck, which in turn should be tied to the lines of your house.

Configuring Planters. It's hard to go wrong with foliage, as long as you can keep it healthy. Any color combination looks great—nature doesn't agonize over paint chips. You can make a planter of the same material

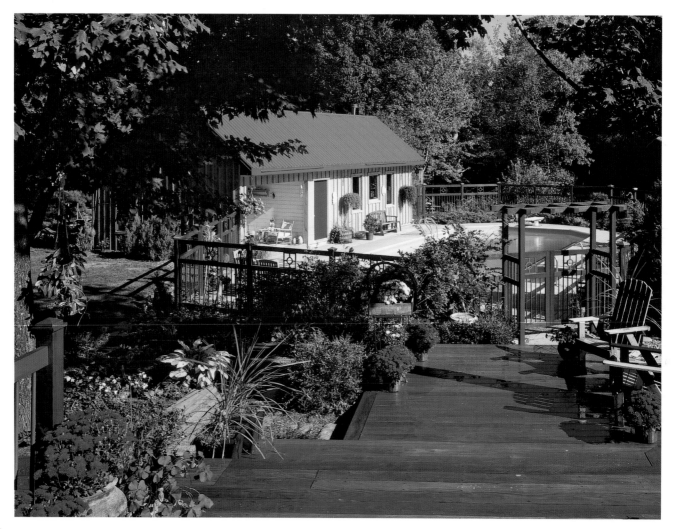

as the deck, and use plants in it that are similar to those in your yard to create a tie-in between deck and yard. And if you can build a planter that harmonizes with the house's exterior, then you can tie in all three elements.

Incorporating Trees. If you have a tree that looks great next to your house, don't cut it down. Build your deck around it, instead, to take advantage of the shade and help the deck blend into the site. Trees near the edge of the deck work well too, forming a sort of arch from yard to house, with the deck in the middle.

💡 SMART TIP

DESIGN FOR SAFETY

Don't forget these elements when designing your deck:
- A railing system that complies with building codes
- Adequate lighting for nighttime safety

A series of broad deck levels, opposite, guides people from the main area down to the pool.

An open deck includes a planting area, right top. Decks give you the option of incorporating shrubs and trees in the design.

Wide steps, right, provide plenty of room for placing container plants and other yard and garden accents.

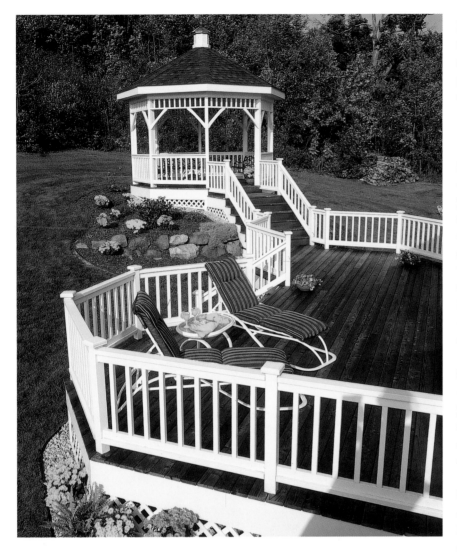

hot tub, a huge potted plant, a series of flower boxes, a well-kept greenhouse, or a statue. Play to your strengths, and position the deck and furniture to accentuate your focal point.

DESIGN CHALLENGES

Every design project hits a snag now and then, whether it turns out that your railing hits the house in the middle of a window or the stairs end in the middle of the driveway, but learn to see these challenges as opportunities to create pleasing points of interesting detail. Solutions to some of these problems are given later in the book, but now is the best time to start thinking about them.

Storage Space. Add storage space by providing access to the area under your deck or by building an attached shed. List the things you need to store, and make sure you have enough room, or they will clutter up your deck.

Lighting. Installing a lighting system adds a lot of charm to your deck, and if you plan now, you can hide at least some of the wires by running them through parts of your deck framing. This is much easier to do before you put the decking down.

Drainage Problems. Drainage will only be a problem in the future if it is a problem now. For minor problems, plan a gravel-filled trench in the ground to collect runoff from your deck and direct it away from the site. If you have major water problems, such as frequent standing water or significant erosion, be sure to deal with them before you build the deck.

Adding an Outbuilding. If a gazebo, shed, or play structure is in your future, include it in your plans now. There may be a simple way to tie it to the deck and the house. For example, make the roof of the same materials as the roof on your house and paint the rest of the structure the same color as your house. Play structures can usually be built of the same woods used to build the deck.

Theme and Variation. The best decks take one or two great ideas and then work out variations on those general themes.

The theme could be a gently curved line that you use in several places, such as the edge of the decking, the railings, and a path next to the deck. Or you may experiment with a unique decking pattern: have three or four sections that break off of each other at similar angles, for instance. If you have a large octagonal-shaped projection, you may be able to add a smaller version of it elsewhere on the deck, or you can echo the shape by building an octagonal table or bench.

The most visible elements of a deck are often those that project vertically. Choose railings or benches to harmonize with the overall structure. Planters should echo the deck structure.

A great deck usually has a stunning focal point, something that immediately grabs your attention. Perhaps you already have one—a beautiful tree, a lovely view, an inviting pool. Or you can supply a new eye-catcher yourself—a

The designer of this deck extended the railing design up to the trim on the gazebo roof, opposite.

If you are planning on adding a shade structure, incorporate it into your plans from the beginning, right.

Pergolas and arbors add vertical visual interest to deck designs, below.

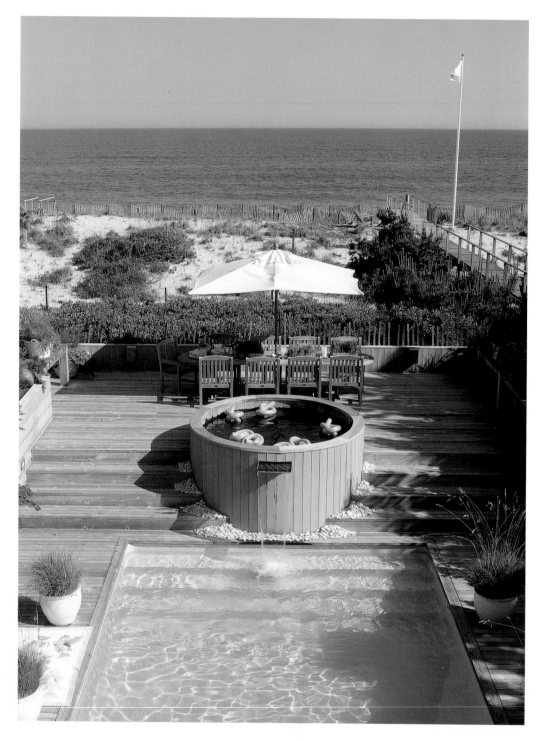

In addition to being compatible with the surroundings, this deck conforms to the site.

Sloping Sites. A sloping site makes the construction process more difficult but also presents an opportunity for an interesting, multilevel deck.

Trees. Trees on a deck site also present a chance to do something stunning, such as building the deck around the tree. Consider the age of your tree and how fast it will grow, and plan to leave ample space.

Pools and Hot Tubs. Building a deck with a pool, hot tub, or spa requires precise planning, engineering, and cutting. Think carefully about how high and wide you want the decking around pools and tubs for maximum sitting and sunning pleasure. Hot tubs usually require a foundation that is separate from the deck structure, such as their own piers.

Shade and Access. If you want some shade but don't have foliage overhead, add some louvered structures or brightly colored awnings. For areas with heavy rainfall, build a roof extension.

Plan access hatches so you can get at plumbing or electrical service junctions underneath the deck, just in case something needs repairing someday. Little trap doors and hatches that would look tacky inside are charming on a deck.

Railings are usually required on any deck over 30 inches above the ground. Plan now if you want to include any custom design features or unusual patterns in your railings. A built-in bench adds visual interest to a long expanse of railing as well.

OVERLOOKED DECK LOCATIONS

Decks aren't always found hugging the ground right next to the back door. An island deck isn't attached to the house at all, so it can go virtually anywhere on your property.

And don't forget to look up when you're searching for the perfect deck location. A rooftop deck usually offers better views, more breeze, and a more private setting.

Almost any patch of flat or low-slope roof can support a roof deck. You can run posts down to ground level, but the easiest system is to make removable platforms that lie down directly on the roof. The panels must be removable because you may have to fix a roof leak at some point. If the decking were permanent, you would have to rip it out to make a roof repair.

One popular option is to build a private deck off the master bedroom and change a window into a door.

A new deck need not be built tight against the house. This section of deck juts out into the garden for a better view of the surroundings.

When planning, think of the various uses for your deck. Here, having a shaded spa was an important consideration.

FINAL DRAWINGS

Once you have made all your decisions regarding site, substructure, decking, stairs, and railings, you are ready to finalize your plans. The finished drawings should be clear: do not rely on scribbled-over and often-erased sheets—take the extra time to draw a clean set of plans because they will be easier to follow.

The set of deck plans at the end of this chapter is a good example of what you'll need to produce in order to get your building permit. After reviewing these drawings and your site plan, your building department will either issue you a permit or ask for some changes.

Plan Drawings

Plan drawings show the deck framing from above. For these drawings, it is common to leave out the railings and decking. Be sure to include the following:

- Correct dimensional drawing of the perimeter
- All joists, beams, posts, and footings
- Dimensions for all lumber
- The distance spanned by beams and joists

- Indication of size and direction of decking (It's not usually necessary to draw this)
- Hardware, such as joist hangers, angle brackets, and bolts
- Exact locations of doors and windows
- Any electrical and plumbing fixtures and lines

Elevation Drawing

An elevation drawing shows the deck in cross-section from the side. Draw at least one elevation, including these elements:

- A detailed drawing of the railing system, including all dimensions that pertain to local codes
- Views of the concrete footings, with dimensions showing how deep and wide they will be
- Hardware list, including sizes of post anchors, tread cleats, and bolts
- Height of the tallest post
- A rough approximation of the site's slope

Detail Drawings

Draw close-up views of complicated spots on your deck. Sometimes you will need to make a detail drawing to

satisfy the building department. At other times, you may need it yourself in order to figure things out. Draw details for situations like these:

- Where the stair railing meets the rest of the deck railing
- Hatchways for access to electrical and plumbing
- Framing around trees or hot tubs
- Changes in level
- Any area of the deck with special framing, such as extra joists under a section of deck that will support a portable hot tub
- Flashing around ledger

SAMPLE DETAIL DRAWING

SAMPLE PLAN DRAWING

SAMPLE ELEVATION DRAWING

DECK BUILDING TOOLS

A fairly modest set of tools is all you need to build most decks. For the most part, they are the tools you would normally find in a homeowner's toolbox. However, building a deck is a big project and some power tools will make the work go faster. Consider investing in good miter and circular saws; they will prove invaluable on the job site. A good-quality drill/driver will make the drilling of holes and the driving of screws go smoothly. Beyond that, you might want to consider additional purchases carefully. If you will rarely use the tool after the deck project is completed, is it really worth the price? And if there's a tool you've just got to try, consider renting it for a day instead of buying it for a lifetime.

TOOLS FOR BUILDING DECKS

The people on TV home-improvement shows always seem to have an endless supply of specialized tools for their projects. If you can find a tool manufacturer to sponsor your deck, you'll probably have a big pile of tools too, but chances are that you'll need to build your deck with the tools you own now, plus a few additions.

Once you decide which tools you actually need to buy, the next decision is how much to spend. Should you buy the $279 cordless drill, or will the $39.99 model work just as well for the kind of work you'll be doing?

Typically, the answer lies somewhere between these two extremes. The high-end, professional model will probably build dozens of decks before breaking down. But you probably don't need that kind of durability if you're working on only a few projects every year. Conversely, a

bargain-basement tool might quit before you finish one project. For most DIYers, a midpriced model is a practical compromise. It will serve on a heavy-duty project, such as building a deck, and still be around for ongoing repair and improvement projects around the house.

You'll need the standard supply of basic hand and power tools, of course, including a circular saw with a sharp blade and a drill-driver (cordless or not). You probably have most of them already. But you may want to check into some of the more specialized tools and gadgets (included throughout the book) that are available today.

SAFETY EQUIPMENT

Common sense should tell you not to do carpentry without first having some basic safety equipment, such as eye and ear protection. Wear safety goggles or plastic glasses whenever you are working with power tools or chemicals. Both earplugs and earmuffs will protect your hearing. Whichever you choose, be sure that it has a noise reduction rating (NRR) of at least 20 decibels. Protect your lungs, especially if you are working with pressure-treated wood. A simple dust mask is good for

short-term use, but a respirator with a replaceable filter is best for toxic dust and fumes from finishing products. Work gloves are nice for avoiding hand injuries—catching a splinter off a board or developing a blister digging post holes is not a good way to start a workday. Steel-toe work boots will protect your feet and prevent injuries from dropped boards or tools. Flexible steel soles will protect you from puncture by a rogue nail.

PROTECT YOURSELF WITH (A) gloves, (B) ear protection, (C) hard hat, (D) knee pads, (E) respirator/dust mask, (F) safety glasses, (G) work gloves, (H) first-aid kit.

EXCAVATION AND CONCRETE

Posthole Digger. Whether you use tubular concrete forms or pour your concrete directly into the ground, you will need to dig deep, narrow holes for your footings. Essentially two mini-shovels hinged together, a posthole digger picks up dirt in "bites" as you spread the handles. This tool allows you to work directly above the hole without creating sloping sides.

Round-Point Shovel. The most basic digging tool there is, the round-point shovel gets plenty of use on a deck site, from excavating to spreading gravel. Use a file to keep the edge of the shovel sharp—it'll cut through small roots like a hot knife through butter.

Hoe. A standard garden hoe is handy for mixing concrete; a special mason's hoe, which has two holes in the blade, works even better.

Wheelbarrow. This is a handy place to mix and transport small amounts of concrete—one 80-pound, premixed bag fits nicely in most wheelbarrows. You'll also use your wheelbarrow to transport gravel, soil, sod, and sand.

Square-Nosed Shovel. The front edge of this shovel is perfect for cutting sod when you need to remove grass from your building site. You'll also find that this is the best shovel for scooping up dirt or gravel from a driveway.

Metal Rake. For spreading soil or gravel, and for sloping a site for drainage, a metal rake, or garden rake, is the best tool.

EXCAVATION TOOLS (A) wheelbarrow, (B) posthole digger, (C) standard garden hoe, (D) round-point shovel, (E) selection of trowels including a finishing trowel and a pointing trowel, (F) square-nosed shovel with a sharp front edge, (G) metal garden rake.

MEASURE AND LAYOUT

Water Level. For some decks you will need to check for level over long spans. For this task, a water level is ideal. The water level is more accurate and more expensive than a line level. It is basically a water-filled hose with clear tubes attached to each end. Because water always seeks its own level, the water in the two tubes always settles out at the same height. This is especially useful when you need to level two spots around a corner from each other.

Angle Square. Often called by the brand name Speed Square, this triangular piece of aluminum is extremely versatile, yet it is tough enough to get banged around on the job and not lose its accuracy. Its triangular shape enables you to lay out a 45-degree angle as quickly as a 90-degree angle; it also enables you to find other angles quickly, though not with great precision. Held firmly in place, your angle square makes a good cutting guide for a circular saw. You will probably find it the most useful of all the squares you may own.

Carpenter's Level. An accurate carpenter's level is crucial when building a deck. A 4-foot level is a good choice; a 2-foot level will probably do, but an 8-footer is often awkward to use. A level made of wood and brass is more durable than the cheaper aluminum levels but not necessarily more accurate. An aluminum model is an excellent choice for the occasional carpenter.

Take care of your level; all it takes is one good drop or a hard hit to make it inaccurate. Test the level regularly, especially before you buy it. To test, set the level on a smooth surface, and note the bubble. Flip the tool end-for-end and put it in the same spot. The bubble should read the same. (Also see laser level, pages 68–69.)

Framing Square. This L-shaped piece of flat metal measures 16 inches along one edge and 24 inches along the other. Use it for laying out stair stringers and also for checking the squareness of your layouts and string lines.

Post Level. If your design calls for any long posts, consider getting a post level. This very specialized but inexpensive tool straps onto the post, so you don't have to keep holding up a level while you are moving heavy material. A post level usually has two bubble vials set at 90 degrees from each other so you can check for plumb in both directions at once. Some post levels use a single, round bull's-eye vial to show perfect plumb instead.

Folding Rule. If you get a folding rule, find one that has a sliding extension on one of the end sections. This is a great tool for getting interior measurements—such as the length of a handrail between two existing posts. Many carpenters prefer a folding rule for short measurements.

Torpedo Level. You will find a 9-inch torpedo level handy for leveling small objects. It fits easily into your toolbox or your pouch.

Combination Square. This square has an adjustable blade that slides up and down. It shows both 90- and 45-degree angles, and the adjustable blade is handy for transferring depth measurements and as a pencil guide for running a line along the length of a board.

Measuring Tape. Purchase a high-quality measuring tape. A 25- or 30-foot tape is preferred, and a 1-inch-wide blade is far superior to one that is ¾ inch wide, since it is more rigid and will not quickly fold when you extend it.

Mason's String Line. You'll pull your string line very tight and it needs to last, so it's a good idea to get the professional stuff—nylon is a good choice.

Reel Measuring Tape. For large decks, where you are laying out long distances, it's helpful to have a 50-foot or 100-foot reel measuring tape. This tool doesn't automatically retract, like your 25-foot measuring tape—you wind in the plastic or metal tape the way you turn a fishing reel.

Chalk-Line Box. The tool that aligned the ancient pyramids, a chalk line will enable you to mark long, perfectly straight lines in just a few seconds. Use blue chalk because the other colors are so permanent that they often can't be washed away.

T-Bevel. If you need to duplicate angles other than 45 or 90 degrees, use a T-bevel (or sliding bevel square). This has a flat metal blade that can be locked into place at any angle.

Carpenter's Pencils. Have plenty of pencils on hand—they have a tendency to disappear. Flat carpenter's pencils are better than regular pencils because they need sharpening less frequently.

Line Level. A line level consists of a single bubble vial that clips onto a tightly stretched string line. When reading the bubble, make sure the string is stretched taut, and place the level near the center of the string line. Check the level by taking it off the string and reversing it. If the reading is the same both ways, then your line level is accurate.

Plumb Bob. To pinpoint the location of posts, you will need to drop a perfectly straight vertical line from a given spot. A plumb bob hangs from a string and tapers to a sharp point. Once the bob stops swinging, gravity ensures that the top of the string and the tip of the point are in perfect plumb alignment. The tapered shape of many chalk-line boxes allows them to double as suitable plumb bobs.

LAYOUT TOOLS (A) water level, (B) angle square, (C) 4-ft. level, (D) framing square, (E) post level, (F) ruler, (G) torpedo level, (H) combination square, (I) measuring tape, (J) string, (K) reel tape, (L) chalk-line box, (M) T-bevel, (N) pencil, (O) line level, and (P) plumb bob.

CUTTING AND SANDING

Power Miter Saw. If you need to make a lot of angle cuts or if you don't feel able to make consistent, precise cuts at all angles, it may be a good idea to buy or rent a power miter saw. These tools (also called chop saws) are simply circular saws mounted on a pivot assembly that allows you to make precise, repeatable cuts. Make sure you get a chop saw that will do the job: a saw with a 10-inch blade will not be able to completely cut a 2x6 at a 45-degree angle.

Another version of the miter saw, called the compound miter saw, makes both miter and bevel cuts in one pass. You probably won't need this ability on a deck, but if you are buying a miter saw and plan to install interior molding, it may make more sense to get a compound miter saw.

You can put together a jig that will help guide 45-degree cuts with a handheld circular saw. But it won't work as well as an adjustable chop saw, and will pay off only if you're using an angled decking pattern where the end of each board needs the same angled cut.

Circular Saw. Most carpenters and do-it-yourselfers prefer circular saws that use 7 ¼-inch-diameter blades. This size will allow you to cut to a maximum depth of about 2 ⅜ inches at 90 degrees and to cut through a piece of two-by lumber even with the blade beveled at 45 degrees.

You can get a rough idea of a saw's power and overall quality from the amperage the motor draws and the type of bearings it uses. A low-cost saw will pull only 9 or 10 amps and will run its drive shaft on sleeve bearings. This will mean less power, a shorter life, a tendency to heat up during continual use, and sometimes less precise cuts because the blade might wobble a bit.

Better saws carry a 12- or 13-amp rating and use ball bearings or roller bearings on the motor's shaft. This combination of extra power and smoother operation makes for long life and more precise cutting. As is often the case, a mid-priced model may well be your best choice.

Worm-drive saws have the most powerful motors and the longest-lasting bearings. They're built like tanks and weigh almost as much. These are primarily professional contractor's tools, and they take some getting used to. They last quite a long time, but do-it-yourselfers should probably avoid them.

A plastic housing is no longer the sign of an inferior tool, because many new plastic composites are actually tougher than metal and highly impact resistant.

Check out the saw's base carefully: if it is made of thin, stamped metal, one drop from sawhorse height could bend it out of shape for good. Look for a thicker base that is either extruded or cast aluminum.

Use carbide-tipped blades in your circular saw. These cost a few dollars more but last up to five times longer than comparable blades made from high-speed steel (HSS). A 24-tooth blade is usually the best choice for deck construction and general use. There is a trade-off between the number of teeth and cut rates and quality: a blade with fewer teeth will cut faster, but the cuts will tend to be ragged. More teeth will produce a finer cut. Have an extra blade on hand; wet wood and dense treated lumber can dull your saw's blade quickly.

Though you can use a file to touch up a damaged tooth on an HSS blade, send it to a sharpening shop when it needs a major tune-up. Take your carbide-tipped blades to a professional sharpening shop as well.

Router. Though by no means essential for deck-building, a router equipped with a chamfering or roundover bit can be quite handy for adding detail to your deck.

Belt Sander. Use a belt sander to clean up your decking and to round off the edge of the deck and railings as a finishing touch. Use this tool with care; it's easy to oversand, especially if you are working with soft wood such as cedar or redwood.

Reciprocating Saw. For demolition and for cutting off posts, a reciprocating saw works well, but don't buy one just for building a deck—a handsaw will work fine for the few cuts of this kind on your deck.

Saber Saw. This is a good choice if you need to make cutouts or if you want to make some curved cuts. If you need to do a lot of this kind of cutting, get a heavy-duty saber saw. With a standard do-it-yourself model, you'll cut through two-by lumber very slowly and the saw will have a tendency to wobble, which produces a ragged-looking cut.

Pad Sander. A vibrating or oscillating pad sander is great for smoothing decking and railings, but a sanding block will often suffice for a deck project.

Block Plane. You may occasionally need a plane for trimming or smoothing wood and straightening irregular edges or bevels. Properly set, a block plane will trim one thin shaving at a time.

Sanding Block. A more common tool for rounding off sharp edges and smoothing splinters is the sanding block. There are several types, and they are all far superior to simply using a sheet of handheld sandpaper.

Handsaw. This tool comes in handy for finishing cuts that a circular cannot finish—such as when you are cutting out stringers or cutting off posts in awkward places.

Hacksaw. Use this tool to cut through nails or other metals. The number of teeth determines the thickness of the metal that can be cut. Hacksaws have removable, adjustable blades.

Chisel. This is useful for cleaning out dado cuts,

finishing notch cuts, and other trimming and wood-shaving tasks. A 1-inch-wide chisel works well for this kind of work.

Aviation Snips. For trimming metal flashing at the ledger, metal snips are the most accurate tool.

CUTTING AND SANDING TOOLS (A) power miter saw, (B) circular saw, (C) router, (D) belt sander, (E) reciprocating saw, (F) saber saw, (G) pad sander, (H) block plane, (I) sanding block, (J) handsaw, (K) hacksaw, (L) chisel, (M) aviation snips.

FASTENING TOOLS

Compressor and Nail Gun. If you plan to frame or fasten your deck with a nail gun, you'll need a compressor to supply the air. Choose carefully—if the compressor is too small, you'll waste lots of time waiting for it to supply enough pressure for the next shot. A typical framing nailer shoots nails from 2 to 3 ½ inches long. Choose one with a restrictive or two-step trigger—this makes it much harder to fire a nail accidentally. Though safe when used properly, a nail gun can cause serious injury in a fraction of a second, so read and follow all safety precautions, especially the part about wearing safety glasses.

Cordless Drill. If it's in the budget, a cordless drill is very useful. Thanks to advances in battery technology, cordless drills have taken over most tasks you'd otherwise do with a corded drill. The most notable exception in deck building is installing decking—a corded drill still makes sense for that task since even today's batteries will soon run out of juice under such concentrated use. You can now buy a powerful 20-volt drill that is quite compact, well balanced, and easy to handle. A good cordless drill will come with a charger and an extra battery so that you'll always have a fresh battery available.

Read the owner's manual carefully, especially the part about charging batteries. Don't wait until a battery is completely dead before you charge it—pop it in the charger as soon as it starts to show signs of weakening.

Pipe Clamps. Pipe clamps are sometimes helpful for holding pieces of lumber in place temporarily—so you can check the level one last time before fastening, for example.

Bar Clamps. Bar clamps do some of the same jobs that pipe clamps do, but are usually a little easier to set up. You can adjust some models with just one hand so you have the other hand free to hold things in place.

C-Clamps. A pair of large C-clamps is useful when you need to reach past obstructions to apply pressure to the center of a board. Squeezing a pair of 2x12s on the outside of a 4x4 post prior to fastening is a good example.

Flat Bar and Wrecking Bar. The flat bar is more versatile, but the wrecking bar (sometimes called a crowbar) gives you more leverage. These are handy for demolition, such as removing siding before installing a ledger board, for

prying deck boards into position, and for moving or breaking rocks you run into when digging holes.

Hammer. Your hammer is always at your side and constantly in use, so get a comfortable one. A 16-ounce hammer is a comfortable weight that will do the job, but the extra weight of a 20-ounce hammer will drive large nails more quickly. A straight-claw hammer is better for demolition work, while a curved-claw is better for pulling nails.

Caulking Gun. Though it is used sparingly on a deck, there are places that benefit from a good bead of caulking.

Cat's Paw. This tool is for pulling framing nails back out of wood. By striking the back of its claw with a hammer, you can drive it under a nailhead, even if the head is below the surface. Then you push or strike the top of the tool to pull the nail out. A cat's paw always gets its nail but often seriously mars the face of the board in the process.

Nail Set. For places where the nails will show, you want to avoid the smiles and frowns caused by the hammer hitting the wood when you strike the nail with that last blow. Use a nail set, a small shaft of metal with one square end and one end tapered to a blunt point. With this, you can either drive nails perfectly flush with the wood or countersink them into the wood.

Utility Knife. No carpenter's apron should be without a utility knife. You'll use this inexpensive tool for all sorts of things: sharpening pencils, slicing away splinters from boards, shaving pieces of lumber, and opening bundles and packages. Get a better-quality, heavy-duty knife. Blades of cheap knives can slip out when you bear down hard. Replace a blade as soon as it gets dull. Be sure to get a retractable knife.

Zip Tool. A zip tool is used to unlock the joints between courses of vinyl siding. You'll find it handy if you are removing vinyl siding to install a ledger.

Ratchet Wrenches. If you will be installing lag screws or carriage bolts, a ratchet wrench with the right socket is much faster than a crescent wrench.

FASTENING TOOLS (A) nail gun and compressor, (B) drill, (C) pipe, bar, and C-clamps, (D) pry bar, (E) hammer, (F) caulking gun, (G) cat's paw, (H) nail set, (I) utility knife, (J) zip tool, (K) ratchet.

ACCESSORIES

Tool Belt or Apron. A tool belt or apron is a definite must; without it, you will spend untold hours looking for that tool you used just a few minutes ago. You can get an elaborate leather belt or a less-expensive canvas one. The belt should comfortably hold those objects you use most during a working day: your square, measuring tape, hammer, chalk-line box, nail set, chisel, pencils, and utility knife; and it should have a pocket for a good-size handful of nails. Be sure you can holster and unholster your hammer, pencil, and measuring tape with ease.

Hammer Holster. When you know you're going to do nothing but drive nails for a while, you might want to drop the full tool belt and put on a simpler tool holder with just one pocket and a hammer loop.

Extension Cord. Always check the wire-gauge number on an extension cord—the phrase heavy-duty on the package doesn't guarantee that it will supply enough current to your tools. In general, an extension cord with 14-gauge wires, designed to handle up to 15 amps, will do the job.

Stepladder. Available in wood, aluminum, or fiberglass, stepladders are a handy tool if you are working on a flat, level surface. A fold-down shelf can hold tools and finishing materials. Stepladders are available up to 15 feet high. As with other ladders, they are rated for the amount of weight the they can hold. Although they are sturdy when extended, do not stand on the top three steps.

Sawhorses. Usually used to set up a temporary cutting station, sawhorses should be strong and stable.

Small Sledgehammer. For driving stakes, a standard 16- or 20-ounce hammer will usually do the job, but a small sledgehammer is faster.

Putty Knife. This is for filling holes in damaged wood or holes left by countersunk screws.

Tool Bag. A tool bag is a great way to transport and organize all those tools that don't earn a permanent place in your tool belt.

RENTING TOOLS

When you need a specialized tool for just a few hours, check with your local rental yard. Chances are they've got what you need and will rent it to you for a day or two. Some yards even rent by the half day, so if you're fast, you can save a little money. Think carefully before renting any tool for longer than a week: after a point, it makes more sense to go out and buy the tool yourself.

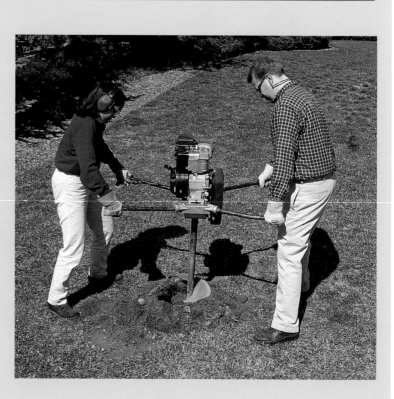

A power auger makes short work of digging holes for posts, but the tools often require two people to operate safely.

SOME USEFUL ACCESSORIES (A) nail aprons, (B) hammer holster and belt, (C) extension cords with GFCI protection, (D) stepladder, (E) leather tool belt, (F) sawhorses, either plastic, steel, or made with 2x4s and metal brackets.

MATERIALS FOR DECKS

While the universe of materials used to build decks continues to expand, pressure-treated lumber is still the most popular choice. The material is relatively inexpensive; it resists insects and rot; and it is readily available. However, many homeowners and professional deck designers are turning to other materials, such as redwood, exotic hardwoods, and synthetic materials, for the decking and railing systems—the areas that are in full view. These products offer a variety of looks that cannot be matched by pressure-treated lumber. In most cases, pressure-treated lumber is still used for the structural portions of the deck, including posts, beams, and joists.

LUMBER

Because your deck is out in the weather all the time, you want to use wood that will resist decay and insects.

There are several choices, but the most popular are treated lumber, redwood, and cedar. Other options include cypress, recycled plastic decking, untreated lumber, and tropical ironwood.

To get the wood that's right for your project, it's not enough to choose a certain species. Other factors that influence a wood's performance include moisture content, method of drying the wood, what part of the tree the lumber comes from, and the quality, or grade, of each piece.

You also want to choose wood that won't warp or check after it's installed. All wood swells when it gets wet and shrinks while drying, so you should expect a certain amount of twisting, cupping, and splitting, but choosing the right type of lumber for the different locations on your deck should keep this problem under control.

Lumber Basics

Most of the lumber you buy is surfaced—smoothed, with rounded edges—on all four sides. This is called S4S, meaning surfaced on four sides. If you want a rough-sawn look (for the fascia or for posts, perhaps), you should be able to find cedar or redwood that is either rough all over or is smooth on only one side. This lumber may be a bit thicker and wider than S4S.

Lumber Sizes. The nominal size of a piece of lumber—for example, 2x4—refers to its size prior to drying and surfacing. So the 2x4 you buy will actually be 1 ½ inches by 3 ½ inches; a 2x6 is actually 1 ½ by 5 ½; a 1x8 is ¾ x 7 ¼, and so on. In most cases, lumberyards carry pieces in 24-inch increments beginning at 8 feet, so you can buy 8-footers, 10-footers, and so on.

Many people use either cedar or pressure-treated ⁵⁄₄x6 ("five quarter by six") boards for the decking and sometimes for the top cap on the railing. This material is actually 1 inch thick and 5 ½ inches wide. Rounded edges minimize splintering. Often only one face will be usable, so choose your boards carefully. To satisfy most codes and to build a strong deck, you will have to space joists no more than 16

LUMBER GRAIN

All trees have two types of wood inside: sapwood and heartwood. Sapwood is located toward the perimeter of the tree and carries sap to the branches. Heartwood comes from the center of the tree and is denser than sapwood because it is older. It is also more stable than sapwood. All parts of the tree can be used, and lumber taken from either the sapwood or heartwood region is graded accordingly. Because a lot of lumber today is cut from younger, faster-growing trees, you may find fewer distinctions between the heartwood and sapwood areas.

Decking products must be able to withstand the extremes of weather.

inches on center to use this material.

Most people choose deck boards that are 5 ½ inches wide, such as 2x6 or ⅝x6, either because they like the wider appearance or because they are less work to install. But the price for wider boards is rising fast because more lumber now comes from smaller trees, so 2x4 decking is becoming a more economical choice. However, lumber prices tend to fluctuate, so it makes sense to price out both types.

Lumber Density. As a general rule, lumber of greater density will be stronger but also more prone to splitting and warping. Likewise, lower-density wood is weaker and may splinter and twist less. This is because lower-density wood can act like a sponge, absorbing moisture when the weather is wet and drying when the sun comes out. Dense wood does not have the ability to transfer moisture quickly, and the internal stresses cause warping and splinters. Treating lumber does not affect density but only adds temporary weight in the form of moisture.

So higher-density wood—Douglas fir or southern yellow pine, for instance—works well for the substructure, where strength is important and splinters and warping do not matter as much. And because you want to avoid splinters on the decking and rails, lower-density wood, such as redwood or cedar, may be a better choice.

Heartwood and Sapwood. The wood near the center of the tree, which is inactive because it has not been growing for some time, is called heartwood. Lumber milled from this portion of the tree is more resistant to rot and insects and less porous than sapwood, which is taken from the area of the tree near the bark. This is a significant difference: decking made of redwood or cedar heartwood will last far longer than will sapwood decking of the same species.

Vertical and Flat Grain. Different sawing techniques at the mill yield different grain patterns on the boards. Lumber generally either has vertical grain, with narrow grain lines running along the face of the board, or flat grain (also called plainsawn), with wider lines that often form rippling V-shapes. Most boards are a combination of the two, and in any given load of lumber, you will find boards that are both primarily flat grained and primarily vertically grained.

Vertical grain is less likely to shrink and warp, and most people think it looks better. But you don't have to go to the extra expense of specifying vertical grain when you order; when you choose boards, just pick as many of the ones with narrow lines as possible.

Moisture. Freshly cut trees delivered to a sawmill have a lot of moisture in them. And after sawing and surfacing, pressure-treated lumber gets saturated with liquid chemicals, making it even wetter. It dries out some before it gets to the lumberyard, but some lumber you buy may have a moisture content of 30 or 40 percent.

Wood that is wet—whether from natural moisture or from chemicals—will shrink as it dries out. Wood shrinks most across its width. The lengthwise shrinkage is minimal unless the board is especially long. Butt joints in a long run

LUMBER GRADES

Number 1 grade of most common lumber has few, if any, knots.

Number 2 grade has more knots and defects than Number 1. It's the type specified as a minimum requirement in most building codes.

Number 3 of most common lumber has many knots and defects. It may not be approved by your local building code.

of decking may open up over time if the boards are installed wet. If your lumber has a moisture content (MC) of less than 20 percent, shrinkage and warping should be minimal.

The grade stamp on lumber indicates the moisture content, but don't trust this number completely; wood can pick up moisture from rain or humidity while sitting in the lumberyard. Your local yard may be willing to check some boards with a moisture meter. If not, try driving a nail into a board and see if any water squeezes out around the shank. If it does, it's too wet.

Lumber Grades. Lumber is sorted and graded on the basis of number, spacing, and size of knots, milling defects, and drying technique.

The highest-quality—and most expensive—lumber is called select structural. This lumber has the fewest knots and other imperfections.

Most often, you will be dealing with common lumber, which is graded No. 1, No. 2, or No. 3. No. 1 is the strongest,

and usually the best-looking wood as well. No. 2 is the grade most commonly used in deck framing. No. 3 lumber is less structurally sound.

Another grading system uses the words Const (for construction), Stand (standard), or Util (utility). These three classifications are generally used to grade 2x4 and 4x4 lumber and No.1, 2, and 3 grade 2x6 and wider stock.

No. 2 is the most common grade and will be fine for most applications. Chances are, your building codes will require "No. 2 or better."

For the railings and other areas that are highly visible, you may want to spend the extra money to get No.1 or even select structural lumber—if you can find it. Good lumber is getting much harder to find these days. Lots of lumber is now cut from corporate forests, where fast-growing trees mature quickly but have widely spaced growth rings and yield less lumber.

Lumber is graded on the size and number of knots, opposite. Clear wood provides the most finished appearance.

LUMBER SPECIES

Redwood

The redwood trees of northern California are legendary for their size and the quality of lumber. Redwood's beautiful straight grain, natural glowing color, and weather resistance have traditionally marked it as the Cadillac of outdoor building materials. It is a pleasure to work with, easy to cut, and sweet-smelling. Unfortunately, overlumbering has made redwood expensive and hard to get.

Because of its high price, you might want to use redwood only for the highly visible portions of your deck, such as the decking and railings. Redwood works for structural support as well, though you may have to use slightly larger joists and beams than if you were using regular pressure-treated lumber.

You can usually tell sapwood from heartwood by color: the sapwood is much lighter and hardly looks like it comes from the same tree. Redwood heartwood has the deep, rich color and is extremely weather- and insect-resistant. Sapwood may start to rot in two or three years if it has contact with the ground or if it will remain wet for long periods of time. Treat sapwood before installing it, and use it only where there will be good drainage most of the year.

If you let redwood "go gray" by not treating it with anything, it will reach a light gray color after a few years and develop a slight sheen that many people find attractive. Or you can treat it with stains and a UV blocker to keep it close to its original color.

In some parts of the country, you can find redwood that has been both treated and stained, which makes the sapwood more decay resistant and similar in color to the heartwood. This is an expensive item, but if it comes with a lifetime warranty, it's worth checking out. Inspect several pieces to make sure you like the color. The reddish-brown will fade after a few years, and the deck will turn a uniform gray unless you restain it.

The Redwood Inspection Service of the California Redwood Association establishes redwood grades. The service has two grading categories: Architectural and Garden. Architectural grades are the best-looking, most expensive grades of redwood. Garden grades are more economical and have more knots. Both categories of redwood are available kiln-dried or unseasoned and are usually surfaced on four sides.

Architectural grades include:

Clear All-Heart. All heartwood and free from knots, this wood is recommended for highly visible applications.

Clear. Similar in quality to Clear All-Heart, except that Clear contains sapwood. Clear is ideal for highly visible applications where the wood won't be subject to decay.

Heart B. Containing limited knots, but no sapwood, Heart B is a less costly alternative to Clear All-Heart.

B-Grade. Similar characteristics to Heart B but contains sapwood; same uses as Clear.

Garden grades of redwood are suitable for most deck-building applications. They include:

Construction Heart/Deck Heart. These are all-heartwood grades containing knots. Both are recommended for work on or near the ground, such as posts, girders, joists, and decking. Deck Heart is similar in appearance to Construction Heart but also carries a grade stamp for strength. Deck Heart is available in 2x4 and 2x6 only.

Many people use more than one type of wood on their deck. Visible areas receive the highest quality lumber.

SMART TIP

STACKING WOOD

When wood is delivered, some of it may be a little wet, which means it can shrink and twist on your deck. You should return any waterlogged lumber that is significantly heavier than other pieces. The rest you can store off the ground on 4x4s with strips of wood laid between layers to increase air circulation and drying.

Construction Common/Deck Common. Containing knots and a combination of heartwood and sapwood, these grades are best for aboveground applications such as railings, benches, and decking. Deck Common is similar in appearance to Construction Common and has the same uses but is also graded for strength. Deck Common is available in 2x4 and 2x6 only.

Merchantable Heart. This is the most economical all-heartwood grade. The rules allow larger knots and some knotholes. It's used for garden walls or utility structures on or near the ground.

Merchantable. Having the same characteristics as Merchantable Heart but containing sapwood, this grade is suitable only for fence boards, trellises, and aboveground garden and utility applications.

Cedar

Cedar has many of the benefits of redwood and usually costs less. Like redwood, it is stable, easy to work with, and rarely splinters or checks. And like redwood, it is the heartwood of the cedar tree that is resistant to decay. Sapwood will decay relatively quickly. You can recognize cedar heartwood by its dark color and the hamster-cage smell you get when you cut it.

Cedar is fragrant and beautiful, though it tends to have a more informal feel than redwood, with its light brown color. Left untreated, cedar will turn gray.

Cedar is not quite as strong as redwood and isn't often used for structural posts, beams, or joists. You may want to use it in places where the structure will be visible—for example, for fascia. In other places, such as the outside and header joists, it is common to use pressure-treated lumber for the structure and then cover it with cedar fascia boards for looks.

However, unlike redwood and pressure-treated lumber, cedar is available in most any size, even up to 12x12 monster posts. So you might use it for unusually sized post-and-beam constructions.

Cedar is widely available and comes in a number of varieties. The most commonly used variety is Western red cedar. You can purchase Clear All-Heart, but this is quite expensive. Chances are, you will want to use No.1 varieties: Select Tight Knot, taken from new growth and containing some sapwood, works well for decking that will not remain wet for long periods. Architect Clear and Custom Clear come from old growth and should be used in places susceptible to rot. Stepping down from these grades you will find Architect Knotty, Custom Knotty, and No. 2. These will contain more knots, but probably have the same amount of rot-resistance. And you may like the look of the knots.

One of the most common decking materials used is ⁵⁄₄ cedar decking. This has rounded edges so you will end up with virtually no splinters. But inspect this lumber for the qualities discussed earlier. Just because some company has labeled it "decking" does not mean it will suit your needs.

Use cedar with one smooth face and one rough face (called S1SE, meaning surfaced on one side and two edges) for fascia. With the rough side turned outward, it has a pleasing rustic appearance. However, water trapped between a fascia board and the lumber it is covering up can promote decay, so treat these pieces well.

Sometimes cedar will develop black, slimy spots. While this could be mold, chances are that it's just natural resin leaching out of the wood. It can be washed away with soap and water.

LUMBER GRADING STAMPS

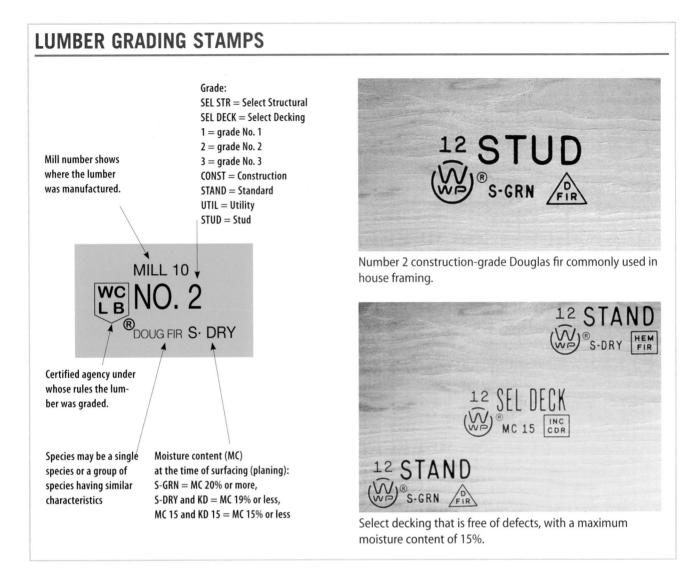

Grade:
SEL STR = Select Structural
SEL DECK = Select Decking
1 = grade No. 1
2 = grade No. 2
3 = grade No. 3
CONST = Construction
STAND = Standard
UTIL = Utility
STUD = Stud

Mill number shows where the lumber was manufactured.

MILL 10

WCLB NO. 2 DOUG FIR S·DRY

Certified agency under whose rules the lumber was graded.

Species may be a single species or a group of species having similar characteristics

Moisture content (MC) at the time of surfacing (planing):
S-GRN = MC 20% or more,
S-DRY and KD = MC 19% or less,
MC 15 and KD 15 = MC 15% or less

Number 2 construction-grade Douglas fir commonly used in house framing.

Select decking that is free of defects, with a maximum moisture content of 15%.

Cypress

Bald cypress is the South's answer to redwood. Native to the swamps and lowland areas throughout the Southeast, bald cypress is similar to redwood in hardiness and strength, although it is not as stable. In the southern United States, local sawmills can be a very economical source for decking lumber. It's hard to get cypress outside of its native region, but your lumberyard might be willing to order it for you.

Treated Wood Products

Pressure-treated (PT) lumber has been used to build wood decks for years. In the past, most lumber was treated with chromated copper arsenate (CCA), which gives the wood a greenish tint that fades over time. The treatment process provided a durable product that went into the construction of millions of decks. However, CCA contains arsenic, a known carcinogen, and safe use of the product required some special handling procedures.

The wood treatment industry has elected to stop producing CCA treated lumber for use in residential applications. Other types of preservatives are now used, including copper azole and alkaline copper quaternary. These and other types of preservatives can affect the look and structural characteristics of the lumber. Be sure to follow the manufacturer's directions for installation, safe handling, and proper uses.

There is nothing wrong with the millions of decks constructed with CCA treated wood. Properly maintained, they will last for years and do not present a risk to those who use them if they follow standard safety practices, including wearing a dust mask, gloves, and eye protection when cutting CCA treated lumber, and washing your hands after handling the wood. Do not sand or burn the wood.

Ironwood

If you have a big budget and a taste for the exotic, you may want to look into South American hardwoods (sometimes called ironwoods), such as ipé and pau lopé. This lumber is extremely strong and durable. In fact, some ironwoods have roughly twice the strength and load rating as similarly sized pressure-treated Doug fir. And the resistance to rot and insects is often five times better than treated lumber found in this country.

As you may expect, these woods are quite expensive; using ironwood for only the decking and railings could well triple the materials cost for your entire deck. Ironwoods are also slow to install—cutting is arduous, and you may have to predrill for every screw or nail.

♀ SMART TIP

CROWNING

Most structural lumber you use for joists and girders has a natural bend, or crown. When you select these beams, sight down the edge to find the bend, and mark an X on the up side. Setting joists and girders with the crowns up counteracts any tendency for the frame to sag.

SELECTING LUMBER

Many lumberyards store structural lumber outside. When it's delivered, you will probably find some high-quality pieces, while others have open knot holes and other defects. Most lumber today is sold in mixed-grade shipments, and unless you're paying for a select grade, you have to deal with it by selecting the best boards for the most visible area of the deck. On the deck surface, don't worry about grain direction, and simply turn the bad side face down.

LUMBER DEFECTS

You probably can't afford to buy clear, select lumber for every part of your deck, so most pieces are going to have some small defects. Some defects are cosmetic and won't affect the strength of the board; others will cause trouble. Here is a list of lumber defects, with descriptions that will tell you whether or not you can live with them.

Bow is a bend in the wood along the wide face, from end to end. It has no effect on strength, and you can use the board on your deck as long as you can straighten it as you fasten it in place.

Cup is a bend across the width of a board. If it's not severe, you can try to flatten it out with nails or screws (for decking) or blocking (for joists). A cupped decking board will hold water if installed cupped-side up, and this will promote rot, so be sure to turn the cupped side down before you flatten it.

Crook is a bend in the wood that makes a hump on the narrow face when you sight from one end to the other. The high portion is called the crown, and joists are always installed crown side up. Most long boards have a small crook, but excessive crooking makes wood unsuitable for framing. When a deck board has a moderate crook, you can usually push or pull it into position before fastening.

Twist is a slight corkscrew-shaped distortion of the wood, and if it's severe enough to be noticeable at first glance, the lumber is unsuitable for decking or framing.

Check is a rift in the surface caused when the surface dries more rapidly than the interior. It produces patches that look like small tears in the surface. These are usually only cosmetic and do not affect the strength. Kiln-dried wood checks less than green wood.

Split is a crack that passes completely through the board at the ends. This is a serious structural weakness. Don't use split lumber on any part of your deck.

Wane is the lack of wood along one edge of a board, usually in a tapered pattern along the length of the board. This occurs on boards cut from the outer edge of the tree—where the bark once was. Wane has little effect on strength. Remove any bark that remains on the lumber because it will promote rot if it stays there.

Knots are the high-density bases of limbs. The knots themselves are strong, but they have no real connection to the surrounding wood. Avoid large knots in decking, which may

come loose over time. Large knots (anything over 1 inch) in the bottom third of a joist could weaken it significantly.

Decay is the destruction of the wood structure by fungi or insects. Don't use decayed wood on any portion of your deck.

Pitch Pockets are accumulations of natural resins on the surface of a board. They have little effect on strength, but will cause discoloration if you paint or stain the board.

SYNTHETIC DECKING

This is the fastest growing category of decking material due to the fact that manufacturers are coming out with increasingly attractive products that are generally easier to install than wood. Synthetics don't have the strength of wood and so are used only for decking and railings, not for framing.

Unlike wood, these products vary greatly from one manufacturer to the next. Also they are available in a range of prices and quality. However, there are three basic types of synthetic decking: composite, solid polyvinyl chloride (PVC), and composite capped with PVC. They all come in wood-like colors, and the more expensive products have color variations and embossed grain-like textures that are quite convincing to the eye, though they don't feel like wood to the touch.

Composite Decking. Wood particles mixed with plastic, usually recycled from beverage containers, are bound with epoxy to create composite decking. It is very stable and won't expand and contract nearly as much as wood. The color is permanent, but over the years it does fade. Faded composite decking can be coated with a stain specifically formulated for the purpose. The biggest problem with composite decking is that it can absorb moisture that allows mold to grow.

Composite decking is usually embossed with a pattern to mimic wood grain. Capped composite (left) can have color variations added to the plastic surface to make it look more like wood.

LUMBER DEFECTS

Bow

Cup

Crook

Twist

Check

Split

Wane

Knot

Decay

Pitch Pocket

Solid PVC. This is the closest to maintenance-free of all available decking materials. Mold won't grow on PVC and periodic washing is all it needs. However, solid PVC is very expensive, more so because stainless steel fasteners are recommended. Also, solid PVC expands and contracts significantly along the length of board. Solid PVC also comes in ¾-inch-thick boards for use as fascia.

Capped Composite. Manufacturers came up with PVC-capped composite decking in an effort to combine the stability of composite with the mold-resistance of plastic. In appearance, it is indistinguishable from solid PVC. As the name implies, it consists of a hard plastic surface bonded to a composite board. In some products the plastic covers just the top and sides of the boards; high-end versions are fully capped all the way around, a better protection against mold. Capped composite costs more than composite alone but less than solid PVC and so has become a popular choice.

CONCRETE

In building your deck, you'll most likely use concrete for footings to support the posts.

Concrete is composed of three elements: portland cement, aggregate, and water. The aggregate is a mixture of sand and gravel that acts to bind the cement paste together, adding strength.

It is important to get the mixture right. Too much water will weaken the concrete; too little will make it difficult to work. So the general rule when mixing your own is to add just enough water to make it workable for your needs. If you use premixed bags, read the label to find out how much water to add, and add it slowly. The mix should be liquid enough to fill all the spaces in a tube form or hole, but if it gets soupy, it's too wet.

The compressive strength of concrete—the amount of weight you can place on it before it crumbles—is determined by the amount of cement in the mix. Occasionally you will get an inspector who requires some sort of proof that you are using concrete that is strong enough.

FASTENERS

The nails, screws, bolts, and hardware you choose hold your deck together, transforming a pile of lumber into a useful, well-built outdoor structure. Some of these choices, such as what size bolts hold your girder to your post, are dictated by building codes; others, such as whether to use screws or nails to hold down your decking, depend more on personal preference than local codes.

Whatever type of fastener you choose, remember this rule of thumb for determining the length you need: the fastener's penetration into the bottom piece should be equal to or greater than the thickness of the top piece. So unless you plan to countersink the fasteners into the top board, they should be at least twice as long as the thickness of the top board. For example, when installing 1 ½-inch boards, you should use 3- or 3 ½-inch fasteners.

Nails

The most common, and usually quickest, way of fastening wood together is to use nails. If you choose the right nails and install them properly, the joint will stay tight for many decades.

The thicker a nail is, the more wood surface it touches, and the more wood the nail's shank displaces, the better it holds.

Nail sizes are described by the term penny, which is abbreviated to the letter "d" (which stands for denarius, an ancient Roman coin—we're talking some very old terminology here). The number originally referred to the cost of 100 nails of that

FASTENERS

Regardless of the type of fastener, use only corrosion-resistant fasteners (hot-dipped galvanized, ceramic-coated, stainless steel, or aluminum).

Nails and screws. Left to right: Galvanized common nail, hardware connector nail, stainless steel ring-shank finish nail, Phillips-drive deck screw, square-drive deck screw, star-drive deck screw, composite decking screw, structural bolt for connectors such as stair brackets, structural wood screw.

Bolts and structural connectors. Left to right: J-bolt for sinking into concrete and connecting to post anchors, carriage bolt, screw bolt with self-tightening cap, lag screw, ledger screw, often used instead of lag bolts.

Hidden deck fasteners. There are many types of hidden deck fasteners, some designed to work with a specific decking product. Here are two common types that lock into a groove in the side of synthetic decking and get screwed down into joists.

size, but today it indicates the nail's length. For fastening two-by lumber together, use 16d nails, which are 3 ½ inches long. For ¾ decking, 3-inch-long, 10d nails work best.

Unless you are working in a place where the nails will not be exposed to weather (something that rarely happens when you're building a deck), it is usually best to use hot-dipped galvanized nails. These have a dull silvery coating that helps them resist corrosion. The coating also has a rough texture, which makes it difficult for the nail to work loose.

Stainless-steel and aluminum nails resist rust more effectively but have slightly less grabbing power than galvanized. Stainless steel is very expensive but may be worth the price in very wet situations. Aluminum nails are soft and bend easily.

A number of "deformed" nails are designed to have greater holding power. Drive-screw nails, also called screw-shank nails, have a slight thread on the shank and actually rotate as you drive them. They hold much like a screw.

Some specialized deck nails have blunted tips to minimize splitting and a knurled or ringed shank for extra holding power. A ring-shanked nail holds very well if it stays completely in place, but loses much of its holding power if it gets pried outward even the slightest bit.

Galvanized casing nails are basically big finishing nails. Originally designed for fastening window and door casings, casing nails do not have the holding power of nails with heads, though they grab a bit better than finishing nails because they are thicker.

Because they lack the holding power your deck needs, casing nails are not usually appropriate for structural connections or decking, even though they look nicer. You might, however, use them for attaching fascia or other finishing touches where less holding power is needed.

Screws

You have a number of good reasons for choosing screws over nails. Screws offer more holding power than nails and can pull a bowed board down flat more easily than nails.

Using screws also eliminates the "smiles" and "frowns" that hammering often produces in the wood. You can also remove them without marring the wood, so that you may not have to throw away a board after making a mistake. If using screws saves even one board, this could make up for the slight extra expense. And once you get the technique down, screwing down decking boards with a good screw gun can be just as fast as nailing.

Wood Deck Screws. These self-driving screws have aggressive threads and a bugle-shaped head. For many years, galvanized deck screws with Phillips-drive heads were standard. These are still available but have been mostly replaced by

ceramic-coated screws with a square-drive or star-drive head. Phillips drives have a tendency to cam out and destroy the recess in the screw head. Square drives rarely cam out and star drives are even better. Never use deck screws to join framing members; they are designed to hold deck boards down, not to support a load across their diameter. For framing, use only structural wood screws or nails.

Composite Decking Screws. Solid wood and composite have different densities. As a result, screws for composite decking have two different threads—the bottom thread is designed to hold well in wooden joists and the upper thread is designed to hold well in composite deck boards. They have a small inconspicuous head that is usually color-matched to the decking. The head is flat on the bottom to prevent the mushrooming effect that happens when bugle-head screws are driven into composite.

Lag Screws. Also called lag bolts, these are thick screws with coarse threads and heads that will accept a socket wrench. Always use a washer or the head will sink into the lumber and will not hold as well. Use them for attaching the ledger board to the house and for other places where you need extra strength but can only reach one side of the connection.

Ledger Screws. As the name implies, these screws are used instead of lag screws to attach the ledger to the house. Unlike lag screws they require no predrilling and are quickly driven in with a drill/driver.

Bolts

Use bolts where connections must be extremely strong. The most common uses on a deck are tying together built-up beams and fastening a post to a beam.

Bolts pass through the pieces of wood they are joining and are secured with washers and nuts. Hexagonal-head bolts are easy to install because you can use a socket wrench on the bolt head. Make sure you use washers under both the head and the nut, or they will sink into the lumber. Carriage bolts have a rounded head and a square shoulder that requires no washer; use them in places where you want a finished look.

Screw Bolts. These structural fasteners are used instead of carriage bolts in applications such as fastening a beam to a post. Unlike carriage bolts, they require no predrilling and they are driven in with a drill/driver. They have a cap nut on the protruding end that tightens when you drive the screw without the need for a wrench.

DECK HARDWARE

Besides screws, nails, and bolts, many other metal fasteners are used in the construction of a deck.

Deck Fasteners

Specialized deck hardware allows you to securely install decking boards with no visible fasteners. There are several hidden-fastener systems, some designed to work with a specific decking product. All of these systems are more expensive than traditional fasteners and they take more time to install, but it may well be worth the extra time and expense to have a clean, nail-free surface, especially if your decking boards are beautiful cedar or redwood.

Flashing

Flashing installation is usually quick and easy—as long as you get the correct material. When possible, buy pre-formed pieces that are in the exact shape you need. You may have to buy a roll of flat sheet metal and form it yourself.

Aluminum flashing will last practically forever, but it has a tendency to expand and contract with changes in weather, causing nails to come loose and leading to leaks.

Make sure you use aluminum nails with aluminum flashing, or you'll have corrosion. Galvanized flashing might develop rust spots after some years, but it is thicker and stronger and does not react to temperature changes as readily as aluminum.

Tension ties. This hardware secures the deck framing to house framing to prevent the joists from pulling away from the ledger.

Hurricane ties. The one at left attaches to one side of the joist and beam. The other type slips under the joist and is attached to both sides of the joist and one side of the beam.

💡 SMART TIP

TREATED WOOD FASTENERS

There is evidence that some of the newer wood treatment chemicals are more corrosive than the traditional treatments for pressure-treated wood. (See "Treated Wood Products," page 58.) Check product information sheets for specific fastener recommendations. Some manufacturers of fasteners are recommending stainless-steel nails or screws when using the newer types of treated lumber.

DECK CONNECTORS

JOIST HANGER

ANGLE BRACKET

ANGLED JOIST HANGER

POST ANCHOR

POST BEAM CAP

POST BOLT CAP

STAIR BRACKET

STAIR CLEAT

CUT STRINGER

There is no one way to build decks—except the way the building inspector prefers. While inspection methods vary, all inspectors zero in on two areas: the piers, to make sure they reach below the frost line, and the ledger, to make sure the deck is securely attached to the house. Of course, there is more to building a deck then simply passing the inspections. The techniques you use will not only make the deck functional but will also contribute to the overall appearance of the deck. This chapter covers basic building techniques, including the laying out and the cutting of curved surfaces on the deck.

MEASURING AND MARKING

Good carpentry begins with accurate measuring and marking. Get in the habit of using the same techniques every time, and your work will be much more precise.

Using a Measuring Tape

You'll use your measuring tape for taking most of the measurements on your project. You will notice that the metal hook at the end of the tape is a bit loose. It is made that way on purpose: it moves back and forth ⅛ inch, which is also exactly how thick it is. This means that you will get the correct measurement both when you hook the end of your measuring tape over the end of a piece of wood, or when you butt it up against something to take an inside measurement.

Make sure you pull the tape straight before you measure. If it curves in any way, you'll get a bad reading. If a helper is calling out measurements for you to cut, make sure that their measuring tape agrees with yours—sometimes the hook gets bent, which can throw your cut off by ⅛ inch or so.

Scribing in Place

When possible, the easiest and most accurate way to measure is not to measure at all, but rather to hold the lumber in place and mark it for cutting. This usually involves butting one end of the board exactly to the spot where it will rest and marking a cut line on the other end.

If you must cut a number of boards to the same length,

SMART TIP

STEP-AHEAD LAYOUT

To inexperienced DIYers, the carpentry technique of marking a step-ahead layout may seem a little simpleminded—after all, you just measure for a modular framing layout (usually 16 inches on center), draw a guideline with a pencil and a square, and then take the extra step of marking a large X beside the line, working in the direction of your layout. However, this way there will be no confusion when it comes time to place joists. If you always cover the X and align the joist to the line, you'll never stray from the on-center layout.

ACCURATE LEVELING

Here are some popular leveling tools.

1. A water level is a basic tool that's great for leveling over long distances. (See page 75.)
2. A carpenter's level normally has bubbles. This one displays a digital readout.
3. Laser levels used to be only for contractors, but some new models have come down in price. The red beam projects a level line against any surface on your site.

cut one and use it as a template for making cuts on the others.

Sometimes it's best not to precut the boards at all, but instead let each piece run wild. It's common to let the decking boards run wild initially, then snap a chalk line and cut them all off in place.

Marking for Cuts

When you make that little pencil mark on the wood indicating the exact length to cut, be sure you know which part of the mark indicates the cut line. Most carpenters make a V, with the bottom point indicating the precise spot. Using your square, draw a line through the V, and make a large X on the side of the board that will be waste. (See "Smart Tip," opposite.)

To mark long lines, snap a chalk line. Have a helper hold one end, or tack a nail and hook the clip onto it. Pull the line very taut, be sure it's in position on both ends, pick the line straight up several inches, and then let go. For long lines or a wavy surface, you may need to first snap your end and then have your helper snap theirs.

For very long lines, tack the far end and have your helper put a finger on the center point, then snap both sides.

There are usually a variety of ways to complete a building task; just be sure the way you pick will meet the local building code.

2

3

CUTTING USING A CIRCULAR SAW

You'll use your circular saw so much in the course of building a deck that you'll soon become comfortable with the tool. But don't let that make you overconfident. When it comes to power tools, complacency can be very dangerous. A circular saw can injure you in a fraction of a second if you are careless.

So take basic safety precautions: know where your power cord is at all times; be sure your blade guard works properly. Avoid kickbacks by correctly positioning the board you are cutting. Don't stand directly behind the saw when cutting—position your body to one side. And keep your blade sharp so that it's less likely to bind.

Test for Squareness

You can't always trust the degree markings on your saw's bevel gauge, so take the time to verify them before you make many cuts.

Set your saw for zero-degree bevel, and crosscut a scrap piece of 2x4. Roll one of the cut pieces over, and butt them together on a flat surface. If your blade is not square to the base, you'll see a gap at the bottom or the top of the cut equal to twice the amount your blade is out of square. (See "Test for Squareness," page 73.)

If you see a gap, unplug the saw, turn it upside down, and loosen the bevel adjustment. Set a square on the base and hold it against the blade. (See "Smart Tip," right.) Hold the square against the body of the blade, not the teeth; the teeth are offset and will throw off your adjustment. Tighten the bevel adjustment when the blade and base bear evenly on the square.

Making Accurate Square Cuts

Work on a stable surface that won't move during the cut. To avoid kickback, make sure that the cutoff can fall away without binding.

Position the Workpiece. If the cutoff will be long, don't just let it fall to the ground. If you do, the weight of the unsupported cutoff might cause the board to break off before you finish the cut, leaving a jagged piece sticking out at the end of the board. Provide something for the cutoff to fall onto that is only an inch or two below it.

Align the Blade to the Line. A spinning saw blade carves a groove through the wood—that groove is called a kerf. One edge of the kerf lines up on your cut line; the rest of the blade's width should be on the waste side of the line. Standard saw blades cut a ⅛-inch-wide kerf, though you

might find thin-kerf blades at the store, too. These blades cut kerfs around ¹⁄₁₆ inch wide. Because they are removing less wood, they require less force to make the cut.

Whatever size kerf you cut, be sure you cut to the waste side of the line so that your board will not end up shorter than you marked it.

Remember that the teeth on a circular saw blade are offset. One tooth veers to the left, the next to the right, and so on in an alternating pattern. Take this into account when you line up the blade to the cut line: first, select a tooth that's offset toward the cut line, and align the saw so that

⚲ SMART TIP

SAW SETUP

To use a circular saw safely, avoid blade binding and kickback by supporting lumber so that the cut opens and the pieces fall away as you saw. Install a new carbide-tipped blade for best results, and check the saw shoe for square.

An arbor lock freezes the blade.

A square checks the blade angle.

the tooth just touches the line. Then look at the front edge of your saw's base to find the alignment notch. Pivot the saw body until the zero-degree mark in the notch lines up with your cut line.

Make the Cut. Squeeze the trigger and saw with a light, steady pressure, allowing the blade to set the feed rate. You might want to use a cutting guide when making your first few crosscuts until you have a feel for the saw, but if you want to make a lot of cuts quickly, you should also learn to cut freehand.

This actually takes only a bit of practice. Get in the habit of keeping your eye on the leading edge of the blade, and become acquainted with the best way to align your saw. When you cut, push through smoothly, without micromanaging the cut by making little turns back and forth. Soon you will easily be making accurate cuts.

For precise cuts, use a guide. An angle square works well. (See page 73, photo 2.) Make sure your saw's base butts up well against the guide and won't easily slide over on top of it. Hold the square in place against the edge of the board, and set the base of your saw so that its edge bears firmly against the edge of the square. Slide the square and saw until the saw blade lines up with the cut line. Make sure the square doesn't slip during the cut.

SAFE CUTTING TECHNIQUES

1. WITH THE SAW UNPLUGGED, adjust your cutting depth so that just the teeth of the blade extend below the wood. This is the safest way to cut efficiently.
2. PLACE THE STOCK on 2x4 scraps to raise it off the work surface. Clamp the board in place so you can use two hands to make a safe and accurate cut. Always run the base of the saw along the supported side of the cut so that the waste can drop away at the end of the cut.

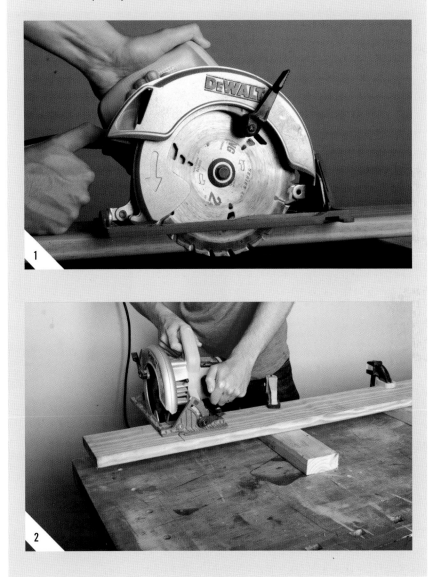

Cutting Miter Angles

A mitered cut doesn't go straight across the board—it angles across the face to leave one edge of the board longer than the other. The most common miter angle used in deck construction is 45 degrees, and it's typically used where the decking or handrails meet at a right-angle corner.

Miter cuts can be hard to get exactly right. Sometimes the blade guard hangs up on the edge of the board at the beginning of the cut, making it difficult to start straight. And you're working in an unusual position, which takes some getting used to. If your decking or railing design calls for a lot of miter cutting, you may want to consider renting a power miter saw.

Built-in seating makes the deck more functional and provides a distinct design touch.

SQUARE CUTTING

Whenever possible, keep two hands on the saw during a cut.

1. Use a square to mark the cut line. Then set the saw with the shoe parallel with the line, align the front guide notch, and start cutting.
2. You can use a square guide to help with precise cuts, but this method leaves only one hand on the saw.
3. Use a rip guide to control long cuts in line with the wood grain. The T-shaped guide is available for most circular saws.

TEST FOR SQUARENESS

Blade Set for Zero-Degree Bevel

Flip this piece.

Zero Mark Inaccurate

Gap Shows Error

Ripping

When ripping lumber with a circular saw—that is, cutting it the long way to make a board narrower—a ripping guide comes in handy. (See photo 3, page 73.) The guide has a shoe that runs along the side of the board as you cut it along its length. This is a steel guide designed to fit your particular saw and usually attaches to the base with a thumbscrew.

Cutting Dadoes and Rabbets

Technically, a dado is a groove cut across the grain of a piece of lumber. A rabbet is similar to a dado, except that a rabbet is on the end of the member. In deck building, you might cut dadoes into railing posts if you want rails to be flush to the post. You might also rabbet the top of a support post to receive a beam.

Kerf the Cut. To make a dado or rabbet, first set your circular saw blade to the exact depth of the cut; experiment on a piece of scrap wood to make sure you've got it right.

The side of a notch that cuts across the grain is called the shoulder—the cut parallel with the grain is the seat. A rabbet at the end of a piece of lumber will have a seat cut and one shoulder cut. A dado has two shoulders and a seat. Mark the shoulders of the dado (or the rabbet's single shoulder) on the piece of lumber (usually a post). Cut the shoulders; then make a number of closely spaced kerfs through the waste area. **Step 1** Use extra caution when making these shallow cuts—the saw's body and handle are higher than usual, which makes the saw less stable.

PROJECT:
CUTTING RABBETS AND DADOES

One step beyond simple butt-joint carpentry, but still short of mortise-and-tenon joinery, lapped or dadoed joints will give your deck a sleek appearance.

TOOLS & MATERIALS
- Sawhorses
- 4x4 post
- Square
- Pencil
- Circular saw
- Hammer
- Chisel
- Mallet

1 Cut a series of closely spaced kerfs with the blade set to the depth of the dado.

2 Use a hammer to break down the strips of wood. Closely spaced kerfs make this step easier.

3 Clear the wood shavings, and smooth down the ridges with a sharp chisel.

Clean up the Seat. Use a hammer or your chisel with the flat side up to knock out the bulk of the waste. **Step 2** The closer together you made the kerfs, the easier it will be to remove the waste.

Finally, use your chisel flat side down to clean up the seat of the dado or rabbet. **Step 3**

Cutting Notches

A notch is essentially a dado or rabbet, but in a board instead of a post or beam. The most common reason you'll need to cut notches in deck building is to fit a decking board around a railing post. The first step is to mark for the notch.

Mark the Notch. Start by putting the board you need to notch on top of the last full board you installed next to the post. Then slide the board over against the post, and mark the width of the notch, defined by the edges of the post, on the face of the decking board. Now measure how deep the notch needs to be, and lay out the notch with your square. Remember to include the spacing between your

decking boards as you lay it out. Keep the board in position while you make your marks so that you can visualize as you go, and you will be less likely to make the common mistake of measuring on the wrong side of the board.

Complex deck designs are attractive, but they usually require the know-how to make a variety of cuts. Practice on scrap lumber before making a new cut.

USING A WATER LEVEL

A water level is a low-tech tool that uses a basic principle of physics: that water always seeks its own level. The inexpensive tool consists of a clear, flexible plastic tube and a couple of clips to fasten the tube in place. To use it, simply fill the tube with water (and a dye to make the level easier to read), and wait for the water to stabilize at the ends of the tube. The center portion of the tube can snake up and down over the site in any direction, and the water at each end will still be dead level.

Find level over distances.

Dyed water is easier to read.

Make the Shoulder Cuts. Start the shoulder cut or cuts by cutting in with a circular saw until the kerf just hits the seat cut layout line. Because the saw's circular blade cuts a curved path through the wood, there may still be some wood to remove at the bottom of the cut. You'll need to finish the shoulder cuts using a handsaw, reciprocating saw, or saber saw. If the cut is a little uneven when you're finished with the notch, try smoothing the cuts with a chisel.

Finish the Notch. For a notch at the end of a board, make the seat cut in the same way. If the notch is in the middle of the board and the wood is straight grained with no knots in the way, make the seat cut with your chisel. Place the chisel along the seat cut line with the flat side facing away from the waste. Make sure the chisel is perpendicular to the board, and give it a sharp hammer blow.

Otherwise, make the seat cut with a saber saw or reciprocating saw. Another option is to nibble away the waste with repeated circular-saw cuts into the seat cut as you did for the shoulder cuts; then clean it up with a chisel.

Making a Plunge Cut

Occasionally you have to cut a hole in the middle of a board. You could drill a pilot hole and use a saber saw, but for a straighter line, use your circular saw to make a plunge cut (sometimes called a pocket cut).

Make sure your power cord is out of the way, and grasp the saw with both hands. Position the saw and raise up the back, using the front of the foot plate as a fulcrum. Now hold the blade guard so that the blade is exposed, and lower the saw until the blade is just above the right spot. When you are sure everything is safe and aligned, squeeze the trigger, and slowly lower the blade down to make the cut. If you do not twist as you go, you will be able to move forward with the saw after you have plunged through the board, but be sure the foot plate is resting fully on the board before you do so.

Cutting 4x4s

A 7 ¼-inch circular saw will not cut all the way through a 4x4 in one pass, so you'll need to cut from two opposing sides. Using a square, draw a line all the way around the 4x4: if the last line meets up with the first, you know your layout lines are square. Then make cuts on two opposite

ATTACHING A LEDGER

Deck Joist

Decking

Band Joist

Bolt

Metal Washers

Joist Hanger

Ledger

Flashing

💡 SMART TIP

LEDGER CHECK

To check the flatness of a ledger or house wall, nail two same-thickness blocks at each end and string a line between them. A third same-sized block should just tuck under the string. Where it doesn't fit, you'll see the margin of high and low spots.

sides. If your blade is square and you cut accurately, the entire cut will be fairly smooth, but don't expect perfection. In nearly every case, the top of a 4x4 gets covered up by other pieces of wood anyway.

If you are cutting off a 4x4 that has a piece of lumber, such as a built-up girder or outside joist, attached to it, first cut whatever you can get at with a circular saw to remove most of the waste; then finish the cut with a handsaw or reciprocating saw. In many cases you can use the second piece of lumber as a guide for the saw.

Cutting notches around posts and making connections with dadoes and rabbets leads to a well-built deck that has crisp, clean-looking joints.

CUTTING POSTS

Most do-it-yourselfers don't have a circular saw with enough capacity to cut through a 4x4 support post in one pass. That leaves two options. You can use a handsaw to cut straight through, or make two passes (from opposing sides) with a standard circular saw. Take the time to make square marks around the post to serve as a guide. And because posts typically are treated lumber, remember to wear a respirator mask, gloves, and safety glasses.

NAILING

Some contractors have a one-question test for new carpenters: they just hand the prospective employee a hammer and watch how he grips it. If the guy wraps his thumb around the shaft, he's in, but if he extends the thumb up the handle toward the head, he's out. The second grip puts less power in each swing and can result in serious damage to the tendons in the wrist. Good nailing technique, once learned, becomes second nature.

💡 SMART TIP

PREDRILLING

Where you have to make a butt joint between boards, predrill each end at a slight angle to avoid splitting the wood as you drive nails. On a long deck, be sure to stagger butt joints so that they don't line up and fall on only one or two joists.

Predrill each board at butt joints.

Nails won't split predrilled boards.

PNEUMATIC NAILING

To make sure your compressor can handle a framing nailer, check out the specs. A nailer needs 3 cubic feet per minute (cfm) of air at 90 pounds per square inch (psi).

1. Air-powered nailers speed work by firing nails from a clip that you slip into a slot below the handle. An air compressor powers the tool.
2. The most important safety feature on a pneumatic nailer is a lock-out safety tip. This keeps the tools from firing accidentally, even if you squeeze the trigger.

Reducing Stresses and Misses

Many handymen and even some pro carpenters do not have good nailing technique. A common mistake is to hold the hammer too stiffly, with the wrist locked in place. Instead, let your wrist flex a little, and finish each stroke with a snap of the wrist. Spend some time practicing; as you gain confidence, you will become more relaxed, and letting the wrist flex will come naturally.

Start with a hammer weight that feels comfortable when you swing it, weighing maybe 16 or 20 ounces. Hold the nail in place, and hit it once or twice until it can stand on its own. Then drive it home with several powerful strokes.

Avoiding Splits

Whenever you are nailing near the end of a board (or near what will be the end once the board is cut off), take precautions to minimize splitting. Remember that any little split you see now will only get larger in time; and some spots that look OK now can develop splits later.

There are two techniques. First, you can predrill each hole. This may seem bothersome, but if you can do a whole row of nails at once, it really doesn't take much time. And the extra 15 minutes you spend now will mean a much better-looking deck for years to come. Use a drill bit that's slightly smaller than the diameter of your nail shaft.

Another less effective but easier technique is to blunt the nail before driving it. Hold the nail upside down against a solid surface, and tap the tip a few times with your hammer to blunt it. This reduces the outward strain that the nail puts on the board.

Skewing

If you're driving two nails through a decking board and into the joist below, skew the nails, or angle them toward each other a little. This creates a stronger connection by hooking the boards together and reduces the possibility of splitting.

Toenailing

Most of the time, when two boards need to be joined at a right angle, you drive a nail through the face of one board into the other.

But sometimes the face into which you would prefer to nail is inaccessible, or the piece you have to nail through is too thick. In cases like this, toenail the pieces together.

Toenailing means nailing at an angle through the end of one board into the face of another. Position an 8d or 10d nail about 1 ½ inches from the end of the board. Get the nail started; then adjust it to a steep angle so the tip will come out near the center of the board's end grain. If possible, drive two nails on each side of the board.

Toenailing works well for nonstructural connections and positioning boards temporarily, but don't depend on toenails to secure a joint that carries loads. Reinforce the joint with framing hardware whenever possible.

💡 SMART TIP

TOENAILING

When you can't nail through the face of one board into the end of another, drive toenails. Start the nail at a slight angle, and after a few blows increase the angle to drive the nail in. Don't rely on toenails alone to make structural connections.

Start a toenail at a slight angle.

Increase the angle as you nail.

Decks are much like any structure: they are only as strong as the foundation on which they rest. In the case of decks, foundations usually consist of footings that reach below the frost line and that support strong posts. If the footings are strong, the joists, decking, rails, and stairs they support are likely to stay where you put them. Footings are the basis of every good deck, and building them begins with some heavy-duty digging.

LAYING OUT THE DECK

The footings will be the least visible element of your deck, so there is a temptation to treat them with nonchalance. But if footings are not set accurately, correcting those mistakes during the rest of the job could be a colossal pain. So take the time to check, cross-check, and recheck every step of the way.

It's best to have a helper for this, not only because you need someone to pull strings taut, hold one end of the measuring tape, and help make adjustments, but also because two heads are usually better than one when working.

Locate the Ledger. The ledger board is usually the primary reference point for the deck. You may even want to install the ledger first and then go on to laying out and digging the foundation. (See "Preparing for the Ledger," pages 105–109.) In any case, to lay out the footings, you first need to mark the ends of the ledger. Account for the outside joists and the fascia board, if there will be any. If you will be applying one-by fascia, for example, your ledger board will need to be 2 ¼ inches shorter than the finished deck on each end (1 ½ inches for the framing lumber plus ¾ inch for the fascia).

Draw a Reference Line. Once you have marked the ends of the ledger on your house, use a level or a plumb bob to bring the line down to a place on the house near the

---

PROJECT: 🐿🐿🐿
LAYING OUT LINES

You can tailor the 3-4-5 method for determining a square corner to suit your project: use multiples of those number, such as 9-12-15.

TOOLS & MATERIALS
- 1x4 lumber
- Saw
- Drill-driver
- Layout strings
- Measuring tape
- Level
- Plumb bob

1 Construct batter boards from the 1x4 lumber. Make pointy ends to drive the boards into the ground.

3 Measure up one leg 3 ft.; measure up the other 4 ft.; in a square corner, the connected points equal 5 ft.

4 You could also measure the diagonals. If they are equal, the corners are square.

ground. If your yard slopes appreciably downward from the house, place this mark near the ground. If the yard is fairly level, make the mark a foot or so off the ground. Attach a screw or nail to this spot so that you can tie a string line to it.

Assemble Batter Boards. For each outside deck corner you will be locating, construct two batter boards. **Step 1** Make these by attaching a 36- or 48-inch-long crosspiece squarely across two stakes. You can buy premade stakes at the lumberyard, or simply cut pieces of 2x4 or 1x4 to a point on one end. Although they are temporary and will be used only to hold string lines, the batter boards must be sturdy—there is a good chance they will get bumped around.

2 Set the batter boards in pairs a few feet outside of the actual contruction zone. Attach lines.

5 Use a plumb bob or level at the intersection of your lines to determine the location of the corner pier.

Lay Out the Perimeter. Measure from the house to determine the location of your posts, and roughly mark lines, using a string or long pieces of lumber. You want this line to run through the center of the posts, meaning that you have to take into account thicknesses of beams and outside joists: a two-by is 1 ½ inches thick, and the center of a 4x4 is 1 ¾ inches from each edge. Pound a stake into the ground or otherwise mark the location at the (again, rough) intersections of the lines.

Establish Centers at Corner Footings. Firmly pound two batter boards into the ground 16 inches or so beyond the stake in each direction. Run string lines from the house to the batter boards and from batter board to batter board in the other direction if necessary. **Step 2** On the ledger, the string line will usually be run 1 ¾ inches in from the outside ends of the ledger location.

Now check for square using the 3-4-5 method: measure along your house or ledger board, and mark a point 3 feet in from the nail holding the string. Now measure along the string and use a piece of tape to mark a spot 4 feet from the house. Finally, measure the distance between the two marks. If this is exactly 5 feet, then you have a square corner. **Step 3** If you have the room, you can be more accurate by using multiples of 3, 4, and 5 feet—for example, 9, 12, and 15.

Double-check the layout for square by taking three pairs of measurements; the two lengths of your rectangle should be equal to each other, as should the two widths and the two diagonals. **Step 4** Once you have established that your lines are square, attach them securely to the batter boards using a nail or screw to make sure that they cannot slip sideways when someone bumps into the string.

Mark for Postholes. Use a plumb bob or chalk-line box, which can double as a plumb bob, or a level to mark the spot on the ground that will be the center of each post—and therefore the center of each posthole. For the corner posts, bring a plumb line down from the intersection of your lines. **Step 5** Hold the line until the bob (or chalk-line box) stops swaying, and mark the spot with a small stake.

The next step is to clear the area of plants and sod that may get in the way of your deck. Be sure to mark the post locations before tackling the landscape work. Of course, you could also remove plants, lawn, and the like before laying out for the deck's posts. If you remove too much lawn or plants, you can go back and fill in with plantings along the deck's perimeter later.

DISTRIBUTING THE LOAD

A deck's footings must support not only the dead load of the deck—the total weight of the framing, decking, railings, benches, and planters—but also the nonpermanent weight called live load—things like snow, people, and furniture. Building codes typically mandate that a deck support 10 pounds per square foot of dead load and 40 pounds per square foot of live load. So your footings must be strong enough to handle 50 pounds per square foot of deck (8,000 pounds for a 10 x 16-foot deck.).

This load is distributed through the framing structure to the footings set in the ground. Typically, the ledger will shoulder its portion because it's bolted to the house and transfers its load to the house's foundation. However, if the house wall itself is cantilevered over the foundation, it may not be designed for additional load. In this case you may need an additional beam to support the joists at the ledger end of the house.

Loose soil may not be able to support much weight—perhaps as little as 500 pounds per square foot—which can mean that you will need more footings or wider footings than you would with firmer soil. By increasing the area of the footpad—the base of the footing where it sits on the undisturbed soil—you can compensate for loose soil. If your soil carries 800 pounds per square foot, a 12 x 12-inch footing can carry only 800 pounds, while approximately the same size footing with a 24 x 24-inch pad, at 4 square feet, can carry a whopping 3,200 pounds.

Some soils, especially those with a lot of clay, may be quite firm when dry but will lose strength when they get wet. If you suspect a problem, ask your town's building department engineer or inspector to assess the situation and make suggestions.

SITE WORK

The shade provided by your deck will usually discourage plant growth, but to be safe, lay down plastic or landscaping fabric and cover it with gravel because it will be difficult to do so after the deck is built. Landscaping fabric is usually a better choice than plastic because it does not trap moisture. If you live in an area where vegetation is extremely lush and tenacious, consider removing the grass, plants, and roots from the site by digging up all of it and hauling it away. Then fill the area with landscaping fabric and gravel. (See "Removing Sod" and "Preparing a Gravel Bed," pages 90 and 91.)

PROJECT:
REMOVING SHRUBS

You may need to remove vegetation to make way for your new deck. Save valuable shrubs and other plants by transplating to another area.

TOOLS & MATERIALS
- Shovel
- Burlap
- String
- Wheelbarrow

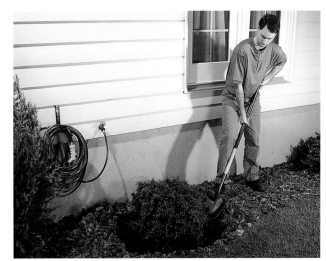

1 Use a shovel to dig under the root of the shrub. Mature plant roots can be difficult to remove.

2 Lift the plant and roots free of the hole, and place the root ball on a piece of burlap.

3 Tie the burlap with string to protect the root area, particularly if the new planting site is not ready.

Solutions for Wet Sites

You may find that your chosen deck site presents you with some extra challenges, usually in the form of water. Here's a list of common problems and typical solutions:

A Site That Is Already Wet. You can build over a moderately soggy site, once you provide drainage to prevent standing water under the deck. The deck may reduce the amount of rain that falls on the ground, but a deck also puts the site in shade, so water will evaporate more slowly, especially if your deck is very near the ground. Any water

standing under a deck for more than a few days breeds mosquitoes and can start to smell horrible on hot summer days.

The simplest way to deal with this problem is to grade the site—to make sure it is sloping uniformly away from the house with no valleys or pits. This can usually be handled simply by shifting dirt with a shovel and rake, although it is back-breaking work. You may find it useful to measure the slope using a tape measure and line level.

Deck height plays a role in the type of piers and posts needed, opposite. Check with the building inspector for code requirements in your area.

PROJECT: 🐾🐾🐾
REMOVING SOD

You can reuse sod if you are able to replant it in a day or two. Keep rolls of sod moist and in a cool place in the yard. The sod will dry out, so replant it quickly.

TOOLS & MATERIALS
- Square-bottom shovel
- Work gloves
- Wheelbarrow

1 Starting about 1 ft. outside of the layout lines, score 16-in.-wide strips of sod with the shovel.

2 Roll the sod out of the way. Include about 2 to 3 in. of soil as you roll.

3 Sod rolls can get heavy, so work with sections that you can easily manage.

Another method is to build the deck so that the deck boards all slope a bit in one direction so that most of the water runs off one edge of the deck. Of course, you'll need to deal with the water at that edge, but you can do this after the deck is built and you have a good idea how big the problem is.

For more severe problems, dig a drainage ditch to collect water and carry it away from your site. Dig the ditch about 12 inches deep at the high end, and angle it down about 1 inch for each 10 feet of trench. Put approximately an inch of gravel in the bottom of the ditch; install a perforated drainpipe (with the holes down); cover with more gravel; and top it off with soil. The far end of the pipe can emerge from the ground if you have a good slope on your property and somewhere to direct the water, or it can pour the water into an underground dry well—a large hole filled with stones and topped with gravel and soil.

Runoff from Heavy Rains. If you have downspouts that dump water on your deck site, plan to change your gutter system so that it will empty out elsewhere.

As a heavy rainfall runs off the deck, you may end up with a little water-filled moat all the way around. This is a problem that's hard to predict before you build, but it's also fairly easy to fix. For minor puddling, try ringing your deck with plants in a wood-chip bed. For larger problems, you may need a bed of gravel 6 inches deep, or you may even need to install a drainage ditch as described previously.

PROJECT: 🐌🐌🐌
PREPARING A GRAVEL BED

This method will stop weed growth, but you can also use a general herbicide in addition to these steps. Be sure to follow the instructions on the label.

TOOLS & MATERIALS
- Rake
- Shovel
- Perforated plastic or landscape fabric
- Gravel
- Wheelbarrow

1 Clear away rocks, roots, and other debris. The ground should slope away from the house.

2 Roll out the plastic. Overlap the edges by 6 in. shingle-style so that water runs away from the house.

3 Dump the gravel in several piles around the site. Rake it out to create an even surface.

Erosion from Water. On a very hilly site, you might have erosion problems; little gullies left where the rain has carried away soil are the usual telltale signs. Severe erosion can undermine your footings, causing them to sink, tip, or fail completely.

Limit erosion by planting suitable foliage to stabilize the site. Check with a local nursery for the best type of plants to use. Or you may need to provide drainage: simple trenches might solve the problem, or you may need to dig a drainage ditch.

Unstable Soil. Any concrete footings or posts sitting in a posthole must sit on undisturbed soil, which is usually reached by 16 inches below grade. However, in cold cli-mates you'll be required to dig deeper to below the local frost line to prevent the deck from heaving in the winter. Check with your building department for the required depth in your area.

Footings placed in unstable or loose soil will settle along with the soil, sometimes unevenly. Swampy soil is likely to be unstable, as is any area that's recently been excavated and backfilled, including within 5 feet of house foundation walls. If you are unsure about your soil's stability, talk with a local soil engineer, an architect, or the local building department. Experts such as these should know a good deal about local conditions and what sorts of foundations work best in the kind of soil on your site.

💡 SMART TIP

MARKING FOR UTILITIES

Before you start digging piers for your deck, check into the location of underground utility lines, such as a natural-gas main or sewer line. On a big job where you're using a contractor to do the digging, the excavation contractor should plot the exact location of underground utilities. But even then it pays to check on them yourself with the local utility company. In most areas, a company representative will come to the site and locate the lines so you can mark them with flags.

You don't see it, but a well-designed foundation will provide years of reliable service.

CANTILEVERS

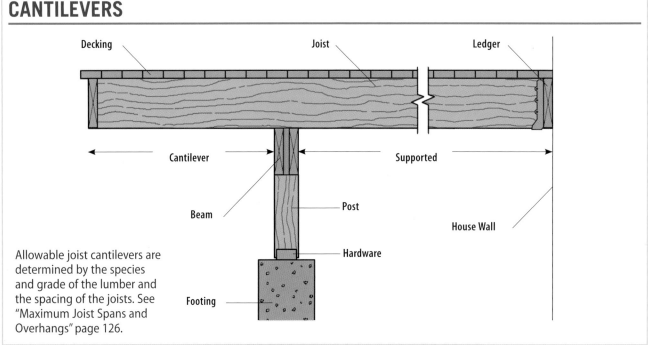

Allowable joist cantilevers are determined by the species and grade of the lumber and the spacing of the joists. See "Maximum Joist Spans and Overhangs" page 126.

FOOTINGS

Most likely you will need to pour concrete and make new footings. Consult local codes and ask the following questions when choosing a footing:

• Is it massive and stable enough?
• If you want to avoid having a floating deck, does it extend well below the frost line?
• Is it raised above the ground high enough to keep the post dry?
• Do local codes require a reinforcing bar?
• Do you need to provide drainage?

Precast Piers. If you have a stable site with little sand and no wintertime frost or you don't connect the deck to the house, you might get away with simply setting precast concrete piers directly on top of undisturbed soil instead of using footings. Remove loose soil, and provide a spot where the piers can rest on level, undisturbed soil. Make sure that this system is code-approved in your area.

Hole-Dug Piers

No Frost Line. In stable soil, you can simply dig a hole that will act as a concrete form. For areas with little frost, a hole that is 12 inches in diameter and 8 inches deep, for instance, will yield a substantial footing. Fill the hole completely with concrete, and taper it upward so that the center is an inch or two above the ground. Insert an anchor or bolt directly into the concrete.

Plan pier locations carefully.

TYPES OF FOOTINGS

Precast Pier

Hole-Dug Pier

Hole-Dug Pier with Form

Hole-Dug Tube Form

Below the Frost Line. Another option is to dig a cylindrical posthole that extends several inches below your area's frost line, and fill it with concrete. Flare the bottom of the hole a bit for stability. This method works best for footings with wide diameters.

Hole-Dug Forms

The top of a footing formed by pouring concrete into a hole is usually flush to the ground, which means that the bottom of the post is near ground level and subject to moisture. You can modify this technique by extending the form above the ground using 1x6s or pieces of plywood.

Precast Pier on Concrete. You can purchase a precast concrete pier and set it into your bed of concrete. It is a good idea to paint the bottom of the pier with concrete bonding agent before setting it 1 to 2 inches into the concrete.

Pouring into a Tube Form. This is an easy and accurate way of pouring a footing. The tubes come in a variety of sizes, though 8 inches in diameter is the most common. The forms are made of fiberboard and are easy to trim to the exact length you need. A tube form has great advantages over just digging a posthole and filling it with concrete: it can be easily extended above the ground to whatever height you desire; it makes inspectors happy because they know the exact dimensions of your footings; and it makes your job easier because you don't have to mix extra concrete. The tubes are waxed, so after the concrete sets you can easily strip away the part that shows above ground.

Post Anchors

With most anchors, you embed one part of the metal in the concrete while it's still wet. Often you just insert a J-bolt or an anchor strap and attach the rest of the anchor later, but some anchors come in one piece and you embed just the

---

POST HARDWARE

PINNED

ADJUSTABLE

BRACKETED

PRONGED

💡 SMART TIP

ALIGNING PIER HARDWARE

When you set and pour concrete piers, you may set the anchoring pin slightly off line. That's one good reason to use adjustable post hardware. Most types have a slot in the base instead of a hole. That allows you to adjust the hardware slightly in any direction to place the base of the post exactly where you want it.

FOUNDATION OPTIONS

There are prefab products that can help you build footings and piers faster. Concrete deck blocks (left) simply sit on the ground, and the deck frame tucks into cuts in the tops of the blocks. The system meets many local codes because the deck floats. It's not actually attached to the house and may even be considered a temporary structure. Be certain to check this kind of system with your local building department. The Bigfoot form (right) is a high-density plastic form that attaches to prefab pier tubes. It adds strength and stability by forming a bell-shaped foot under the pier, and sheds water away from the footing.

💡 SMART TIP

CONTINUOUS POSTS

In some situations you can set posts directly into a concrete form—for example, to help support the end of a stairway railing where it's not practical to pour another pier. But the most durable design is to set posts in hardware on top of piers.

lower portion. Look for an anchor that you can adjust laterally. Adjustable anchors give you an inch or two of play in all directions so that you can compensate for small layout errors.

Continuous Posts

You can also extend posts down into postholes. It may seem that doing this adds a lot of strength to the structure, but in the case of a mostly horizontal structure such as a deck, that is rarely the case. Nearly all the lateral strength of your deck—what will keep it from swaying—comes from the way it all ties together. Every nail, screw, and bolt you install makes it a bit firmer. In addition, you will probably gain rigidity by tying the deck to your house. So unless you are building a freestanding deck that is raised more than a couple of feet above the ground, concrete-set posts do not

add significant lateral strength.

And there are drawbacks to posts sunk in concrete or gravel: first, there's no correcting of mistakes. Second, posts set into the ground are more likely to rot. And third, they are very difficult to replace in case they get damaged. So unless you have special reason to use them elsewhere, use this type of post only for the stair rails, which often need a little extra lateral support.

However, continuous posts are required in some areas subject to earthquakes. They are also sometimes called for when the deck is raised high above the ground to make sure the post bottoms won't move. Continuous posts are often simply set into postholes that are backfilled with concrete. They can also be inserted into a large-diameter, concrete-filled tube form.

DIGGING POSTHOLES

If there are just a few holes to dig, you can do the work yourself using a posthole digger. For larger projects, however, you'll thank yourself for renting a power auger to speed up the job. Some are designed for one-person operation (though it certainly wouldn't hurt to have a helper), and the larger ones require two fairly brawny people.

Dig the Holes. Once the marker stakes are all firmly established, remove the string lines to give yourself room to dig. Whether you are using the auger or a posthole digger, if you run into a rock, you'll need a wrecking bar (also called a breaker bar or a crowbar) to break up stones or pry them loose. If you run into roots, chop at them with your posthole digger or shovel, or use branch pruners. In extreme cases, you may have to go in there with a handsaw.

Tamp the Bottom and Reattach String Lines. The bottom of your footing hole should be firm. Even if you have reached undisturbed soil, an inch or two of dirt crumbs will be left over from the digging process, so tamp the soil down with a piece of 4x4. Put your string lines back in place, recheck them for square, and double-check your footing locations.

Install the Forms. Once you have dug the holes, install the concrete forms of your choice, making sure they are secure. If you are using a fiberboard tube form, you can usually just backfill outside it with dirt to keep it stable. Some designs call for leveling all the footings with each other. To do this, first backfill all the tubes, then mark them with a water level and cut them off with a handsaw.

DIGGING OPTIONS

Working in rocky soil, you will find it handy to have a pickax, or at least a heavy-duty wrecking bar to help dislodge rocks.

1. Using a shovel is the basic and sometimes back-breaking way to dig piers. But you'll wind up moving more dirt than you need to.
2. A posthole digger has two handles that work in a scissors action to cut and scoop dirt. They make a neater hole with a smaller diameter.
3. The power auger is a tool you can rent. There are one- and two-person models that churn through the dirt. Both are a handful to operate, but they are efficient.

Add Gravel and Rebar. Pour 2 to 3 inches of gravel into the bottom of the concrete form.

If your building inspector requires reinforcing bar, this is the time to add it. Usually, this means pounding a long piece of the rebar into the ground at the bottom of the hole so that it runs through the center of the form. Do it carefully so the rebar will be at or near the center of the concrete. Be sure it does not stick out of the form and will not interfere with the part of your post anchors that you'll embed into the wet concrete. Ask the inspector to specify a size for the rebar; also inquire about rebar spacing.

POURING CONCRETE

Now it's time to begin forming a permanent part of your deck. Though backfilled footings aren't too impressive looking, they are important to the overall stability of your deck.

Estimating

Concrete is sold by the yard; a cubic yard is 3 feet by 3 feet by 3 feet, or 27 cubic feet, and there are 1,728 cubic inches in a cubic foot.

For box forms, multiply the inside length times the inside width times the depth, all measurements in inches. Divide the result by 1,728 to convert into cubic feet, then divide by 27 to convert into cubic yards.

PROJECT: 🐾🐾
MIXING CONCRETE

To make this dusty work go smoothly, pour in about two-thirds of the water to start; then mix and add the rest slowly. Follow the directions on the bag for mixing.

TOOLS & MATERIALS
- Concrete mix
- Work gloves
- Wheelbarrow
- Hoe
- Bucket
- Water

1 Whether you use premixed ingredients or combine them yourself, do the mixing in a wheelbarrow.

2 Mix the dry ingredients with a hoe. Create a crater in the center of the pile.

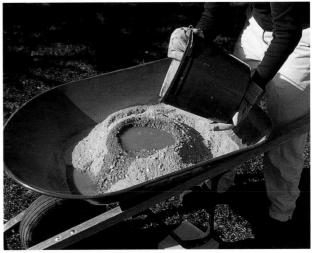

3 Pour in the water slowly, following the directions on the bag. Too much water ruins the mixture.

To find the volume of cylindrical footings, the formula is: volume = $\pi r^2 h$. That means that you multiply pi (3.14) times the radius squared times the height to get cubic inches. Then you convert that into cubic feet by dividing by 1,728; then divide by 27 to obtain cubic yards.

Getting Concrete

There are two basic ways to get concrete ready to pour on site: you can add water to premixed bags or mix your own from piles of raw materials. (See the "Smart Tip" opposite for dealing with large amounts of concrete.)

Using Premixed Concrete. You can buy bags that have the cement, sand, and gravel already mixed. A wheelbarrow makes a good container for adding water and mixing. Each bag yields about ⅔ cubic foot, so a typical 8-inch-by-42-inch cylindrical footing will take two bags, and ½ cubic yard will require about 20 bags.

Mixing Your Own. For in-between amounts or for sites where truck delivery would be difficult, consider mixing your own concrete in a wheelbarrow or on a sheet of plywood. Or, for larger amounts, you can rent an electric mixer.

Mixing and Pouring

The basic technique is the same here whether you are using premixed concrete in bags or combining your own dry ingredients. You can build or buy a mixing trough, but the easiest method is simply to mix right in the same wheelbarrow you will use to transport the concrete. (See "Mixing Concrete," page 97.)

Mix Dry Ingredients. If you're mixing your own dry ingredients, shovel them right into the wheelbarrow. Use three shovelfuls of gravel, two of sand, and one of cement. Mix the dry ingredients thoroughly with a concrete hoe even if you are using premixed bags. If you have a large wheelbarrow, try mixing two premixed bags at once.

Add Water. Hollow out a hole in the center of the dry ingredients and pour in some water. Mix thoroughly; then slowly add more water, testing the concrete as you go for the right consistency. Don't make it soupy, even though more water makes mixing easier. It should be just fluid enough to pour into your form.

Pour and Strike Off the Concrete. Pour the concrete directly from the wheelbarrow, or scoop it into your forms with a shovel. Clean up any excess as you go. Poke a 2x2 or a piece of rebar deep down into the concrete in several places to get out any air bubbles. Once you have filled the form, strike it off with a scrap piece of 2x4 to obtain a smooth, level top surface.

Install Post Anchor Hardware. Install your J-bolt or post anchor immediately. Wiggle it a bit as you place it to get rid of air bubbles. Then line up the hardware with your string line and a plumb bob to ensure it will be in the center of the post. Be certain that it is sticking up the right distance out of the concrete, and use a torpedo level to make sure it's plumb. Loosely cover the top of your footings with plastic so they won't dry too quickly. You can start to build on the footings after 24 hours. But remember that concrete takes three weeks to fully cure, and it will be prone to chipping if you bang into it during the first few days.

PROJECT: 🐿️🐿️
BUILDING PIERS

Backfill fiberboard forms once they are in the hole to hold them steady, eliminating the need for braces.

TOOLS & MATERIALS
- Form tubes
- Level
- Concrete
- Trowel
- Post anchor hardware
- Wrenches

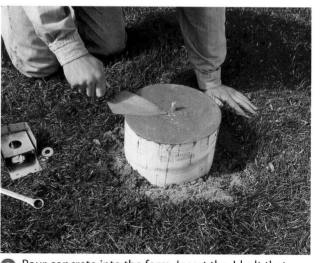

3 Pour concrete into the form. Insert the J-bolt that comes with the hardware into the center of the form.

Installing Posts in Postholes

If you choose to sink your posts into the ground, give the buried section an extra dose of preservative, especially the open end grain.

Dig Flared Holes. For additional stability, flare your holes so that they are 3–4 inches wider at the bottom than at the top. Throw 2–3 inches of gravel in the bottom for drainage. Another option is to use a large-diameter concrete tube form and put the post inside before pouring the concrete. This makes more efficient use of concrete and makes it possible to bring the concrete several inches above grade.

Check and Brace the Posts. You will let the posts run wild and cut them to their exact height after the concrete is set.

For now, however, use a line level to make sure that all the posts are sitting high enough. Align them with your layout strings, and plumb them in both directions. Then attach two braces to each post.

Pour the Concrete. As you pour, poke a long pole or piece of reinforcing bar into the concrete on all four sides of the post to release any air bubbles. This is especially important when the post extends down inside the footing and the concrete forms a long, narrow ring around the post. Stop pouring and do this a few times until the form is filled with concrete.

Use a trowel to slope the top of the concrete upward, creating a small incline so that rainwater drains away from the wood.

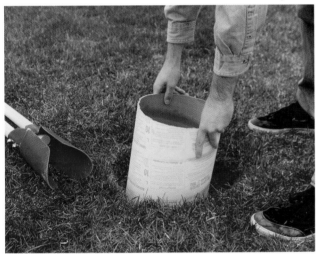

1 Place a cut tube in the hole. The top of the tube should project 6 in. above grade.

2 Level the tube, and backfill to hold the tube steady. Check for level while backfilling.

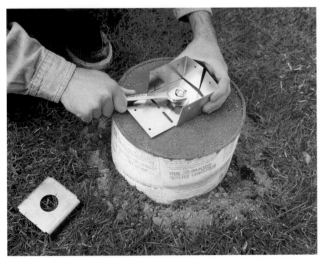

4 After the concrete cures, attach the rest of the post anchor hardware.

💡 SMART TIP

DELIVERY BY TRUCK

If you need ¾ cubic yard or more, you may be better off having it delivered in a truck, even if the concrete yard's minimum is 1 full yard. You need to be completely prepared before the truck arrives. Map out where the truck will park and where the chute of the truck will reach to fill the wheelbarrow.

The ledger, posts, and beams are the components that secure the deck to the house and the ground. They carry the structural load of your new deck. In most cases, looks are not important because these components are usually hidden, but what is important is selecting the right materials to do the job and installing these elements correctly.

Once you have the ledger and beam in place, the deck's joists should go down smoothly. Install a solid layer of joists, and the decking that rides across them will be solid underfoot.

For help with selecting the right tools and materials for the project or to brush up on some of the construction techniques deck building requires, see Chapters 2, 3, and 4.

FRAMING BASICS

In nearly every case, pressure-treated lumber is the best choice for framing a deck. Treated wood is infused with chemicals that resist rot, and it costs only a little more than untreated framing lumber. For highly visible areas such as outside joists, you can pick the best-looking boards in the pile. Or you can hide treated outside joists behind fascia boards made of redwood, cedar, or composite boards.

Redwood and cedar are occasionally used for framing. These woods are naturally rot resistant and more attractive than treated wood. But they are more expensive and not as strong, so these woods are typically reserved for visible areas such as decking and railing.

A basic deck frame is made of posts, a beam, joists, and a ledger. Posts rest on your footings and are usually made of 4x4s; for a raised deck, 6x6s usually are required. The main beam usually rests on top of the posts, although to create a ground-hugging deck, it can also rest directly on level footings. This main support beam can be a solid four-by or two or more two-bys. Joists that support the decking usually rest on top of the main beam on one end, and are attached to the ledger board at the other end. Joists and ledgers are made of two-by lumber and are generally of the same width. The ledger is attached to the house.

Connections at the ledger, posts, and girders will determine the stability of your new deck.

SMART TIP

SPACING OPTIONS

Spacing of framing members must be approved by the building inspector, but you have a lot of leeway in the design stage. Generally, if you use fewer piers and posts, you will need a larger beam to span the spaces between them. This approach can be an advantage on sloping sites and where digging even two piers is a difficult job. Conversely, if you use more piers and posts in the design, a smaller beam will be strong enough to span the shorter distances between supports. Practical issues such as lumber costs can have a big impact on spacing, but you can alter the framing plan based on looks, too.

SAFETY

SAFE HANDLING OF MATERIALS

Get product data sheets for any of the materials you use on your deck. Many materials, such as treated lumber, require extra precaution when cutting, sanding, and disposing of the material. The data sheet should outline any special requirements.

SIZING AND SPACING FRAME MEMBERS

The required span for a piece of lumber is the distance it can safely traverse without being supported underneath. If you exceed a required span, your deck will feel flimsy and there is a good chance it will sag over time. It is also unlikely to pass final inspection by the building department.

The charts "Dimension Lumber Deck Beam Spans for Joists Framing from One Side Only" and "Maximum Joist Spans and Overhangs" on pages 123 and 126, are based on the International Residential Building Codes (IRC), which have been adopted by most building departments in the United States.

Use the span charts to help you plan the deck, for example to decide whether you want a massive beam with only a few post supports or a smaller beam with more posts. Before designing the structure of your deck, however check with your local building department to make sure your municipality adheres to the IRC—while unlikely, it is possible your municipality has different code requirements. For example, the deck designs included at the end of this book were approved by building departments in the municipalities in which they were built. It's possible that some of those decks may not comply with the IRC or the code used in your area.

Also remember that the same sizes of different wood species can have different requirements. Not all 4x12s have the same ratings. Generally, stronger woods such as Douglas fir can span greater distances than weaker woods such as cedar.

You'll also find that the suggested spans in this book (and in literature from your building department) are based on normal loads. If you plan to place heavy objects on your deck, such as soil-filled planters or a hot tub, you'll need to reduce the spans or beef up the lumber sizes, or both.

You will need to determine the span of the beam and the span of the joists. Then you can select the right materials for the job. Once you have determined the spans, spacing, and species of your beams and joists, include this information on the drawings you'll submit to the building department to get your permit to build the deck.

Joists

In planning your joists, keep in mind the size and lumber type of the joists, as well as how far apart they will be spaced. This is called the on-center, or o.c., measurement.

Cantilevering. It's common practice to have joists cantilever over a beam by a foot or two as a way of hiding the beam and its supporting posts, or just making them less prominent. Codes specify maximum joist overhangs based on the wood species, spacing, and dimensions of the joists with a maximum cantilever of one-quarter of the joist's allowable span—the distance between the beam and the other end of the joist. As a practical matter, there's usually no good reason for a long cantilever. The chart "Maximum Joist Spans and Overhangs" on page 126 specifies the cantilevers allowed by the International Residential Code, but check with your local building department in case it adheres to a different code.

Beams

House framing may contain several types of major beams, although on almost all decks there is only one that supports the outer ends of the joists. You can sometimes reduce the beam size by adding a post or two, thereby saving money in lumber. But that savings is likely to be overshadowed by the extra labor of digging and pouring additional piers. Allowable beam spans depend on the size and type of the lumber, as well as the span distance of the joists that rest on it.

Bear in mind that the building department may consider a beam made of two 2x8s to be just as strong as a 4x8, or they may consider it weaker. Built-up strength also depends in part on how the built-up beam is constructed.

Posts. Unless your deck will carry an unusual amount of weight, 4x4 posts will work if your deck is 4 feet or less above the ground. Larger 6x6 posts may be required for decks over 4 ft. high, and code in some areas now require posts to be at least 6x6 in all cases.

Ledger

The ledger usually makes the best starting place for laying out the whole deck, so you may want to install it before you dig your footing holes. It is a major supporting member, so it must be firmly attached to the house. Make your ledger of the same two-by material as your joists. Pick a straight board that is not cupped, so the joist ends can fit snugly against it. This piece of lumber is crucial because it does two jobs. It carries a lot of weight and connects the deck to the house. There are several ways to install a ledger, but the most important consideration is safety. You must be sure that the ledger is securely bolted to the house framing, typically to the system of floor joists. You can't secure deck ledgers to siding or sheathing alone. And you can't secure ledgers through siding unless it is flat plywood.

LEDGER OPTIONS

No matter what kind of siding you have, there is a way to attach a ledger board securely. But you need to be sure that water will drain past the ledger, and not into the house. Do this by flashing the ledger so that water drains off the front face or by adding spacers between the ledger and the house so that water drains straight through. You also need to be sure that the ledger is solidly connected to the framing of the house.

DIRECTLY ON SIDING

FLASHED ON SHEATHING

LEDGER DESIGNS

The ledger can be a trouble spot because rain and snow can collect between it and the house and damage both. In particular, if you have beveled horizontal siding or shingles, simply attaching the ledger onto the siding is an invitation for trouble because water will collect in the V-shaped channel between the siding and the ledger. To prevent these problems, consider one of four common methods for attaching a ledger. (See below.)

If you will be attaching to a flat surface (either siding or masonry), simply attach the ledger tightly against the house so that water cannot seep behind it. This is the simplest solution, and it works well if you can really squeeze the ledger tightly to the house. However, there is a good chance that your inspector will want a more water-resistant detail with flashing.

For joining a ledger to a wall with siding (either flat or beveled horizontal), cut out a section of siding, and fit the ledger into it. In this case, you need to provide flashing that keeps water out of the opening in the siding and forces it to run down the face of the ledger.

For stucco or masonry surfaces, cut a channel above the ledger where you can tuck in the upper edge of flashing.

Another option is to install several washers or shims of treated lumber behind the ledger at each lag screw, thereby providing a space between the ledger and the house. This way water runs easily between them and the ledger, and the house wall can dry out between rains.

All these methods have proved successful in various parts of the country. Opinions vary on which solution is best, and your inspector may favor one or another. If he orders you to do it a certain way, it's a good idea to just do what he says. The point is to avoid having moisture trapped against the ledger or the house framing for long periods.

Preparing for the Ledger

If any of the following steps do not apply to the method of installing a ledger that you're using, just skip to the next step.

Locate the Ledger. It may sound like a good idea to have your deck surface level with your interior flooring, but if you do so, you will be inviting rain and snow to seep under your threshold and into your house. So plan to have a small step down. Even 1 inch will go a long way toward keeping your home drier in most regions. You can make a larger step, but it should be no more than the step in a standard interior stairway. Anything over 6 inches may feel awkward.

But the main consideration should be to locate the ledger where it will be easy for you to bolt it directly and securely into the house floor framing. This should be possible with a step down of only an inch or two. If the step is much greater, the ledger may line up against the house foundation instead of the floor framing. You can still attach it securely, but the job is much easier when you can bolt wood frame to wood frame.

To locate your ledger, measure down from the level of your house floor to the level of the decking. This is the amount of your step. Then add in the decking thickness:

WASHER STANDOFF

PLYWOOD STANDOFF

Spacer Detail

1 ½ inch for nominal two-by decking; 1 inch for nominal ¾ decking. Mark this level, and extend it along the house wall to mark the length of the ledger. You want this line to be perfectly level. (See "Smart Tip" on page 113.) For purposes of drainage, you usually want the deck to slope away from the house rather than alongside it.

To make marks that will ensure that your ledger is level throughout its length, either use a water level or set your carpenter's level atop a straight board. (Because few boards are perfect, it is best to place the level near the center of the board.) You can also use an electronic level. Some of these project a beam of light that is easy to mark.

Once you have made several marks, snap chalk lines between them, and double-check those lines for level.

Mark for Outer Joists, Fascia, and Decking. It helps to visualize all the dimensions of your finished deck, so mark for every lumber piece that will go up against your house. This means adding 1 ½ inches for the outside joist, plus ¾ inch for fascia (if any), plus the distance you plan to overhang your decking (if any) on each side of the deck.

Cut Out the Siding. If the ledger installation requires removing some of your siding, mark an outline for the cutout, taking into account everything that will fit into it: the ledger, the end of the outside joists, an extra ⅛ inch in width for the flashing (if any), and possibly the end of the fascia—but not the decking. Marking will be easier if you

tack a piece of ledger-width material in place and draw a pencil line around it.

Cut the line with a circular saw. If you have aluminum or vinyl siding, follow manufacturer's directions; often it works best to reverse your circular saw blade when cutting these materials. Set the blade so that it cuts just through the siding and not much more. You will need to make a plunge cut to start. For wood siding, use a hammer and chisel to neatly finish the cutout at the corners. For vinyl siding, finish the corner cuts with a utility knife. Use snips for aluminum. When making a vertical cut across horizontal beveled siding, it may help to tack on a piece of 1x4 to provide a level guide for your circular saw. Seal up the area you have just cut out with felt (tar paper) or ice and water barrier so that no bare wood sheathing is exposed.

Check for Straightness. Check the surface against which you will be placing the ledger by holding a string against its length. If anywhere along the length, there is a gap of more than ¼ inch between the string and the wall, tack shims to the house so that when you attach the ledger it will be straight. You can also use a string with blocks to check the flatness of your ledger once it's installed. (See "Smart Tip" on page 113.) Remember that unless you cut every joist to fit (a job that you don't want to do), the front edge of your deck will follow the contours of your ledger.

Install Flashing. If you have cut out a section of siding,

(Text continues on page 108.)

LEDGER INSTALLATION

LEAK-PROOF DESIGN — No Drain Gap — No Flashing — Open Seam

WEATHERPROOF DESIGN — Flashing — Rabetted Joint

💡 SMART TIP
LEDGER SETUP

You can tack joists to marks on the ledger and install hangers later or set hangers ahead of time.

PROJECT:
REMOVING SIDING

You have some leeway in placing your ledger on the wall. The step down from house level to deck level can be between roughly 1 inch and 6 inches. Set the ledger where you can bolt it securely to the house framing.

TOOLS & MATERIALS
- Water level
- Pencil
- Circular saw
- Wood shims
- Gloves
- Hacksaw
- blade
- Prybar or hammer

1 Establish the ends of your ledger; then find level points at each end and snap a chalk line.

2 Set your saw to cut through the siding but not the sheathing. Make cuts at each end of the ledger.

3 Pry the siding up, and insert wedges to hold it up. Use a hacksaw blade to cut nails.

4 Make the horizontal cut with your saw. Set the blade to siding depth to avoid cutting the sheathing.

5 The siding should come out easily. If it does not, use a pry bar and hammer to ease it out.

(Continued from page 106.)

install flashing that is the same length as the cutout. (It will cover the top of the outside joists as well, so snip the front edge to make it fit over them.) Tuck the flashing up under the siding. Before you slide the flashing in, make sure you have a clear path for it by prying the upper siding piece loose and removing all nails in the flashing's path. Handle the flashing carefully because it bends easily. Gently renail the siding back into position to hold the flashing in place.

In situations where the ledger is attached over the siding instead of cutting out the siding, you might be tempted to simply set the flashing over the ledger and then glue it in place with roofing cement or caulking. But this will leave you with a problem spot: the cement will probably come loose over time, and it will be difficult to repair because decking will be in the way. So it is best to find a way to tuck in the upper flange. For beveled horizontal siding or shingles, you may have to buy extra-wide flashing, depending on how far above your ledger the next piece of siding or row of shingles is located.

For stucco or masonry, buy or make flashing that has an extra bend so that a lip can be tucked straight into the side of the house. Using a masonry blade on your circular saw, cut a straight line into which the flashing can be inserted.

Depending on the hardness of your siding material, this may require several passes. Be sure to wear protective eyewear. Over stucco or masonry, it's often easier to put the flashing in place after the ledger is installed.

A variety of ready-made flashing is available. One of the most practical has a Z-shape that bends twice—once to slide up under the siding and once to cover the face of your ledger. This last, front-most portion of the flashing need only be wide enough to keep water from wicking between the flashing and the top of the ledger. Remember that the joists will be smashed up against it, so it is best if the flashing comes down the ledger at a right angle to protect the horizontal surface of the ledger.

Cut and Mark the Ledger. Cut the ledger, which runs at one end of the joists, and the header joist, which runs at the other, to the same length. If your deck is not rectangular, they will not be the same length, of course.

Because the ledger and header joist run parallel with

For a tight seal, tuck flashing under the siding and over the top of the ledger.

each other, and the joists are perpendicular to them both, it makes sense to cut the header joist and ledger at the same time, and to mark them both for the joist locations before you install the ledger. After marking the tops, use a square to extend the lines down the faces of the ledger and header. Don't forget to make an X indicating on which side of the line the joists will be installed. (See "Smart Tip" on page 106.)

ATTACHING THE LEDGER

Whether you are attaching to wood, masonry, or stucco, it is important to fasten the ledger securely. Remember that the ledger bears a lot of weight. While about half of the entire deck load away from the house may bear on the main beam and support posts, the remaining load bears on the ledger. Without a beefy beam and a row of posts for support, the ledger must be strong enough to transfer the

LEDGER BOLTS

When you lag the ledger to the house frame, you can recess the washers and lag heads flush to the ledger surface, so it won't matter if one of the joist hangers falls in the same location. Drill the counter bore first; then drill the pilot hole for the lag screw or bolt shank. Be aware that some codes don't allow recessing lags. In this case, you'll need to plan your bolt locations so they don't fall behind joists. Also, code often requires predrilling to two diameters—first with a ⅜-inch bit all the way through the rim joist so the bolt threads will bite into the joist. And then with a ½-inch bit so the bolt will slip through the ledger without a chance of splitting it.

💡 SMART TIP

FLOATING DECKS

Some decks, including decks built next to cantilevered house walls, don't have a ledger and aren't connected to the house, although they might look as though they are. An island deck built right next to the house gives the illusion of a standard deck but skips the ledger work and adds an extra beam near the house. Be sure to check local codes about floating decks.

POSITIONING THE POSTS

When installing posts you have choices to make about how they will be supported at the bottom and how they will be attached to beams. At the bottom, you can either sink posts into holes the way you might with fence posts and secure them with concrete poured into the holes, or you can set them on concrete piers. Local codes may specify one method over another, and of course that's the final word. But using concrete piers generally provides more stability and durability. It's the way most houses are built, with a concrete footing and foundation to support the structure above. Concrete piers also keep the post a few inches above ground, which reduces the possibility of rot.

You have three methods to choose from for attaching beams to posts. One is to bolt the beams through the post. Typically with this method the beam consists of two pieces of lumber with the top of the posts sandwiched between. With this method the bolts bear the load, and some local codes require the addition of -L-brackets bolted to the post and under the beam members. A more common method is to cut the posts to height so they form level supports directly under the beams. The third method is a hybrid: the top of the post is notched to accept the beam. (See "Cutting Dadoes and Rabbets" page 74.) The beam is through-bolted to the posts. (See "Attaching Beam to Notched Post," opposite.)

Here is a rundown of the basic procedure for the most common and probably the most durable system.

PROJECT: 🦫🦫🦫
INSTALLING LEDGERS ON WOOD

For the most secure connection, bolt through or lag into framing. Don't secure the ledger to the siding alone.

TOOLS & MATERIALS
- Ledger board
- End joist
- Clamps
- Combination square
- Pencil
- Saw
- Flashing
- Drill and bits
- Props
- Ratchet wrench
- 4-in. lag screws

1 Transfer the layout marks for the joists from the ledger to the end joist.

2 Predrill and countersink holes for fasteners. This will guarantee clearance for joist hangers later.

3 Prop ledger into position, and drive lag screws with a ratchet, or install carriage bolts if possible.

ATTACHING BEAM TO NOTCHED POST

When beams are attached to the side of a post, they must be fastened with a bolt that goes all the way through the members with a nut on the other side. Traditionally, ½-inch carriage bolts were used for this purpose. Now you can use screw-bolts that require no predrilling. You place a special washer over the screws then drive them through the beam and post (top). Then you place a cap on the other side (bottom). Drive the screw a bit more and the cap tightens without putting a wrench on it.

💡 SMART TIP

LEDGER CHECKS

You need to check for level, of course, but also for flatness against the wall. Do this using three blocks. Tack one at each end, connected by a tightly drawn string. Use the third to check the margin between the string and the ledger. If the ledger is flat, the margin will be the same all along the ledger.

Check the ledger for level.

Check the ledger for flatness.

Beam on Pier-Supported Post

Check for Rough Length. In most situations, you will cut the post to exact height later. But first make sure that every post will be tall enough. Use a line level, water level, or long piece of lumber with a level on top to find out how high each post needs to be. (It is best to slope your deck slightly down coming away from the house, but this measurement is too small to worry about at this point.) Give yourself at least a few extra inches and you won't have to worry.

Locate and Attach Post Anchors. If you are using adjustable post anchors, now is the time to fine-tune their positions. Most hardware has a slot or some other way of making an adjustment. This way, if the threaded anchors fixed in the concrete piers are not exactly in line with each other, you can slide the post hardware one way or the other before fastening them in place.

The best way to do this is to confirm your measurements from the house wall and double-check for square. Then string a line or snap a chalk line between the outermost piers. Center one post anchor (which may not be exactly centered relative to the anchor bolt), and tighten it in place. Most hardware has a platform inside the bracket, which keeps the post slightly elevated and out of standing water. Typically, you fasten down the base plate before inserting the platform. But you should follow the manufacturer's directions. Then repeat the process at the other end, and use your string line to make sure that any intermediate anchors fall into line.

Insert and Fasten the Posts. Make a square cut on the bottom of each post to be sure that it seats firmly in the anchor. If you are not using pressure-treated lumber, even though that is the best policy on posts, it will help to flood the freshly cut end grain with wood preservative.

If the posts are short, they may stand by themselves in the hardware. But on most projects, you'll need to attach a few temporary braces. You don't need to plumb the posts exactly at this point; just keep them roughly plumb and stable as you fasten the anchors.

The procedure may vary from one manufacturer to another, but a typical anchor has one open side (so you can slide in the post). When the post base is in position, you simply bend up that metal flap with pliers. Then drive a few nails through the perforated holes in the hardware flaps to lock the post in place. Even though the post is roughly in place, you may want to wait until it is set and braced before driving all the nails. (See "Anchoring Posts," page 116.)

You don't want to pound away on the nails and possibly dislodge the anchor or, worse yet, crack the concrete pier. To guard against this, you install the anchors with structural wood screws. Or you can back up the post with a heavy hammer as you nail on the other side. The extra

(Text continues on page 117.)

PROJECT:
PLACING RAISED-DECK POSTS

Ground contact can foster rot; use treated wood that is rated for ground contact, even if you plan on installing post anchors to hold the post above ground level.

TOOLS & MATERIALS
- 2x4
- Level
- Pencil
- String
- Batter boards
- Posthole digger
- Posts
- Clamps
- Drill & bits
- Stakes & braces
- Sledge hammer
- 2 ½-in. screws

💡 SMART TIP

PLUMBING POSTS

Plumbing posts can be challenging because you need to manage a level, a brace, and a clamp at the same time. In most cases, you must adjust a pair of braces while adjusting the posts and the level. A handy tool called a post level clips onto the post and reads in both directions at once, so you can make adjustments and add braces with both hands free.

1 To locate the posts, start from a reference point on the house and plumb down.

2 Extend layout strings from plumb marks to batter boards. Mark the hole locations.

3 Remove the strings, and start digging the hole. Dig below the frost line.

4 The type of footing that supports the post will be determined by the local building code.

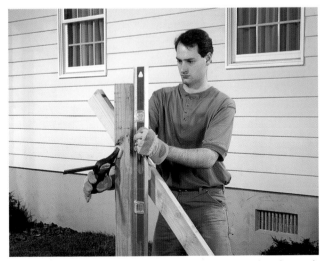

5 To brace the post, attach a 2x4 to a ground stake and clamp it to the post.

6 Brace the post in two places to keep it steady. Plumb the post and secure the braces to the stake with 2½-in. screws.

PROJECT: ANCHORING POSTS

With pier and post anchors, wood stays off wet ground that can cause rot. It is important to square off the bottom of the post so that the post is plumb when in position.

TOOLS & MATERIALS
- Post
- Sawhorses
- Square
- Circular Saw
- Post hardware
- Wrenches
- Hammer
- Nails

1 Square off the bottom of the post so that it seats securely in the post anchor.

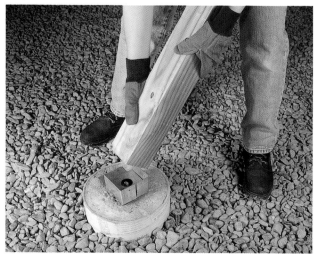

2 Set the post in the anchor. Adjustable hardware provides some play in the anchor position.

3 Close the anchor around the post, and drive nails through the anchor into the post.

💡 SMART TIP

BRACING

Even short 4x4 posts for a deck beam near ground level need to be braced securely in two directions. Drive pointed stakes into the ground about 2 feet away from the post as shown. Attach a 2x4 to each stake, and extend it up the sides of the post at a 45-degree angle. Secure with screws.

(Continued from page 114.)

weight, say, from a sledgehammer that you hold in one hand, absorbs a lot of the impact and keeps the post from shifting as you use a standard hammer in your other hand.

Plumb and Brace the Post. This job is easiest with two people because there is a lot to do at the same time. You need to release the temporary braces, fine-tune the plumb position of the post (checking and rechecking in two directions), and lock up the final position with a clamp before securing the braces.

Ideally, you can have one person check the level and, once the post is perfectly plumb, tell the other person to drive in a screw attaching the brace. Do this again for the other brace, and then recheck the first direction. Don't be surprised if you have to redo things once or twice. But once you have achieved perfect plumb, drive in more screws for stability—at least two for each attaching point. Then you can drive in the rest of the nails to hold the post anchor to the post.

(Text continues on page 119.)

POST ALTERNATIVES

The most common setup is a series of posts topped with a beam. But there are other options. For example, you can make a sandwich with the beam by attaching boards to opposite sides of a post. With the boards level, you can drill through the sandwich and bolt the components together. In this design, you need to cut the post flush with the tops of the boards. Another approach is to let the post run long. You can use the extension of several feet to support other parts of the deck, such as railings and built-in benches.

Y-BRACING

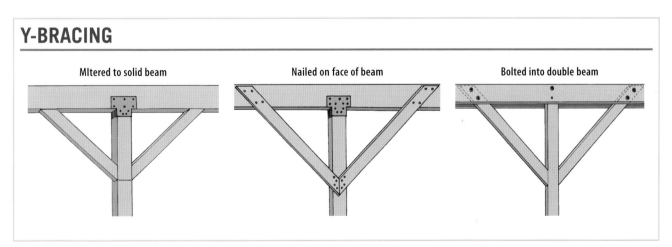

| MItered to solid beam | Nailed on face of beam | Bolted into double beam |

PROJECT: 🐀🐀🐀
ESTABLISHING POST HEIGHT

Few homeowners have levels long enough to span from the house to the posts. Extend your 4-ft. level by placing it on top of a straight board.

TOOLS & MATERIALS

- 2x4
- 4-ft. level
- Joist & beam stock
- Pencil
- Combination square
- Circular saw
- Post-cap hardware
- Drill & bits
- 1 ¼-in. deck screws or 8d nails
- Hammer

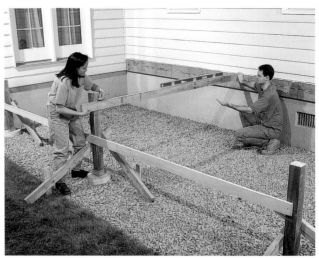

1 Use a straight 2x4 and level to mark the elevation of the ledger on the posts.

2 Use a section of joist stock to measure down from the mark to find the bottom edge of the joist.

3 Using beam stock, measure down to find the bottom of the beam. This will be the top of the posts.

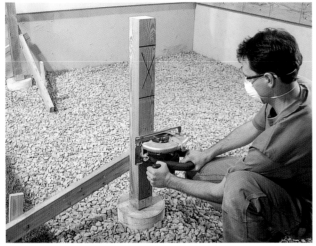

4 Mark a cut line with a square. Use a circular saw to cut the posts.

5 Install the post caps to each post, and secure with screws or nails. Predrill nail holes.

(Continued from page 117.)

If you are working solo, set up ground stakes and 2x4 braces at 90 degrees to each other. Drive a screw through the base of the 2x4 into the stake, pivot the brace onto the post at about a 45-degree angle, and secure it with a clamp. The idea is to use the clamp as your helper. Keep enough tension on the clamp to prevent the brace from falling, but not so much that you can't tap the post slightly one way or another as you make minor adjustments to bring the post plumb. When the post is plumb, tighten the brace, work on the other side, and finally lock the braces with several screws to hold it secure. Remove the clamps. (See "Smart Tip" on page 116.)

MAKING AND INSTALLING BEAMS

There are several things to consider when you choose the main beam for your deck. Sometimes one characteristic outweighs all others. For example, if it will be difficult to dig through rocky soil on your site, you may want the largest possible beam and only two piers. More often, several factors go into the final decision about how big and what kind of beam to use.

Beam Size. First, think about space, particularly the amount of vertical room that the beam and joists will use together. If your deck is built close to the ground, you may not have room to put a large beam on top of posts with a layer of joists on top of it. If you need to save room, it can

Lattice panels hide the beam in this deck.

make sense to use more posts and a smaller beam or to bolt the beam to the posts.

Another option is to use the beam itself as the header joist. You might need a large beam made of several 2x12s, for example. But instead of resting the joists on top of it, you can use framing hardware and butt the joists into its side. This way the beam is at the same level as the joists. You'll save almost a foot of vertical space.

Beam Appearance. Next think about whether the beam will be visible, and if so, what it will look like next to a stairway or an entrance to the house. No matter what type of wood you use, an evenly spaced layout and nicely installed bolts on a built-up beam can look good. A massive timber can have a classy yet rustic look. But availability comes into play. It may be that you can't get a good-looking 4x8, for instance.

But you have many ways to dress up a beam. You can cut a 45-degree angle off the bottom corners to create a floating effect or chamfer or rout the edges in a decorative detail. You can coat the lumber with stain to dress up the appearance of treated wood or cover the rough construction lumber altogether with a finished fascia board.

If the beam needs bracing but you don't want to use galvanized hardware in an exposed location, you can add 2x4s or 2x6s to the sides of the support posts and extend them up along the sides of the beam. This makes a neat structural sandwich that you can lock up with bolts.

Beam Weight. Lastly, consider weight. A 16-foot length of treated southern yellow pine 4x12 can be a real back-breaker. And things can get downright dangerous if you have to lift the beam high in the air. So in some cases, it is simply easier and safer to use a built-up beam.

Types of Beams

You can use several types of beams as a main support beam under deck joists. Here is a rundown of some of the most common types.

Solid. This is a beam made of a solid piece of four-by lumber, generally set on top of 4x4 posts. This has a classic, clean look, but there is little leeway for correcting mistakes, and it can be difficult to find a straight, good-looking piece of four-by lumber.

Built-Up. This is a beam made of two two-bys (photos page 124), sometimes with spacers sandwiched between (photos page 121). Before you add spacers, be sure to check the thickness of the posts on which the beam will sit—actual post thicknesses can vary a bit. This built-up as-sembly can actually be stronger than a solid-timber beam and is usually less expensive. But it does take some extra time to fabricate. Once you assemble the pieces, it may be just as heavy and difficult to maneuver as a conventional solid beam.

Spaced. This is another two-part beam consisting of two pieces of two-by lumber attached to opposing sides of the posts. (See "Making Spaced Beams," page 125.) Though time-consuming to build, this beam may be best for the do-it-yourselfer because it involves little heavy lifting and is easily correctable during construction.

Laminated. This is likely to be a special-order item be-cause the beam is made of many two-by boards that have been joined together with screws or nails and glue. You can build one yourself, of course. But this option is best reserved for special load conditions where you need a very large beam that is easier to assemble board by board than to buy in one piece.

There are other types of manufactured beams—for example, large timbers made from interwoven strips of wood. Because they are built and not grown, you can order one in almost any size.

Let-In. This is a beam set into notches in the posts—usu-ally with the top of the beam flush to the top of the posts. Notching allows the beam to bear directly on the post while also allowing you to bolt through the side of the beam into the post.

Beam Locations

Joists can either rest on top of a beam (usually the simplest solution because you can hide the beam by cantilevering the deck) or be attached to the side of the beam with joist hangers. Both attachment approaches will meet codes if you use large enough lumber with the proper spacing. All but one of the beam types discussed above can accom-modate either method—the exception is sandwich beams, which can't be hung from the side because only one side of the beam would support the joists.

Attaching to the Top. Where joists cross the top of a beam, you can space them out on your layout lines and tack them in place with a few toenails. This keeps them from shifting, although being attached to a ledger, header, and bridging makes it difficult for them to shift at all. But there are small pieces of hardware (galvanized straps with a twisted shape) that you can use to tack the joist to

the beam without toenails. In some areas, your building department may require these tie-downs to help resist special loads.

Attaching to the Side. By attaching joists to the side of the beam, you can run the joists at the same level as the beam. In fact, the beam takes the place of the header joist and so will be cut to exact length and marked for joists in conjunction with the ledger. As always, make sure the beam is crown side up when you mark for the joists. All beams have a tendency to sag when they are loaded, and installing the crowns up provides some extra resistance to sagging.

💡 SMART TIP

CLAMPING CROWNS

While most structural lumber has a crown, or slight hump along one edge, it's not likely that you will find two with exactly the same curved shape. Even if you nail together a girder with both crowns up, one board may be a little higher than the other. To bring the top edges into alignment and provide a uniform base for the joists, you can drive a few toenails. But you are likely to get better results with a clamp. Set one end on the low board, the other end on the high board, and tighten to bring the two boards into line.

Beam Assembly

You can use lag screws and washers to assemble the components of a beam, or predrill and bolt all the way through. But most carpenters simply nail them, and reserve lags and bolts for attaching the ledger and connecting sandwich-style beams to posts.

Some inspectors will look closely enough at your work to see how many fasteners you're using for a particular job. In most cases, if you drive nails with a hammer (or screws with a drill-driver), you'll be fine with rows of three fasteners about 12 inches apart. For even more strength, you can flip over the beam and install some fasteners through the other face as well.

Be sure to use nails or screws that penetrate all the components without poking through on the other side. For example, you could use 8d (2 ½-inch) nails on a basic two-piece beam that is three inches wide. [Some carpenters use 10d (3-inch) nails and drive them at a slight angle to keep them from protruding.]

Installing a Beam

The following is the basic sequence you can use to place your main beam in the right position.

Mark the Corner Posts. Use a level and a long, straight piece of lumber, a line level, or a water level to mark the location of the beam on the posts. It's wise to mark the two corner posts first, and check and double-check your marks from the ledger and between the posts themselves. Once the corner posts are marked, you can string a line between them to mark any other posts in line under the beam. You want to find the spot on the post that is level with the top

---

PROJECT: 🐾🐾🐾
PACKING OUT BEAMS

Some codes require beams to be the same thickness as a 4x4 post. Use treated lumber for the spacers.

TOOLS & MATERIALS
- Beam stock
- ½-in. treated spacers
- Clamps
- 10d nails
- Hammer

1 Cut spacers from treated wood. Use treated lumber even if the beams are not treated.

2 Tack the spacers to one side of one beam. Set the spacers 16 in. on center.

3 Place the other board on top to create a spacer sandwich. Secure with 10d nails.

BEAM CONNECTIONS

POST TO SOLID BEAM

POST TO SANDWICHED BEAM

POST TO JOIST AND BEAM

of the ledger. If you want the deck to slope slightly for drainage, measure down from that mark 1/16 inch for every foot of joist travel. But most builders do this only on decks with closed surfaces—for example, tongue-and-groove boards you might be more likely to use on a porch floor. Because typical decks have spaces between the boards, there is more than enough area for water to drain. From the mark that indicates where the tops of the joists will be, measure down the depth of a joist to find the top of the beam. Follow these steps on both corner posts, and check the post marks for level.

If you plan to butt the joists into the main beam, remember not to make the last measurement. When you level across from the top of the ledger, you will be marking the tops of the joists and the top of the beam at the same time.

Mark the Rest of the Posts. Use a chalk line to extend lines between the marks you made on the corner posts. You might double-check the line marks with a level to be sure you will be cutting in the right place.

In case of a mistake, you can add a shim to the top of a post. But if you take the extra time to verify your level lines, shimming the post should not be necessary.

Once you are certain of the marks, use a square to extend lines onto all the faces of your posts. You'll need these when you cut because most circular saws can't cut deeply enough to go through a 4x4 post in one pass. (See "Cutting Posts" on page 77.)

Cut Off the Posts. To make your cuts safely and accurately, be sure that the posts are securely braced. Double-check your circular saw to make sure it cuts at a perfect right angle.

Because this is an unusual cut and you have to hold the saw sideways, get into a comfortable position with solid footing. Try to keep the same margin along the marked lines—for example, leaving the pencil line on and cutting just up to it. This will help you get a flat surface on the post even though you need to make two or three passes.

Cutting the Beam. If the beam will be low to the ground, you don't want to let the piece run long and cut it in place. You should probably recheck your measurements. But at this point your posts should be locked in proper plumb position in a line that is squared up with the ledger on the house.

If you are using a spaced-type beam and plan to build it up in pieces along several posts, be sure that the splices will fall over the centers of the posts. You'll need to be careful making these connections. Predrilling is essential to avoid splitting the beam pieces and the post.

If you need to make multiple splices on your beam, plan the lumber lengths so that you splice one side of the beam on one post and the other side on another.

Attach the Beam. If you have a heavy beam to set, arrange for plenty of help and be sure that any ladders you use are stable. There is an extra step you can take to be sure that the beam won't topple off your posts during assembly.

The idea is to temporarily but securely screw a piece of 2x4 or 2x6, called a scab, onto the corner posts with at least 6 inches projecting past the top. As you get the beam into position, it will bear down on the posts, of course, and now it won't tip because of the scab. You can have a clamp at

the ready and use it to pin the beam to the scab as soon as you set the heavy timber in place. This approach can help even if you install galvanized hardware connectors on the posts. This hardware may be required by local codes unless you install permanent wooden cleats or braces to keep the beam from tipping.

A typical connector has two flanges that fit over the post, and two that rise up around the beam. When the timber is in place, you can tack through perforated holes in the fastener to lock the pieces together. If you prefer to use wooden cleats, you can clad opposing sides of your posts with 2x6s. If you extend them all the way down to the piers, you will end up with a very strong built-up post, plus a reinforced pocket past the top of the post.

DIMENSION LUMBER DECK BEAM SPANS FOR JOISTS FRAMING FROM ONE SIDE ONLY

Species	Size	6'	8'	10'	12'	14'	16'	18'
		JOIST SPANS (L) LESS THAN OR EQUAL TO:						
Southern Pine	Two 2x6	6' 8"	5' 8"	5' 1"	4' 7"	4' 3"	4' 0"	3' 9"
	Two 2x8	8' 6"	7' 4"	6' 6"	5' 11"	5' 6"	5' 1"	4' 9"
	Two 2x10	10' 1"	8' 9"	7' 9"	7' 1"	6' 6"	6' 1"	5' 9"
	Two 2x12	11' 11"	10' 4"	9' 2"	8' 4"	7' 9"	7' 3"	6' 9"
	Three 2x6	7' 11"	7' 2"	6' 5"	5' 10"	5' 5"	5' 0"	4' 9"
	Three 2x8	10' 7"	9' 3"	8' 3"	7' 6"	6' 11"	6' 5"	6' 1"
	Three 2x10	12' 9"	11' 0"	9' 9"	8' 9"	8' 3"	7' 8"	7' 3"
	Three 2x12	15' 0"	13' 0"	11' 7"	10' 6"	9' 9"	9' 1"	8' 7"
Douglas Fir-Larch Hem-Fir Spruce-Pine-Fir Redwood Western Cedars Ponderosa Pine Red Pine	3x6 or Two 2x6	5' 2"	4' 5"	3' 11"	3' 7"	3' 3"	2' 10"	2' 6"
	3x8 or Two 2x8	6' 7"	5' 8"	5' 1"	4' 7"	4' 3"	3' 10"	3' 5"
	3x10 or Two 2x10	8' 1"	7' 0"	6' 3"	5' 8"	5' 3"	4' 10"	4' 5"
	3x12 or Two 2x12	9' 5"	8' 2"	7' 3"	6' 7"	6' 1"	5' 8"	5' 4"
	4x6	6' 2"	5' 3"	4' 8"	4' 3"	3' 11"	3' 8"	3' 5"
	4x8	8' 2"	7' 0"	6' 3"	5' 8"	5' 3"	4' 11"	4' 7"
	4x10	9' 8"	8' 4"	7' 5"	6' 9"	6' 3"	5' 10"	5' 5"
	4x12	11' 2"	9' 8"	8' 7"	7' 10"	7' 3"	6' 9"	6' 4"
	Three 2x6	7' 1"	6' 5"	5' 9"	5' 3"	4' 10"	4' 6"	4' 3"
	Three 2x8	9' 5"	8' 3"	7' 4"	6' 8"	6' 2"	5' 9"	5' 5"
	Three 2x10	11' 9"	10' 2"	9' 1"	8' 3"	7' 7"	7' 1"	6' 8"
	Three 2x12	13' 8"	11' 10"	10' 6"	9' 7"	8' 10"	8' 3"	7' 10"

Note: Be sure to check all allowable spans between supports and all lumber requirements with your local building department.

PROJECT:
MAKING AND SETTING A BUILT-UP BEAM

Find the crowns on your lumber, and assemble the beam with the crowns up.

TOOLS & MATERIALS
- Clamps
- 10d nails
- Hammer
- Level
- 2x4 braces
- Stakes
- Drill & bits
- 1 ¼-in. deck screws

1 Sight down the stock and locate the crown. Place the crowns side by side.

2 Screw or nail the boards together; use groups of 3 fasteners 12 in. on center.

3 Put the beam in the post caps crown side up. You may need a helper.

4 Plumb the beam. Braces help keep the posts from shifting.

5 Secure the beam with a series of braces. Drive screws through the post caps into the beam.

PROJECT: 🪚🪚🪚
MAKING SPACED BEAMS

A sandwich beam can be easier to make than a built-up one because there is less nailing. Trim the post once the beam is in place.

TOOLS & MATERIALS

- Level
- Braces
- Stakes
- Clamps
- Drill & bits
- 2-in. screws
- 7-in. carriage bolts or screw bolts
- Washer
- Rachet wrench
- Handsaw

1 Start with plumb posts. Use braces and a level to make sure the posts are plumb.

2 Use props and clamps to hold the beam stock in position as shown. Level the boards.

3 Drill pilot holes through the beam stock and the posts about 1 in. from each edge.

4 Insert carriage bolts or screw bolts (check with building department for bolt diameter). Use washers under nut and bolt.

5 Use a handsaw or reciprocating saw to trim the posts flush to the top of the beam.

MAXIMUM JOIST SPANS AND OVERHANGS							
		JOINT SPACING (o.c.)					
		12"	16"	24"	12"	16"	24"
Species	Size	Allowable Span			Allowable Overhang		
Southern Pine	2x6	9' 11"	9' 0"	7' 7"	1' 0"	1' 1"	1' 3"
	2x8	13' 1"	11' 10"	9' 8"	1' 10"	2' 0"	2' 4"
	2x10	16' 2"	14' 0"	11' 5"	3' 1"	3' 5"	2' 10"
	2x12	18' 0"	16' 6"	13' 6"	4' 6"	4' 2"	3' 4"
Douglas Fir-Larch Hem-Fir Spruce-Pine-Fir	2x6	9' 6"	8' 4"	6' 10"	0' 11"	1' 0"	1' 2"
	2x8	12' 6"	11' 1"	9' 1"	1' 8"	1' 10"	2' 2"
	2x10	15' 8"	13' 7"	11' 1"	2' 10"	3' 2"	2' 9"
	2x12	18' 0"	15' 9"	12' 10"	4' 4"	3' 11"	3' 3"
Redwood Western Cedars Ponderosa Pine Red Pine	2x6	8' 10"	8' 0"	6' 10"	0' 9"	0' 10"	0' 11"
	2x8	11' 8"	10' 7"	8' 8"	1' 5"	1' 7"	1' 9"
	2x10	14' 11"	13' 0"	10' 7"	2' 5"	2' 7"	2' 8"
	2x12	17' 5"	15' 1"	12' 4"	3' 7"	3' 9"	3' 1"

Note: Be sure to check all allowable spans between supports and all lumber requirements with your local building department.

MODULAR JOIST LAYOUTS

Every part of a deck needs careful layout, of course. But when it comes time to plan out and install the joists, you need to be sure to account for the decking that will cover them. Because you will most likely be using decking in stock lengths, generally in 2-foot increments, you want to make a modular layout that makes the most efficient use of the materials you buy.

Modular framing layouts for most decks (and for most house frames) work in multiples of 16 inches. That's the distance from the centerline of one joist to the centerline of the next one in line. Two units make 32 inches, and three make 48 inches, which is another basic building block of construction that matches the width of drywall panels, plywood, and other sheet materials.

As a practical matter, if you didn't maintain the 16-inch module, there wouldn't be a joist where you needed one at the end of a deck board. You would wind up wasting a lot of wood.

Planning Lengths of Deck Boards. Oftentimes your deck boards won't be long enough to reach from one end joist to another. If for example, the deck is 29 feet, 2 inches wide, you might use a 16-foot deck board and a 14-foot deck board for each course. In this case, the boards meet at the center of a joist. That's why the modular layout is from center to center, so that each board is supported by half a joist's width. By the way, it's a good idea to stagger the joints in this situation—start one course with the longer board and the next course with the shorter board so the joints fall on different joists. This looks better and also knits the deck together more strongly. Typically you'll let the ends of the decking boards "run wild" when you install them, then snap chalk lines to cut them all to final length with a circular saw.

Spacing the Joists. Because the joists are 1½ inch thick there will be 14 ½ inches between each set of joists. The exceptions, as you will see in the next paragraph, are the rim

☝ SMART TIP

JOIST ASSISTS

When large joists are too heavy to set yourself, this add-on makes the job possible. Temporarily screw on a strip of wood that overhangs the joist. When you wrestle the joist into place, the strip rests on the ledger and carries the weight.

joists and the joists closest to each one.

Although you want the joists to be 16 inches on center, a centerline would be covered by the end of the joist, so you'll actually strike a line at the location for one side of each joist, and then mark an X at the side of the line where the joist will be. Because the joists are 1 ½ inch wide, the side marks will be ¾ inch from the center of each joist. Fortunately no math is needed to allow for this when doing your layout. Just hook your tape measure over one end of the ledger or beam and strike a line at 15 ¼ inches to mark the side of the first joist in from the outermost joist. (The 16-inch on center spacing starts from the outside of the rim joist, so the spacing between it and the next joist will be 13 ¾ inches.) Tape measures have special marks to indicate 16-inch intervals, so all you need to do is strike a line ¾ inch to the same side of each interval to indicate the side of each joist. The distance between the second-to-last joist and the other rim joist will be whatever is left over—for example, for a 31-foot-2-inch-wide deck, it would be 11 ¾ inches.

No matter how beautiful the finished project looks, all well-built decks start with a carefully constructed post, beam, and joist support system.

FRAMING HARDWARE

Galvanized metal connectors play a big role in making modern decks strong and safe. In fact, in some applications connectors are required by code. For example, building codes usually require joist hangers to be used to attach joists to ledgers. Joist hangers may or may not be required to connect joists through the header. When the joists are cantilevered over a beam, local code may allow you to nail through the face of the header into the end of the joists. Check with your local inspector.

To meet code, joist hangers must be installed with the approved fasteners. The hangers have a flange that goes against the ledger or header. The flange must be attached with 1 ½ in. connector nails or 1 ½ in. structural connector screws that are specifically designated for the purpose. (See "Fasteners," page 62.) The part of the hangers that wrap around the joist have angled holes on each side to guide 10d common nails or 2 ½ inch approved connector screws at an angle through the sides of the joists into the ledger.

Deck Tension Ties. A recent addition to many building codes is a requirement to install lateral load connectors. This requirement stems from research showing that the majority of deck collapses occur because the ledger pulls away from the house. Special deck tension ties (See page 64) meet the code by tying the joists through the ledger into the house framing. Code requires using these connectors on four joists per deck—you can buy a kit that includes the four connectors and required screws.

Hurricane Ties. These are another connector that usually is required on any deck that has joists resting on a beam.

PROJECT: 🦇🦇🦇
SETTING THE OUTER JOIST

It's important to have a good, clean, square cut on the outer joist—if only because it will probably be the most prominent on the deck.

TOOLS & MATERIALS
- Joist material
- Measuring tape
- Pencil
- Framing square
- Circular saw
- Hammer
- 16d nails
- Corner bracket & nails

1 Measure out from the beam to determine the amount of overhang.

3 Cut the outer joist using a circular saw. This is usually a prominent area, so make a clean cut.

4 Before nailing, make sure the deck frame is square and the two outside joists are equal.

There are two types, both of which are installed with 1-½ in. approved connector nails. One type has two flat surfaces at right angles to each other. One surface is nailed to the side of the joist and the other to the side of the beam below. The other type slides up over the joist and has flanges that are nailed to the joist and the header. (See page 64.) Check with your building inspector to see if he requires one type or the other.

SPECIAL CASES

Some decks may have to step over an existing set of concrete steps or change levels to accommodate a sloping yard. (See "Changing Levels," page 140.)

Demolishing concrete steps with a sledgehammer and hauling away the rubble is a lot of work. As long as the

2 Use a framing square to draw a cut line on the joist. Leave beam and post braces in place.

5 Drive a toenail through the joist into the beam. Reinforce this with a twist fastener.

💡 **SMART TIP**

STRAIGHTENING JOISTS

Given the conditon of lumber today, it's likely that you will get a few twisted timbers in a load of deck joists. You may be able to return the worst of them. But there will be some twists and turns that won't line up with your square layout lines. To get rid of a small twist, secure a clamp near the end and use the handle for leverage. To increase your leverage, use several clamps to attach a 2x4, and use it as the handle.

A twisted joist won't square up. Use a clamp to pull it into position.

Nail the joist into its final position.

top step is lower than the top of the deck joists, it's usually easier to leave the steps in place.

If the concrete is sound, stop the ledger at both sides of the steps. Treat the end grain of the ledger board with water repellant before setting it in place. Notch the joists to fit over the top step and rest on the second step. (See "Framing Over Steps," below right.)

INSTALLING JOISTS

In the majority of decks, joists are attached to the ledger on one end and are cantilevered over a beam with a header joist nailed to their ends to form the outside of the deck frame. There are various approaches to installing joists in this situation. One of the most common is to first install the two joists that meet the ends of the ledger, cut them to length, make sure they are square to the ledger, and then tack them in place by toenailing into the beam. (See "Setting the Inner Joist," page 129 and "Setting the Outer Joist," page 130.)

Then you can install all the other joists, letting the lengths run wild past the beam. After squaring those joists, you'll tack a temporary brace across them to hold them in position while you'll stretch a chalk line between the two joists you already cut (the inner joist and the outer joist if you are building into a corner of the house). Next snap a line on the top of all the other joists. You'll transfer this line to the side of the joists. By cutting them all off at this line you'll know they are the right length without having to measure each one.

Attach the Header Joist. If your end joists sit on top of the beam, attach them flush to the ends of the beam. Attach the header to the joists with three 16d galvanized nails through the header into the ends of the joists. Remember that stock-sized lumber does not always have a square cut at both ends. You also may find some rough spots or cracks that can be trimmed away to create tight joints at the critical corners of the frame.

Install Joist Hangers. As mentioned, code usually requires joist hangers at the ledger but may or may not require them at the beam. It's a good idea to install them at the beam even if they are not required. You can install each joist and joist hanger as shown in "Setting Joists," opposite, or you can install all of the hangers and then go back and install the joists.

Take a short block of joist material, and hold it in place--it should touch the line and cover the X, but most importantly, its top edge must be flush with the top of the ledger or header. Slide the joist hanger up against it so that it touches on one side only. There are pointed tabs on the

(Text continues on page 134.)

A simple deck becomes an intimate seating area in this garden. Even simple designs require a good support system.

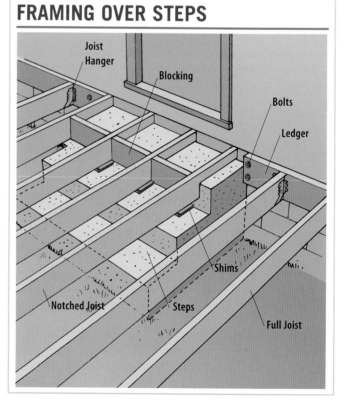

FRAMING OVER STEPS

Joist Hanger

Blocking

Bolts

Ledger

Shims

Notched Joist

Steps

Full Joist

PROJECT: 🐿🐿
SETTING JOISTS

Make the joists and ledger flush; then install joist hangers. Some codes require the use of joist hangers.

TOOLS & MATERIALS
- Joists
- Square
- Pencil
- Gloves
- Horses and saw
- Hammer
- Scrap wood
- Joist hangers
- Twist fasteners
- Measuring tape
- 1x4 brace

1 Make a square cut on the ledger-end of the joists. Allow the other end to run long for now.

2 To help support the joist, nail a strip of wood with a small overhang to the joist.

3 Slip the joist hanger around the joist. Check for level and drive nails through the joist hanger.

4 For added stability, add a hurricane tie where the joist crosses the beam.

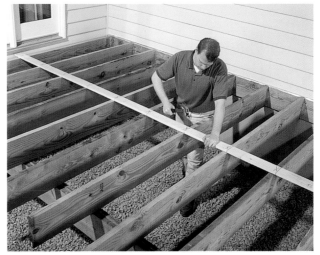

5 Copy ledger layout lines to a brace. Tack to joist at midspan, bringing joists to your marks.

133

(Continued from page 132.)

hanger; pound them in to hold the hanger position. Drive two nails through one side of the flange to secure the hanger. Double-check to make sure the block is still accurately in place, then close the hanger around it and fasten the other side with the recommended number of hanger nails.

Slide the Joists in Place. The joist ends must butt tightly against the ledger or header at all points. So before you measure for cutting the joists, be sure that the end you are measuring from is cut square. (Sometimes the lumberyard will give you ten that are square-cut and one that isn't, so look at them all.) Cut the joists to length.

Right now you're probably itching to make some real, visible progress in a hurry. But at this point it's a very good idea to take a little time first to seal the open grain of the cut ends with some sealer/preservative.

Install each joist crown side up. This is a two-person operation. If things are tight, you may have to slide both ends down at the same time. A little pounding is fine, but if a joist is so tight that it starts to bend, take it out, measure again, and recut it.

If you have the kind of flashing that makes a 90-degree turn to cover the face of the ledger, just set the joist against the turned edge. If your flashing makes only a slight downward turn, you could tuck the joists under the leading edge. But don't dislodge the metal (or tear it) by bending the flashing up as you install joists.

Finish Fastening. Eyeball the framing to see that everything looks straight and parallel. Finish installing the screws or nails in the joist hangers—put one in every hole. Where joists rest on a beam, toenail or drive a screw to minimize

twisting. Hurricane ties provide extra hold-down strength. They may be required by code, but even if they are not, it's a good idea to install them.

Bracing

Decks that are raised above the ground—more than 4 feet for 4x4 posts; more than 8 feet for 6x6 posts—need extra

Y-braces add lateral support.

1 Measure out from the ledger on each of the end joists. Mark the top of the end joists.

PROJECT: 🐾🐾🐾
TRIMMING JOISTS

Snap a line, and the cut joists will form a dead-straight line. Trim the joist ends using a circular saw.

TOOLS & MATERIALS
- Measuring tape
- Pencil
- Chalk-line box
- Framing square
- Circular saw

lateral support to keep them from swaying. An on-top solid beam has less lateral strength than a bolted-on beam and may need bracing even if it is lower.

If you will be installing solid skirting (siding panels that enclose your deck below the deck surface), that will provide a good deal of lateral support and can take the place of bracing. Lattice skirting, however, is much less effective. Guidelines on bracing vary greatly from area to area, so check with your inspector if you think you may need it. In most cases, bracing can be added after the deck is built.

Bracing can add a classic, handcrafted look, and for less work than you might think. The only tricks are making accurate 45-degree cuts and making sure that the braces are in symmetrical relation to each other and are exactly the same size, for a uniform look.

Y-Bracing. In most cases, simple Y-bracing is sufficient. To brace a solid beam on top of a post, cut pieces of post material (4x4 or 6x6) to go under the beam and against the sides of the post, or use 2x4s or 2x6s and attach them to the face of the post and beam. For beams attached to opposing sides of a post, sandwich the braces between the beams, and secure them using lag screws, bolts, or carriage bolts.

Other Bracing Patterns. Larger projects may require more elaborate bracing patterns. These are all best done with 2x4s or 2x6s on the face of the post and beam. When building these sorts of structures, first make marks on the posts and beam; then hold up the braces for marking rather than using a measuring tape.

💡 SMART TIP

REMOVING BRACES

As the deck takes shape and the job progresses, it's natural to want to remove the hodgepodge of braces and clean up the working area. Resist the temptation. On the 4x4 support posts, for example, it's wise to wait until they are completely locked in their final position by the main girder and joists.

2 Line up the chalk line; the string should touch each joist. Snap the line.

3 Draw a cutting line with a framing square. Trim each joist using a circular saw.

Braces that will span 6 feet or less can be made of 2x4s; for longer spans, use 2x6s. Consider traffic patterns when deciding on your bracing. If you need to walk under the deck, a simple Y may be the best way to go; if you need more elaborate bracing, you may be able to leave one section unbraced if you really beef up the other sections.

Raised Decks

If you are building a deck that's 8 feet or more above the ground, most of the layout will be the same, but your work methods might differ dramatically. Most operations will take twice as long to perform, as you spend lots of time wrestling with ladders, carrying things up and down, and being extra careful.

PROJECT:
INSTALLING TENSION TIES

These ties will prevent the deck from pulling away from the ledger. In most situations, code requires that four of these be installed. You can buy a kit with four ties, all the screws you'll need to install them, and hex-head bit for your drill/driver. Note that code requires that the ties be fastened to interior framing but not the rim joist that's usually behind the header. Usually this means attaching to the doubled two-by plates just under the rim joist.

TOOLS & MATERIALS
- Tension tie kit
- Drill/driver
- ⅜-inch hex bit
- #20 star bit

1 Stick a screwdriver in one of the holes in the breakout washer and pry the washer out.

4 Put the long screw through the smaller hole in the breakout washer and put the screw through the hole in the body of the tie. Use a ⅜-inch hex bit in a drill/driver to drive the screw into the house until the head is slightly away from the washer.

5 Use a #20 star bit in a drill/driver to insert two screws into each vertical leg.

Decking, ledgers, joists, and beams have all the same requirements as decks built low to the ground. However, there are a few key differences that you should take into account. For example, decks near the ground may not need a railing, which could alter your plans for post and joist placement. You should check with the local building department to be sure, but decks within 30 inches of the ground often do not require railings to prevent falls. (Of course, you may want them for looks in any case.)

Bracing the Posts. To prevent shifting, you also may need lateral bracing, such as an X-pattern of 2x4s or 2x6s that ties together several long posts. Generally, concrete piers that extend below the local frost line offer the most solid

(Text continues on page 139.)

2 Put a long screw through the tie and use its head to pivot open the legs of the tie to about a 45-degree angle.

3 Slide the legs of the tie over the joist, just beyond the joist hanger. Pinch the legs together so they stay in place.

6 Drive screws into all six holes in the brace strap.

7 Tighten the long screw until it's snug against the breakout washer—don't over tighten.

PROJECT: 🔨🔨
SETTING THE HEADER JOIST

Adding a header joist is the last step before installing bridging. Save time and keep an accurate layout by marking the ledger and the header joist at the same time. They should be the same size.

TOOLS & MATERIALS
- Joist material
- Clamps
- Scrap wood
- Hammer
- 16d nails
- Corner brackets
- Joist hangers
- Joist hanger nails

1 The header joist holds the ends of the joists in place and helps maintain proper spacing.

2 Create a temporary shelf for the header by clamping strips of wood to the bottom of three or four joists.

3 Making sure the top edge of the header and the tops of the joists are flush, nail the header in place.

4 Install corner framing hardware where the header meets the end joists.

5 To reinforce the deck framing, install a joist hanger where the joists meet the header.

(Continued from page 137.)

NAILING THE HEADER JOIST

When you box in the free ends of the joists, you may find that some are a little high or a little low, even though they all sit on the same beam. Help bring them into line by working with a helper who can raise or lower the free end of the header joist as you work down the row. Even a small amount of leverage will help you align the tops of the opposing timbers. And the tops need to be flush for your decking to lie flat. You will lose leverage as you connect more joists, but this trick can save you some planing or trimming work.

and durable support for deck posts. And with this system, the posts sit a couple to several inches aboveground (locked in place with galvanized hardware), which greatly reduces the possibility of rot due to ground contact. (See "Anchoring Posts," page 116.) Use 2x4s or even 2x6s for temporary bracing. Pound the stakes deep into the ground.

If your inspector will allow it, wait until the framing or even the entire deck is completed before pouring the concrete around the posts. This will make your footing stronger because it will not get banged around during the construction process, which could loosen the concrete's bond with the post or with the earth. Also, doing it this way gives you the luxury of being able to make small adjustments to the posts, if necessary.

Notching the Post. Though not recommended elsewhere, notching the post for a beam is the best method when you have 6x6 posts. This approach provides better attachment

than setting the beam atop the posts, and it helps prevent the beam from twisting. After you have cut the post to height, use your angle square to mark for the beam; the best design is to notch it completely in, so that the face of the beam ends up flush with the face of the post. To do this, first set your circular-saw cutting depth to equal the thickness of the beam—for example 3 inches for a beam made of doubled two-bys. Make the seat cut first. Then, with the circular saw set to the same depth, cut kerfs every ½ inch or so between the seat cut and the top of the post. (The kerfs need not be square or perfectly spaced.) Finally, use a chisel and a hammer or mallet to chop out the kerfed area, using the bottom of the kerfs as a depth guide.

Attach the beam with through-bolts such as carriage bolts or screw bolts rather than lag screws. Apply siliconized latex caulk to the joints, and give the exposed end grain of the post a healthy dose of a preservative-sealer.

Step Decks

Some decks can have several levels, which means you'll have at least one step where deck platforms meet. These steps must be comfortable. Generally, each step should be no greater in height than a normal 7 ½-inch stair rise. Because the actual width of a 2x8 is 7 ¼ inches, often the easiest way to accomplish a level change is to place a 2x8 joist on top of the frame below. Remember that even a simple step-down between two large platforms can count as a step and be governed by building codes. As always, be sure to check the specifications for level changes with your local building department.

When planning and building a change in level, take care that no decking pieces will be left unsupported at their ends. One approach is to make a second framing box. For small raised areas, the simplest method is to first build the main deck, then construct a box of framing that sits on top of it. This is not cost-effective for larger raised areas, however, because double framing is under the raised section.

Another approach is to create shared beam support. This way, the upper level partially overlaps the lower so that they share the support of the same beam on one end. The end joists of the upper platform can fall directly over the end joist and beam below or it can overlap the level below by about 12 inches. Each level will have its own support at its other end. (See "Changing Levels," page 140.)

example. The idea is to set the brace along your ledger and transfer the joist layout. Then set the brace near your chalk line and bring each joist into line on your layout marks.

You should be able to rely on the measurements, but it pays to take a look down each joist from the outer end of the deck to make sure it's straight. You need only one nail through the brace into each joist, and you don't need to drive it home.

The next step is to pencil-in square lines on the sides of the joists where the bridging will fall. This will help you set the bridging correctly. Remember that in one bay the bridging needs to ride on one side of the lines, and in the next bay it needs to ride on the other side.

The final step is straightforward once you have prepared the job. Just cut the blocks, tap them into position on your marks, and drive at least two nails into each end. If you find that the bridging blocks are not exactly the same size as the joists, keep the tops flush with the tops of the joists. That's where the decking will ride, so you want all the framing components to be in one flat plane.

Moving Joists

There may be one or two joists that have a big twist that is difficult to correct. You probably should have left them at the lumberyard, but sometimes a crooked board or two slips by, and you have to find a way to use it.

To push or pull a joist into place on the layout marks of your temporary brace, you can use other joists as a backstop for a 2x4 and force the crooked timber into place. In extreme cases, you can use a handy tool called a come-along, or winch. This ratchet-action cable tool will even pull a series of joists into place as long as the other end of the cable is solidly anchored.

If you need to untwist a joist, say, to line it up with your square mark on a header, use a lever to help with the untwisting. One approach is to securely clamp a short 2x4 onto the joist and simply pull it to one side or the other until the joist corrects. You may need a helper to hold the position while you drive several nails. With a minor twist, you may be able to use the clamp itself as a lever. It's a good idea to overcorrect slightly because the joist will likely slip back slightly. (See "Aligning Joists," page 144.)

FRAMING FOR A CURVED SECTION

After installing the beams, let the joists run wild at the curved section. Mark them for cutting only after you've secured all of them in place. You'll need a laminated header

3 Each joist bay will get a section of solid blocking, but you will need to offset them for nailing.

for the curved section.

For V-pattern decking, lay out the joists, as shown on page 145. Start in the middle. Establish the joist where the tip of the V-shape in the decking will fall. Next, measure 16 inches on center to either side of this joist. Install the joists using joist hangers secured to the ledger. Install the two short header joists, allowing them to run longer than needed. For the curve, splice the joists over the beam, and allow them to run wild past where they will be cut. Double the thickness of the center joist by scabbing on pieces of 2x4. Make sure that you attach the joists firmly in place.

1 Find the centerpoint of the two outer joists. Snap a chalk line between them.

2 Transfer the marks to the sides of the joist. Use a square that will reach the bottom of the joists.

4 Cut bridging from joist stock, and install between joists. The brace helps maintain proper spacing.

5 Drive two nails into each edge of the bridging. Remove the brace when bridging is installed.

If your deck will contain decking running in one direction only, there is no need to add the doubled-up center joist.

Mark the Curve. To mark the joists for the curve, make a beam compass, or trammel. For the dimensions shown here, drill two holes exactly 8 feet apart in a 10-foot length of 1x4. Use a ³⁄₁₆-inch bit for one hole and a ¼-inch bit for the other. To establish the centerpoint of the radius, tack a nail through the smaller hole and into the center of the doubled-up joist. Place a pencil into the other hole, and then swing your compass around the arc to mark the top of each joist. Adjust the size of the compass to fit the dimensions of your deck.

Use a square to mark plumb lines down from the com-pass marks, and cut each joist with a circular saw. Note: adjust the bevel of the saw for each cut to make sure that it follows the compass mark on top of the joist.

Curved Fascia. To make a curved header/fascia, resaw 2x4s into ⁵⁄₁₆ x 3 ½ inch pieces using a table saw. Then laminate five or six of these strips together. Cut the 2x4s longer than you'll need so that the fascia won't end up short.

To make a gluing form, cut pieces of plywood that match the curve of the deck. Then laminate the strips together using epoxy, clamping them to the curved form every 6 inches. You'll need to use lots of clamps. Cover every strip thoroughly with epoxy, or the slats may delami-nate. Allow the assembly to dry for 24 hours, then belt-sand the edge to produce a finished appearance.

PROJECT: 🐾🐾🐾
ALIGNING JOISTS

Instead of laying out a new series of marks on your brace, transfer them from the marks on your ledger.

TOOLS & MATERIALS
- Square
- Pencil
- 1x4 brace
- Hammer
- 10d nails
- Clamp

1 When you attach your brace (page 133), you will probably find some joists out of alignment.

2 Push or pull the offending joist into alignment. Use clamps or spreaders for this job.

Set the pieces in place, and fasten them to the ends of the joists, driving two nails into the edge of each joist. Once you've stacked three of these assemblies on top of one another (for 2x10 joists), you'll have a strong laminated fascia.

DECKING OVER A SLAB

Concrete patios have two problems. Many slabs eventually develop so many cracks that they basically look broken. And after you patch the cracks, the repairs stand out, making the slab look even worse. You could keep patching, or jackhammer the slab into oblivion and start from scratch with more concrete. Here's another alternative: covering the cracked concrete with wood decking. This approach uses sleepers—supports that serve in place of conventional joists. If you plan to use composite decking over the sleepers, check with the manufacturer—some require more ventilation underneath than this design provides.

Design Advantages

You'll see many advantages to this approach. **First,** you don't have to remove the slab, which is quite a job physically, and can add considerably to the cost of the project. That's mainly because concrete is heavy, and carting costs are generally based on weight.

Second, even an old slab with an unsightly surface can serve as the foundation for the deck. It won't matter if the

💡 SMART TIP

RECESS BOLTS

On some parts of a deck project, extra steps pay off later on. For example, when you bolt the main ledger to the house framing, it's wise to drill shallow counterbores that can accommodate the bolt heads. When you install joist hangers, the bolts won't be in the way.

FRAMING FOR CURVES

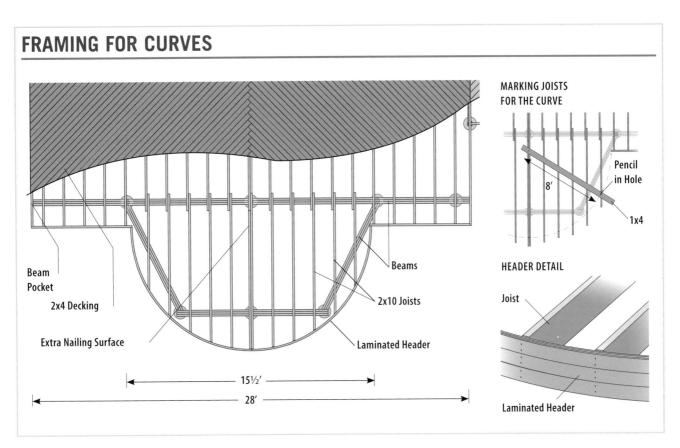

Beam Pocket

2x4 Decking

Extra Nailing Surface

Beams

2x10 Joists

Laminated Header

15½'

28'

MARKING JOISTS FOR THE CURVE

8'

Pencil in Hole

1x4

HEADER DETAIL

Joist

Laminated Header

surface is pitted or cracked on the surface, because you won't see it under the new layer of wood.

Third, the deck boards, generally 2x4s in this kind of project, are more flexible than concrete. That makes them more comfortable to walk on and provides a little resilience that can absorb some seasonal heaving in the slab. With concrete, even slight movement can cause splitting. And once a crack opens, water can enter, freeze up, and expand in winter and make the split even wider, which lets in more water in a cycle of ever-increasing deterioration.

The basic plan is to install wooden nailers on the concrete and a finished deck surface on the nailers. To prevent rot, use pressure-treated wood on the slab. To fasten the nailers, a contractor uses a special nail gun that fires a small explosive charge to drive a hardened nail through the wood and into the concrete. Using one of these tools can be dangerous if you're not experienced. It's not really a do-it-yourself tool, and you may have trouble even finding a dealer who will rent one to you. But you can get by without one and use a manual-powered hammer. The job may take a little longer, but it will be safer. Here's how to safely install sleepers to a concrete pad.

For more on laying out and cutting curves, see pages 82 and 83.

A curve adds an interesting design element. Finish with a curved fascia, or leave the end open for low-level decks.

145

Nailing Sleepers

Once you establish your layout, including boards around the perimeter and interior boards spaced about 16 inches on center, determine the material you'll use. You could use 1x4 nailers, but 2x4s provide more nailing substance for the surface boards. Thin nailers offer plenty of support but split too easily as you nail.

It's also wise to lay out the sleepers perpendicular to the main house wall. This will allow water to drain away from the house.

Remember that it's a good idea to use a respirator mask when cutting treated wood, particularly when you use a power saw. Even outdoors, this operation makes a lot of sawdust.

Also be sure to wear safety glasses while nailing. Because the concrete is so much harder than wood, nails sometimes can snap, and pieces of metal can fly up unexpectedly. You may not stick to safety glasses for odd jobs around the house, but this is one case where eye protection is essential. Unlike nailing in wood, where the force from a misdirected blow causes a bend, a mishit concrete nail can snap and ricochet off the slab into your face, packing quite a wallop.

Use hardened nails, often called cut nails, or masonry nails to fasten the sleepers. You'll find that standard common nails used on wood framing will bend over before penetrating the slab.

Be aware of another phenomenon peculiar to concrete nailing called hammer rebound. The hardened nail may hit a piece of stone in the slab, at which point all the force from your hammer blow comes right back off the nailhead and makes the hammer jump up in your hand. Try a few nails to get the feel of it—notice when the nail is penetrating and when you've hit an immovable object and are forced to move over an inch or so.

With those caveats in mind, simply proceed to attach the nailers, say, 16 inches from center to center across the slab. Keep nails a few inches away from the edges of the concrete to avoid splitting off small chunks.

Here's one more reason for using 2x4s instead of 1x4s for your nailers. Although it may take more time to fasten the larger lumber (and cost a bit more, too), you can level out some irregularities in the slab. While thinner boards would bend up over the rises and dip a bit into the low spots as you nail, pressure-treated 2x4s will bridge most of the gaps.

If you have a few major depressions in the slab, nail the sleepers at the high spots and insert shims (wedge-shaped

DECKING OVER A SLAB

House Wall

Drainage Gap

Gravel Base

Concrete Slab

Compacted Soil

Decking (parallel with house)

Sleeper (perpendicular to house)

pieces of pressure-treated wood or cedar shingles) to keep the 2x4s level as they ride over the low spots.

Planning the Deck Surface

Now comes the nice part of the job—installing the surface decking. Because the surface 2x4 (or 2x6 if you like) decking doesn't sit directly on the concrete, air will circulate around the wood. That means you don't have to use pressure-treated wood, even though treated boards are likely to last longer than fir, redwood, or cedar out in the weather.

Some people just don't like the look of wood after it has undergone the chemical treatment. Most treated products lose their original look over time; others will keep their original look. You can use treated boards and coat them with a semitransparent wood stain to kill the tinge, or use standard construction framing timbers and apply a water-resistant surface sealer to protect the wood.

Nailing the Deck

To make the surface look really nice, take care with the spacing between boards needed for drainage through the deck surface and nail placement through the surface timbers into the sleepers. The old-fashioned and reliable

system is to use the shank of a common nail as a spacer between boards. Or you can insert any convenient spacer that will allow something like ⅛-inch clearance to start with. (Some products shrink considerably. Check product data sheets or with the manufacturer for specific nailing instructions.)

Each surface 2x4 or 2x6 should get two nails. Be sure to select a galvanized common nail that reaches through the deck boards and most of the way into the sleeper but not into the concrete.

ROOF DECKING

There is another, more exotic application where sleepers take the place of conventional joists: on a flat or very low-slope roof. If you don't have much of a view or a breeze in the backyard, why build a deck at ground level when you might have an airy perch on the roof? This is not a great idea for turreted Victorians or steeply sloped Capes. But almost any flat or very low-slope roof can be covered with a wood platform that is more durable and more inviting than asphalt.

The first concern, of course, is safety. Although you can build or rent a scaffold and work from the edge of the roof,

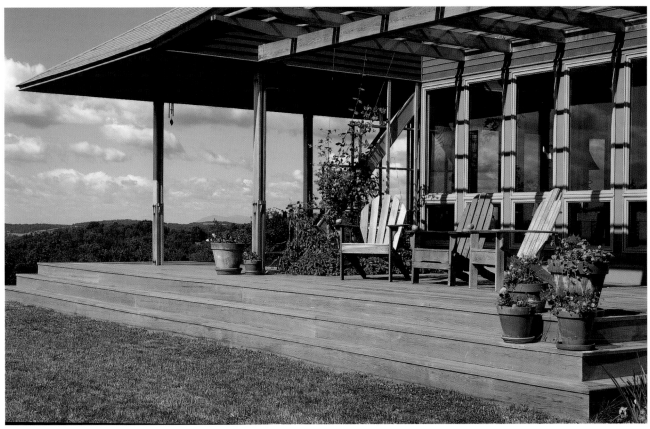

Ground-level decks transition easily to the yard.

it's generally easier (and safer) to haul materials and tools through the house. This leads to the first step in most roof-deck projects: building an opening and installing a door.

Door Location. Many factors can influence the door location. You want an opening that creates easy access, say, from a second-floor bedroom or hallway right out to a garage or first-floor roof. But you also want a stretch of wall free of pipes, wires, and ducts. Rerouting these mechanical systems can make a straightforward door installation much

more complicated. Often, changing out an existing window for a door is the most practical approach.

Door height is another wrinkle. Most doors are just under 7 feet high, which poses no problem in standard, 8-foot-high walls. But the floor level inside usually is too close to the roof level outside, and creates a leak-prone seam that is almost impossible to flash. So instead of cutting the opening down to floor level, roof access doors generally are installed on a curb, which is simply a narrow section of the house wall that you don't remove. Construc-

Roof-top decks afford views and privacy that ground-level decks cannot. Here a dormer window was replaced by French doors to connect the deck with the bedroom inside.

148

tion details will differ depending on the type of roof you have and how it joins the house wall. But if a well-flashed curb winds up creating an awkward step, build raised landings inside and outside the door.

The most practical deck system over roofing is a series of interconnecting panels, called duck boards, that are 4 or 5 feet square. The platform sections have boards about a foot apart that rest on the roof (the sleepers that serve as joist supports), and a top layer of closely spaced boards screwed at right angles to the supports below. To prevent your fasteners from puncturing the roof, drive brass or stainless-steel screws up through the sleepers into the surface boards. (See drawing below.)

Check Building Codes. Even well-built panels will be a little rickety compared with a ground-level deck with rows of 2x4s nailed or screwed into large joists. Roof panels have to be strong enough to keep foot traffic and chair legs from

damaging the roof but light enough to remove.

Check your local building codes for all details on this kind of deck project. All roof decks require a railing. Be sure to observe the rules about railing height and spacing between balusters that enclose the deck space.

ROOF DECKING

Drainage Gap
Hidden Panel Seam
Panel Section
Deck Boards
Roofing
Sleeper
Overlapped Boards
Drainage Bay
Removable Panel

FASTENER DETAIL
Deck Board
Sleeper
Scews (brass or stainless steel)
Overlap
TWO-PANEL OVERLAP
Sleeper

INSTALLING DECKING

Now comes one of the most rewarding parts of building a deck: adding the decking. This is the part of your project that will show the most, so take your time. Maintain even spacing between boards, and follow the manufacturer's directions if installing synthetic decking. If you haven't decided on material, see "Materials for Decks," beginning on page 50. To brush up on deck building techniques, including cutting and attaching decking materials, see "Building Techniques," page 66.

MAXIMUM DECKING SPANS

⁵⁄₄x6 Southern pine or Douglas fir, perpendicular	16"
⁵⁄₄x6 Southern pine or Douglas fir, diagonal	12"
⁵⁄₄x6 redwood or cedar, perpendicular	16"
⁵⁄₄x6 redwood or cedar, diagonal	12"
2x4 or 2x6 Southern pine or Douglas fir, perpendicular	24"
2x4 Southern pine or Douglas fir, diagonal	16"
2x6 Southern pine or Douglas fir, diagonal	24"
2x4 redwood or cedar, perpendicular	16"
2x4 or 2x6 redwood or cedar, diagonal	16"
2x6 redwood or cedar, perpendicular	24"

Note: Be sure to check allowable spans between supports and all lumber requirements with the local building department.

💡 SMART TIP

WHICH SIDE UP?

Installing deck boards bark side up is a well-known rule of thumb of deck building. The bark side is the side of the board that faced toward the outside of the tree. Because of the round shape of trees, the bark-side grain has a convex shape that would seem to be good for shedding rain.

The idea seems to make sense because if the nonbark or dry side gets wet, the reasoning goes, it will trap water. But there are some major problems with the rule.

First, if you install boards that are still wet, or green, they will shrink as they dry out. And a green board installed bark side up is likely to dry into a U-shape, which means water will be trapped on the boards.

Second, if you use good lumber—especially cedar, redwood, or Douglas fir—there is little chance of significant cupping. And a small cup is not

really a problem because no end grain is exposed to the water. In fact, the United States Department of Agriculture has determined that it doesn't matter whether boards are laid bark side up or down. So unless you are using very wet or very dry treated lumber for your decking, just pick the side that looks the best.

DECKING OPTIONS

Laying the decking is the most gratifying part of building a deck. The work proceeds quickly because most of the layout work is completed at this stage. With a helper or two, you can cover the framing on a deck in a day, even if it has some angles or finishing details at the edges.

These can take the form of trim that covers the rough end grain of deck boards, fascias that cover rough joists or girders, and skirting that conceals the area under the deck and makes the structure blend in with the yard.

You may be anxious to finish the project at this point, but it pays to take the time to carefully space the surface boards and to drive your nails or screws the same way (with the same edge margins) over the entire surface. Of course, you should also take the time to examine boards; discard lumber with excessive twisting, cracking, or other problems; and set the best side up.

Plan for the Railings

Before you start laying deck boards, make sure that the installation will work with the railings. In most cases, you can install railings after the deck boards are set, even if you have to create notches in the outer board. If the decking overhangs the frame, you'll need notches for the railing support posts to sit flush against the joist. However, in some designs, especially those that incorporate benches, you must install posts or other supports before the decking. But you can take another approach: installing the posts first and notching deck boards around them as needed.

Also take into account the location of the fascia boards and skirting panels if you're using these finishing details. Because these components are generally nailed onto the outer joist or header joist, you will need a generous overhang on the deck boards to cover their top edges.

There are several factors to consider when you think about how to deck over the joists. Some of the options are limited at this point, of course, because you need to use decking lumber and a surface layout that will work with the joist spacing. On most decks, that's 16 inches on center. But there are plenty of choices. You still need to select a species of wood, its width and thickness, the decking pattern, how the decking will be fastened, and, in some cases, where and how to install the fascia boards and skirting.

Types of Decking

As manufacturers improve the appearance and performance of their products, synthetic decking has become an increasingly popular alternative to wood. It's a durable product that doesn't need finishing or periodic refinishing like wood does. Pressure-treated decking is another popular choice—it's rot resistant but made from southern yellow pine, which tends to twist, cup, and split. Cedar and redwood are naturally rot resistant and less prone to twisting, cupping, and splitting than treated wood. Cedar and redwood are also much more expensive. Synthetic decking prices range from slightly more than pressure-treated to nearly as much as cedar or redwood.

Lumber Dimensions

Most often, ⁵⁄₄x6 wood or synthetic decking is used. These materials are actually about 1 inch thick and 5 ½ inches wide. Whether wood or synthetic, ⁵⁄₄ comes with nicely rounded edges. You can also use wood 2x4s (actual dimensions 1 ½ inches by

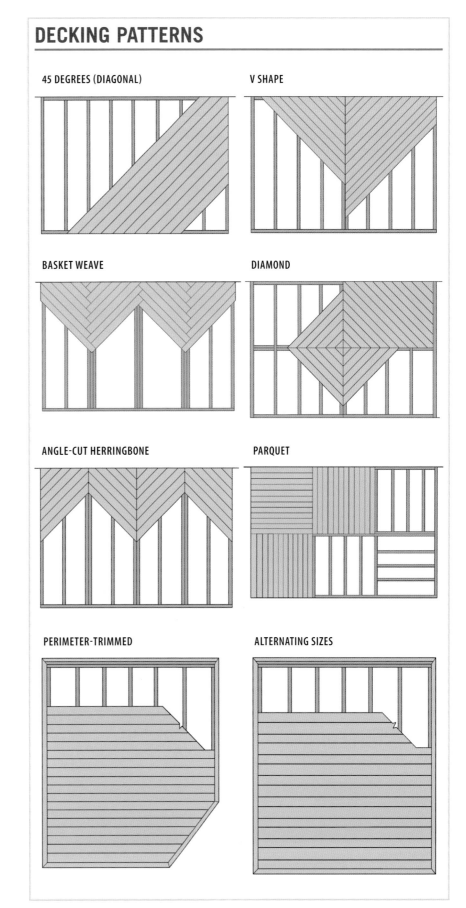

DECKING PATTERNS

45 DEGREES (DIAGONAL)

V SHAPE

BASKET WEAVE

DIAMOND

ANGLE-CUT HERRINGBONE

PARQUET

PERIMETER-TRIMMED

ALTERNATING SIZES

3 ½ inches) or 2x6s (actual dimensions 1 ½ inches by 5 ½ inches). Boards that are wider than 2x6 will expand and contract more and have a greater tendency to cup.

Generally, 2x6s cover more ground and make the work go faster. They may be less prone to twisting than 2x4s, which are often cut from smaller, younger trees. When you run into a knot in a 2x4, you've got a nailing problem, whereas a 2x6 is wide enough to give you room to work around a knot.

Patterns

Most decks look best with boards running parallel with the longest house wall. Straight runs that cross the joists at right angles are also the easiest to install. There are many pattern options, but they often require extra framing and more cutting and predrilling on the deck boards. If there are a lot of angle cuts or a pattern of mixed sizes, count on ending up with extra waste lumber, too. Some herring-

On most decks, the decking runs parallel with the house. But installing the decking on an angle to the house often creates an interesting design element.

1 Set a ½-in. strip of plywood against the house and set the first board in place. String a chalk line.

2 Use a scrap piece of decking to make sure that there will be a gap between the first board and the house.

3 Set out the boards and spacers if necessary. The end board should overhang the framing.

bone and parquet designs can eliminate a lot of angle cuts. But bear in mind that these patterns may run wild along the edges of your deck and make the overall pattern look incomplete. If your deck has different levels, you can create a basic pattern contrast by running the decking at a different angle for each level.

Fastening Systems

You can attach your decking with 10d or 12d galvanized common nails. Or you can use galvanized ring-shank or spiral nails, which have more holding power. However, for maximum holding power you can't beat deck screws—the best ones are ceramic-coated against rust. Today's deck screws use square or star-shaped bits that are much less likely to strip out the X-shaped Phillips bits. Using a power drill/driver, driving screws is easier than hammering nails, and screws are easy to withdraw if you make a mistake. There are also hidden fastening systems. (See "Fasteners," page 62.)

Fascias and Skirts

Both fascia boards and skirting tuck under the decking that overhangs the outer joists. This method is easy and is rot resistant because there are no places where water can be trapped against open grain.

With fascia boards, you might also cut the decking flush to the edges of the joists and cover both the joist and the decking with the trim boards. This detail calls for straight cut lines and high-quality lumber that won't twist or shrink over time. Even then, the seam where the butt ends of the decking meet the fascia can trap water and foster rot.

PROJECT: 🐿🐿🐿
DECK BOARD SPACING

Spacing requirements vary with the material. Some will follow the directions shown here, but other products require no spacing between boards.

TOOLS & MATERIALS
- Common nails
- String
- Decking
- Measuring tape
- Fasteners

ESTIMATING MATERIALS

You could just figure out your square footage and then order enough lumber to cover it, plus 15 percent for waste. And the lumberyard would love it if you did because it could unload the lengths that are overstocked. To minimize waste and time-consuming butt joints on the deck surface, though, take the time to make a plan of your deck surface that shows every piece. Then you can determine the lengths that will work most efficiently and result in less waste.

To figure decking that will be cut at a right angle, start with the width of the deck to find out how many deck boards (or rows of deck boards, if the deck is longer than the longest deck boards you can buy) will be needed. Divide the total width of your deck by 5.6 (for 2x6 or ⁵⁄₄x6 decking) or 3.6 (for 2x4 decking). This figure adds about ¹⁄₁₀ inch for the space between boards. Once you know how many boards you will need, be sure to order the correct lengths to save money.

Estimating is more difficult for angled patterns. Start by calculating how many total linear feet of decking you will need. Divide the deck's square footage by 0.47 for 2x6 decking or 0.3 for 2x4. Add 5 to 10 percent for waste, and you will have a good general figure. Now look at your drawing, and estimate the most-efficient lengths you will need.

Sometimes it's possible to avoid making butt joints by buying extra-long pieces of decking—18 feet or longer. These may cost more per foot, but they're worth it: you'll have fewer rot-prone butt joints, and the installation will be easier and quicker. Where you do need butt joints, be sure to stagger them over different joists. It looks best to keep the joints at least two joists away from each other.

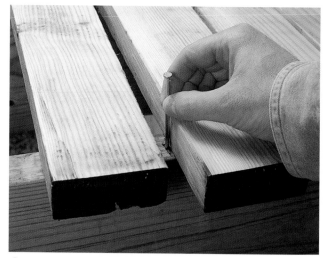

1 A common nail makes a good spacer for kiln-dried lumber. Position the board, and remove the nail.

2 String a chalk line from one end of the deck to the other. Check for bulges and depressions.

3 Measure from the ledger frequently. This helps keep the courses square with the deck frame.

Better synthetic decking, such as the capped composite decking shown here, has color variations and texture that does a good job of imitating the look of imitating wood.

EDGE DETAILS

No matter what kind of deck boards you use, there are three basic choices for fastening them along the edges of your deck. You can cut them flush, box them in with a fascia, or let them extend past the joists an inch or so. You can make a case that any one of them looks better than the others. But to build a durable deck, overhanging boards are best because they shed water and do not create water-trapping seams where wood can rot.

FLUSH

Boxed in

overhanging

INSTALLING WOOD DECKING

Before you start nailing, it makes sense to sort through the boards, square-cut them, and seal all the surfaces. Then you can set the first board next to the house. Its position is important because it sets the starting point for the other boards. You can then lay down the decking, repeating your nailing patterns and spacing to make a uniform surface. Finally, you make the trim cuts and add the finishing touches, such as edging that covers exposed end grain, fascia boards, and skirting.

Preparing the Boards

Sort through the stack of lumber, and choose which side will be up for each piece. Weed out any boards with bad cracks, twists, or other damage. If you have a number of different lengths, stack them accordingly so it will be easy to find the boards you want.

If the boards are long enough, you can let them run over the outer joist and trim them later. Wherever a board end needs to be butted, you can make the cuts ahead of time or wait to see how the boards fall on the joists and make the cuts as you go. This is the way most carpenters do it. Cutting butts ahead of time seems to make sense, but it can get you into trouble if the on-center measurements are a bit off. You need to be sure that butted boards join in the center of a joist, which is only 1 ½ inches wide. If you find that boards are splitting because you have to nail them too close to the end, you can predrill those holes. Or an easier solution is to nail 2x4s along the length and flush to the top of joists where two decking boards will meet. Then you can nail one board to the joist and the other to the 2x4.

Unless you are using treated lumber, you may want to keep a can of preservative handy so that you can coat the freshly cut butt ends.

As you get ready to install the decking, lay out ten or so boards on the deck as they will go down—for example, with the lengths positioned to stagger butt joints. This keeps the work moving and provides a temporary surface to stand on.

Installing Starter Boards

Straight Runs. For decking that runs parallel with the house, pick a straight board and cut it to length, allowing for the overhang. Measure out from the house at both ends of the run, and mark the width of the decking board plus at least ¼ inch to leave a drainage gap. Snap a chalk line or string a line between your end marks, and check at several points along the wall with a block of decking to be sure you have enough room. (See "Laying Out Decking

Boards," page 155.) If the house wall bows in or out, you may need to increase the margin. Don't make the mistake of twisting the board to conform to the house wall. You want the deck boards to be straight. For decking butted to the house, you should follow the same basic procedure.

Diagonals. If you are installing a diagonal pattern, don't start with a short piece in a corner. Start with a straight board at least 6 feet long instead, and set it on a 45-degree angle by measuring equal distances from the starting corner. Before you fasten it, measure from the center of the board to the corner, and use blocks to check how the boards will fall. You don't want to end up with a tiny piece in the corner.

Parquets. To keep track of things when you have boards running in both directions, tack at least four starter boards in place, and measure carefully to make sure that all your decking boards will come out right. Then drive the screws or nails home. With complex patterns, you may want to lay out all of your decking boards, including spacers, to see how the pattern will fall on the framing.

Herringbones. With a herringbone pattern, you need to account for the repeats. Generally, it looks best to use a pattern of full boards centered on the deck and equal-size partial lengths where the pattern meets the edges. Provide adequate nailing surfaces by doubling up deck joists where decking boards meet.

Fastening the Decking

If you nail by hand, expect your arm to tire after a few hours. There's not much you can do about that except use a pneumatic nailer. But because a lot of deck work is best done on your knees, you may want to make the work easier by investing in knee pads.

Position and Cut the Boards. As you place each board in position, make sure the long end hangs over far enough to trim squarely and still cover fascias or skirts. For angled, herringbone, and parquet designs, you will need to measure and cut at least some of the boards as you go. When possible, hold the boards in place to mark them.

You may want to cut a few boards next to the house to length. But when you make trim cuts with a circular saw, you can get pretty close to the house wall and then finish the cut with a handsaw.

(Text continues on page 160.)

PROJECT: 🐾🐾🐾
INSTALLING DECKING

The house wall may bow in and out, but your first board should be straight. In severe cases, you can cut the first board from a larger timber and scribe it to conceal irregularities.

TOOLS & MATERIALS
- Decking
- Chalk-line box
- Measuring tape
- Fasteners
- Hammer

1 The decking should overhang the outer joist plus any fascia or skirting by 1 to 2 in.

2 Set the first board on the chalk line drawn earlier. Maintain the gap between the board and house.

3 For professional results, keep nails spaced evenly. Use the shank to locate each nail from the edge.

4 Drive nails an inch from each edge. Protect deck with scrap wood when pulling bent nails.

5 Lay out 10 to 12 rows as you work. This will help you keep butt joints several rows apart.

(Continued from page 158.)

Fasten Nails and Screws. You can set all your fasteners as you go (the way most pros do it) or set only a few to locate the boards and come back later to drive the rest. This can be an advantage if you discover mistakes later. But it's not hard to pick the best face of a board as you install it and take care of spacing and fastening in one shot. (See "Installing Decking," page 159.)

Use Nails as Spacers. You might try a thicker 16d nail if the wood is dry already, or a thinner 8d nail if it is still relatively wet. You can simply hold the spacer nail against the last nailed board, and tap the head with a hammer to hold it as you set the next board in place. You should then be able to release the spacer by hand and tap it into place on the next spaced edge.

You drive a pair of nails where each board crosses each joist, about ¾ to 1 inch in from each edge. Some people like to angle their nails slightly toward each other. The idea is that it provides increased holding power. But if you need more holding power you should use larger nails, or screws, instead of nailing incorrectly.

Pros generally drive nails or screws straight in to leave a flat head on the surface. An angled head can tear one side of the wood and create a small water trap. It's also difficult to seat an angled nail without digging your hammer into the surrounding wood.

You don't want to mar the deck boards with mis-hits, of course. But deck work is not trim work. Hit the nails hard, giving one final whack to set the heads flush with the surface. Don't tap lightly and use a nail set to seat the heads, or you will be there on your knees forever.

For appearance's sake, it's not much trouble to keep your nails evenly spaced on the boards and in a straight line across the deck. You can use a string line for a guide, draw a pencil line, or just look up to follow the line of set nails.

Predrilling to Prevent Splits. Even if you use screws, be sure to predrill near the ends of all deck boards to avoid splitting. Screws don't exert as much splitting force as nails because they have thinner shanks and turn their way through the wood, but within an inch or two of the end of a board, it helps to have a pilot hole. One rule of thumb is to use a pilot bit that is two-thirds to three-quarters as thick as the shank of your nail or screw.

If you see a crack start to open as you're working on a butt joint, back out the screw or nail and increase the hole size or move to another location. Any small split that appears now will only get larger with time.

Using Deck Board Hardware. Deck clips or continuous deck fasteners allow you to fasten decking from below and leave the wood surface with no visible nail or screw heads. They are a bit more expensive than screws and take some extra time to install, but they may be worth it if you have beautiful decking boards that you want to show off to their full advantage. Check the manufacturer's recommendations about using the hardware with deck boards subject to substantial shrinkage. And, of course, be sure you have enough room to work on the deck from below.

There are several types of deck-board hardware. (See page 335.) Some require you to put nails into the sides of the deck board and the joist, while others require nailing into the joist only and use a spike on the hardware to lock the deck board in place. You can screw through one side to fasten the hardware to the joist, and through the other to fasten the deck board to the hardware. Some call for toe-nailing one side of each deck board; others do not. All of them automatically space the boards.

💡 **SMART TIP**

STRAIGHTENING BOARDS

To bring a bowed board into line, you can use a specialized tool such as the Bowrench, **Step 1** which locks onto the supporting joist for leverage. Or you can dig a flat bar into the joist and pry against the board. **Step 2**

PROJECT: 🐾🐾🐾
FITTING BOARDS AROUND INTERIOR POSTS

If your posts are attached to the inside of the rim joists, you'll need to notch deck boards to fit around them. This can be a little tricky if, as shown here, the boards meet the posts at an angle. Your cuts won't need to be perfectly accurate if you use bases that slip over composite posts. Start by cutting the board to approximate length and letting it run wild on the other end. (See page 62.)

TOOLS & MATERIALS
- Decking
- Pencil
- Tape measure
- Angle square
- Post offcut
- Jigsaw

1 Measure from how deep the notch will be, then transfer the measurement to the board to be notched.

2 Use an angle square or combination square to draw a diagonal line from the post depth point to the edge of the board.

3 Place an offcut of the post material along the line, then scribe the other side of the notch.

4 Cut the notch with a saber saw or handsaw and check the fit. Let the board run wild past the notch, to be cut off later with the other boards.

5 With the notch fitted around the post, mark where the board meets decking on the other side, draw a line, and make the cut.

Straightening as You Go. Every third or fourth board, check the run for straightness. You can do this by holding a taut string line along one edge of the board, or by eye. But it's also wise to measure back to your starting row against the house at several points. This keeps the boards square to the frame.

You can straighten most bends by pushing them into position. You may need to use a chisel or pry bar for the tougher ones. (See page 160.) Start at one end and fasten as you proceed down the board. Keep all your spacer nails in place until the whole board is straightened. Anchor the straightened parts of the board securely with two fasteners at each joist so that the straight part doesn't get bent while you work.

Making the Final Cuts

Measure out from the last joist to allow for an overhang of about an inch, and to account for a fascia board or skirting panel if you use one or the other. Measure the overhang at each end; snap a chalk line as a guide; and make the trim cut with a circular saw. Set your blade about ½ inch deeper than your decking thickness. (See "Edge Trimming," below.)

PROJECT:
EDGE TRIMMING

To get a smooth cut along the deck edge, use a sharp blade and set the saw depth slightly deeper than the thickness of the deck boards.

TOOLS & MATERIALS
- Measuring tape
- Pencil
- Chalk-line box
- Circular saw
- Handsaw

1 The overhang should cover the end joist and the fascia by about 1 in.

2 Snap a chalk line from one end of the deck to the other. This will be your cut line.

3 Run the circular saw along the cut line with the saw's shoe resting on the deck.

PROJECT: BREADBOARD EDGING

This detail is a favorite of furniture builders who use it to conceal and secure the end grain on wide planks that are fitted together to make a table.

TOOLS & MATERIALS
- Decking
- Table saw
- Construction adhesive
- 8d finishing nails
- Hammer
- Drill & bits
- Belt sander

1 Rip ¾-in.-wide lengths of breadboard edging from decking material.

2 After trimming the deck boards, apply construction adhesive to the board edges.

3 Install the trim to the edges of the deck board using finishing nails.

4 Predrill nailholes at the ends of the breadboard trim to keep the wood from splitting.

5 Because some deck boards may be higher than others, trim the surface with a belt sander.

COMPOSITE FASTENING SYSTEMS

In general the fastening systems for synthetic decking aren't much different that those used for wood. The main difference is that synthetic decking is never nailed. Whether screwed or attached with hidden fasteners, each product has its own fastener specifications. Often, composite decking is simply face-screwed to the joists, much in the same way as wood. (See "Installing Composite Decking," opposite.)

Some composite decking is tongue-and-groove. In this case the tongue is screwed at an angle into the joists and covered by the groove (1). In another system, capped composite is grooved on each side. The decking is secured by proprietary fasteners that are fitted into the grooves and then screwed to the joists (2).

Don't install synthetic decking with deck screws designed for wood. Screws for synthetic decking have two sets of threads—the bottom threads are designed to hold in the wooden joists and the upper threads hold well in synthetic materials. Also, the bugle-shaped heads of wood deck screws will cause the synthetic material to mushroom up when you sink the screws. Screws for synthetic decking have smaller heads that are flat on the bottom to prevent mushrooming.

INSTALLING SYNTHETIC DECKING

Nothing quite matches the beauty of a wood deck, but synthetic materials are getting mighty close. And homeowners love the fact that synthetic decking doesn't warp, splinter, or require periodic refinishing. As you'll realize the first time you pick up a floppy piece of synthetic decking, it's not structural like wood decking is. It'll follow the contour of what it's fastened too, so it's extra important to get your joists straight and level. See "Synthetic Decking," page 60, to learn more about the different products available.

💡 SMART TIP

QUICK DRIVING SYSTEM

If your deck is not large, you can use any corded power drill/driver to screw the decking in place. (A cordless drill will run out of power too quickly.) However, using a screw gun designed to accept screws that are collated like machine gun belts will save you a huge amount of time and work. You insert the belt of collated screws and then just press the tip of the tool against the surface to shoot the screw. The tool comes with an extension so you can use it standing up—a great back saver. Your local rental center probably has one available.

PROJECT: 🦇🦇🦇
INSTALLING COMPOSITE DECKING

If your deck will be a simple rectangle, lay it out as shown in "Laying Out Decking Boards," page 155. Here's how to lay out and install boards if your deck will include boards with angle cuts, as well as boards that overlap opposing rim joists.

TOOLS & MATERIALS
- Decking
- Tape measure
- Pencil
- Circular saw or power miter saw
- Drill/driver
- 2 ½-inch ceramic-coated screws for composite decking

1 Put each board that will be cut at an angle in position to measure the approximate length you'll need. Then cut a board to approximate length with a 45-degree cut on one end.

2 Lay out the deck boards that will run wild on both sides of the deck.

3 If a board needs to be notched squarely around a post, put it in place as shown so you can mark the edge where it meets the post. Then measure the depth of the notch and use a post offcut and a square to lay out the cut.

4 Install the first board. This typically will be the one against the house, but in this case it abuts an existing deck. Use two 2 ½-inch ceramic-coated screws into each joist. Here, a special driver with collated screws speeds the work (see "Quick Driving System," opposite), but you can use any drill/driver with a star bit.

5 Typically you want about ⅛ inch between deck boards. You can use 8d nails as spacers, or you can use spacers designed to fit conveniently over joists. Use spacers as needed—usually one on every other joist.

6 Finish screwing the boards to the joist. Then, as shown in "Edge Trimming," page 162, snap a line and cut off the boards that are running wild.

⚲ SMART TIP

HIDING COMPOSITE ENDS

Composite boards have their color throughout, so you can leave the ends exposed if you like. However, there's no end grain, so the cut end of a composite board is not particularly attractive. For this reason it's common practice to cut the decking flush to the fascia boards and then run a 1½ inch or 2-inch wide rip of composite decking as trim board flush to the top of the decking as shown here.

This type of trim board is a must for capped composite because the plastic cap is a different color than the composite core. For capped composite, a solid PVC trim board is often used to match PVC fascia.

FASCIA BOARDS AND SKIRTING

If you select good-looking lumber for the most visible joists and install fasteners neatly in an even pattern, the deck frame may look fine. To improve the look of rougher framing, you can add a coat or two of stain or clad the exposed lumber with fascia boards.

Fascia boards consist of one-by boards tucked under the overhanging portion of the deck boards and are attached to the perimeter joists. They can be made of pine and stained or painted or they can be made of the same wood as a redwood or cedar deck. You can also use one-by polyvinyl chloride (PVC) boards—as is typically done with synthetic decking, which would clash with the treated framing below.

Installation is straightforward. First, cut the board to length and miter any corner joints. Then sand the boards as needed, predrill for screws or nails to avoid splits, and fasten the fascia in place. You may want to add construction adhesive and decrease the number of nails for appearance sake. (See "Installing Fascia," opposite.)

(Text continues on page 168.)

⚲ SMART TIP

SCRIBING ANGLES

Deck framing doesn't always come out perfectly square. As a result, it can be tricky to get fascia miters to meet perfectly at the corner. The problem only gets harder if you are making an octagonal deck. To solve the problem, temporarily tack one fascia board in place, letting it run a bit long. Put a scrap of fascia material on top of the board and against the meeting joist. Scribe the angle as shown bottom left. Untack the fascia and slip a narrow scrap under it and against the meeting joist. Scribe the angle of the meeting fascia as shown at bottom right. At the miter saw, cut the first fascia along its scribe line and then use the line on the narrow scrap to set the saw for the cut on the meeting fascia.

PROJECT: INSTALLING FASCIA

Select a fascia board that is one size up from the joists—for example, a 1x10 to clad a 2x8.

TOOLS & MATERIALS
- Fascia
- Measuring tape
- Pencil
- Circular saw
- Sander
- Drill & bits
- Construction adhesive
- 8d finishing nails
- Nail set
- Hammer

1 Set your saw to cut 45-deg. angles, and miter the ends of the fascia boards where they meet at corners.

2 Before installing the boards, dress the exposed surface with a random-orbit or belt sander.

3 Predrill near the ends of the fascia to avoid splitting the wood. This will be a highly visible joint.

4 Because you will be using finishing nails, apply construction adhesive to the end joists.

5 Finish the installation using finishing nails. Use a nail set to seat the nails and avoid marks on the wood.

(Continued from page 166.)

Adding Skirting

There are several types of skirting material and a number of ways to close off the space between your deck framing and the ground. Lattice is the most common material, although you can use closely spaced 1x2s or fencing materials to create a similar effect.

One approach is to add a support frame near the ground and set the skirting along the outermost edge of the deck. This requires a fair amount of extra framing work because you have to hang the new supports from the joists. It's often easier to use the supports you already have: the row of piers and posts, and the beam that rests on them.

To avoid rot (even if you use pressure-treated lattice or 1x2s), it's best to keep the skirting an inch or two above the ground.

Assemble the Lattice. One good approach is to buy large sheets of prefab lattice and cut them to size. Then you can build simple frames around the panel sections to strengthen them and dress up the edges. Some lumberyards and home centers sell slotted trim designed to work with lattice, but any reasonably stiff frame will do the job.

To mount the panels, apply them to the front of your posts or add nailers on the sides of the posts so that the panels will tuck between them. (See "Installing Skirting," right.)

It's wise to do as much work as possible on the panels, including jobs such as staining and predrilling, before you have to crouch under the deck overhang and finish the installation.

Decking around a Tree

When you are installing decking at a framed opening in the deck for a tree, take the same approach as you do on the deck edges: let the boards run long, and make the final trim cuts all at one time. This is the best way to get a neat edge, and it saves the time of cutting each board to the exact length you need as you nail it down.

You may have to slice off the end of a board at an angle just to get it in place, but try to get all the boards close to the tree. Once they are fastened, it's time to figure how to make your final cuts. For most trees, you'll want to leave a gap of at least 2 or 3 inches between the tree and the decking. You can always leave more. Depending on the overall shape of your deck or the area of the tree, you may want to cut a square or a rectangle. Generally, a simple square

PROJECT:
INSTALLING SKIRTING

Even on a relatively low deck, skirting can conceal the barren area beneath the framing.

TOOLS & MATERIALS
- Measuring tape
- Pencil
- Nailers
- Drill-driver & bits
- 2-in. screws
- Power miter saw
- Framing material
- Exterior glue
- Hammer
- 6d finishing nails
- Lattice panels

SKIRTING SUBFRAME

Brace

Nailer

Girder

Nailer

Subframe Board

Apply lattice directly to subframe.

Nail Plate

3 Miter the corners of the frame material. The frame stiffens the lattice and hides its edges.

shape with a roughly even margin around the tree looks best. But you also can use a saber saw and cut a contoured shape that mirrors the tree trunk. In all cases, cut the boards so that they overhang the box framing around the tree.

Cutting a Circle. If you prefer to cut a circle, use the framing that you can see around the tree for reference. (If the tree weren't there, of course, it would be easy to scribe a circle from a centerpoint.) If you want to be precise, establish four or eight equidistant points on the circumference of the circle. Or simply set a hose or extension cord around the tree.

Decking Curves

On most decks that have a curved corner, you lay the deck boards to overhang the framing, tack a nail at the radius of the circle, and mark the corner cut with a pencil and string that swings from the nail.

The easiest way to trim decking for a curve is by using a trammel to trace the curve on the ends of the decking. (See "Framing for a Curved Section" on page 142 and "Laying Out and Cutting Curves" on page 82.)

On small platforms—at the head of a stairway, for example—you can form a curved pattern by cutting 2x6 lumber on a diagonal. By placing the narrow ends near the radius, the wide ends will spread out in a fan shape. This system requires extra support framing.

1 Measure between the posts to determine the length of the skirting panel.

2 To recess the panel, attach a nailer to the sides of the posts. Install the panel flush to the post edge.

4 Join the frame sections at right angles using glue and nails. Some frames have slots for the lattice.

5 Attach the frames to the nailers on the posts. Use screws for easy removal.

Any deck set above grade level will require stairs to provide a transition between the deck and the yard. Well-built stairs are comfortable and safe to use, and they add a distinctive design element to the deck.

A railing provides a measure of safety, some privacy, and a place for displaying plants. Possible railing designs are endless, and the right design can enhance the look of your deck. Local building codes vary, but generally, decks built more than 30 inches aboveground will require a railing. The building code will specify minimum requirements for the design of the railing, including the railing height and the spacing of the balusters and posts.

Platform Design

A platform can break a long drop into two more manageable sections and serve as a landing beside the main deck. Platforms should be framed like the deck itself, generally with the same-size joists. You can include a platform landing in your deck frame or build it separately and bolt it in position.

Stringer Design

Use 2x12 lumber for your stringers. If you have two-by treads that are longer than 36 inches, or if you are using ¾ wood or synthetic decking for your treads, you will need a middle stringer, or carriage. The outer stringers can be notched to support the treads, or they can be solid with the treads supported by metal hardware or wooden cleats.

Notched Stringer. These are cut into a saw tooth pattern so that each tread has a flat support. You need to be sure of the layout because cuts can't be corrected. On older decks it was common to run the treads an inch or so over the outer stringers. But now, as explained in "Building Code for Stairs," opposite, you'll likely be required to enclose the outer stringers with fascia boards to close the spaces under the balustrade.

Notched stringers require careful cutting, but for some designs, especially when using synthetic decking and railing, the one-by fascia will look less clunky than exposed solid stringers. Besides, stairs that are wider than 36 inches will need a notched middle carriage anyway. With careful

work, you can build a stairway with notched stringers that will last for decades.

Many do-it-yourselfers will get the best results using precut notched stringers that are available at lumberyards and home centers. If the exact location of your bottom pad doesn't matter, you can adjust its position to accommodate store-bought stringers. Before buying, figure your rise and run to be sure you won't end up with a bottom step that is more than ¾ inch different from the rest of the steps. Ideally the last step to the landing pad should have the same rise as the wooden steps.

Solid Stringer. Also called a housed stringer because treads are contained within the angled framing, this type of stair support is used with metal hardware or wooden cleats that support the treads. You still have to make a layout with equally spaced steps, but you don't have to cut the pattern into the stringers.

And if you make a layout mistake, it's easy enough to shift tread hardware or cleats. The best hardware is L-shaped galvanized metal brackets that won't decay the way wood cleats can.

If your stairway is wider than 36 inches, one practical approach is to first cut a notched stringer (carriage), which will support the treads in the middle, and use it as a template for locating your tread brackets on the housed stringers. (Check your local codes about tread spans on stairs.) Just set it up against the housed stringers and mark the positions for the

(Text continues on page 178.)

STRINGER OPTIONS

Most do-it-yourselfers find it easiest to work with solid, or housed, stringers. You simply buy a few straight 2x12s, lay out the tread pattern on the sides, and screw on galvanized metal brackets to hold the treads. Notched stringers are more complicated to lay out, but many home centers and lumberyards sell precut string-

ers. The proportions are generally set to provide a 10- or 11-inch tread and a 7- to 7 ½-inch rise. The angle is fixed because the tread supports of the sawtooth pattern must be level; just cut the bottom edges to fit your site.

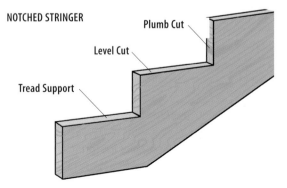

NOTCHED STRINGER

Plumb Cut

Level Cut

Tread Support

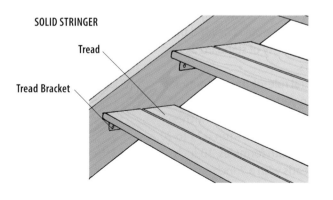

SOLID STRINGER

Tread

Tread Bracket

BUILDING CODE FOR STAIRS

The International Residential Codes (IRC) has in recent years added some new safety requirements for deck stairs. Most municipalities follow the IRC, but not all, and the code does change. That's why it is always a good idea to check your local code before building. Here are three IRC deck stair requirements to be aware of:

Any stair with four or more steps must have a guardrail.

On all guardrails—whether on the deck itself or on a staircase, the spaces between balusters must be small enough to prevent a 4-inch ball from passing through. The four-inch-rule is designed to prevent children from getting their heads stuck.

The 4-inch-rule also applies to the space between a deck and the bottom of a guardrail. However, if you are planning an open stringer with a guardrail, the triangular opening formed by the bottom of the guardrail, the riser, and the tread must be small enough to prevent a 6-inch ball from passing through. For most stairs with guardrails, this means you'll need to use closed stringers or a fascia on the sides.

It once was common to use open risers. However, that space is now also covered by the 4-inch rule. So, unless you have an unusually short rise of less than 4 inches, it also precludes risers that are completely open.

Any stairway with 4 or more steps must have a smooth graspable handrail. The top of the handrail must be between 35 inches and 38 inches above the nosing of the

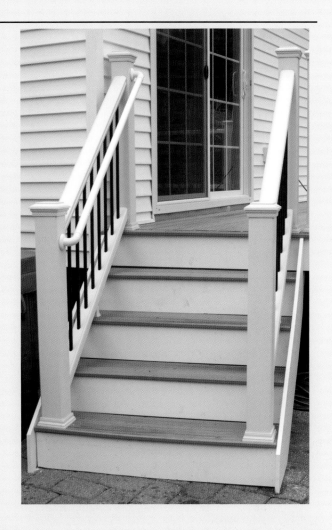

stair tread. It must run continuously and it must return on both ends so that nothing can get caught on it. The handrail must be no less than 1 ¼ inch in diameter and no more than 2⅝ inches in diameter.

As you can see, the 2x4 or 2x6 top rail typically used to construct a deck stair guardrail does not qualify as a handrail. You can make your own handrail—some carpenters rout a groove in a 2x4 and round over the top to create a code-compliant profile. But The easiest way to make the inspector smile is to purchase a handrail kit that can be cut to fit and includes the returns and approved attachment screws.

PROJECT: 🐾🐾🐾
FRAMING A PLATFORM

Use the same techniques on a stair platform that you use on a main deck, matching the joist size and spacing. Put aside good lumber for the exposed sides, and use screws for extra holding power.

TOOLS & MATERIALS

- 2x lumber
- Circular saw
- Square
- Clamps
- Drill-driver & bits
- 1 ¼-in. & 2-in. screws
- Brace
- Hammer
- Nails

1 For clean edges, make square cuts on the platform framing lumber. Allow for overlaps on the corners.

2 To assemble, check for square and then clamp the frame together. Use a brace if needed.

3 Predrill for screws at the corners to avoid splitting the wood. Secure the framing using deck screws.

4 Reinforce the corners with galvanized deck hardware. Add joist hangers to interior joists.

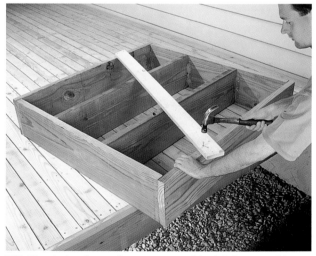

5 Check the frame for square, and lock it into position using a diagonal brace.

PROJECT:
SETTING A PLATFORM

Attach the landing platform to both the deck and the house for support. Sink posts as you would for the main part of the deck.

TOOLS & MATERIALS
- Scrap lumber
- Clamps
- Level
- Flashing
- Bolts
- Wrenches
- Measuring tape
- Drill-driver & bits
- 3-in. screws
- 4x4 posts

1 Clamp the platform to a temporary post. Use clamps to hold the platform against the deck.

2 Check for level in all directions, and make adjustments as needed.

3 Using lag screws or screw bolts, attach the platform to the ledger board against the house.

4 Attach the platform to the deck framing using screw bolts or carriage bolts.

5 Install permanent posts as needed. Screw the posts to the frame, and trim the tops of the posts.

(Continued from page 174.)

brackets, as well as the bottom plumb and level cuts.

To handle unusual stair loads—for example, where stringers are more than 8 feet long—you can use double stringers or laminate a cut stringer to each solid stringer.

Landing Pad Design

Stringers must have something solid to support them at the bottom and protect them from ground contact. You can provide the support in several ways. On a small stairway, you can build two extra piers (one for each stringer). On a larger stairway, it's often more economical to build a concrete slab, which must be at least as wide as the stairs and at least 36 inches wide in the direction of travel. Of course, you also can combine piers with a landing pad made of bricks, gravel, or other material that does not have to support the stringer.

INSTALLING A PLATFORM

There are many ways to include a platform in your stairway. For example, you can support it with four posts and piers to stand away from the deck so that one run of stairs reaches from the deck to the platform and another reaches from the platform to the ground.

Another approach is to attach a platform to the deck to make a step-down landing. This works well if you want the stairs to tuck in next to the side of the deck instead of extending out into the yard. As you climb alongside the deck, you need a transition area, like a landing on indoor stairs, where you can turn and take the last step up onto the deck.

Incorporating a platform landing into your stairs is often easier (and better looking) than extending part of the deck to serve as a landing. This approach also allows you to build the frame independently, complete with joists and fasteners, and bolt the landing frame to the deck frame. In most cases, you will need at least one new pier to support a post at the outer corner of the platform. You may need two, but not if the side of the platform bolts to the deck and the back bolts to the house framing.

Platform Framing

The platform needs to be as strong as the deck. You should plan to frame it with the same lumber you used for the main joists, but pick good-looking lumber for the exposed sides. Set the joists with the typical deck spacing, and secure the connections with galvanized frame hardware. In addition to standard joist hangers, also use L-brackets to reinforce the outside corners of the platform frame. (See "Framing a Platform," page 176, and "Setting a Platform," page 177.)

INSTALLING A LANDING PAD

Whatever design and material you choose for a landing pad, it's wise to build it somewhat oversized. This provides a margin of error of several inches in each direction when it comes time to install and bolt down the stringers. If you live in an area subject to frost, you may need to go below the frost line with your pad foundation. Be sure to check local codes for requirements. Here are some of the options.

Concrete. Use this material to make the strongest landing pad. The area is small, so there isn't too much work involved, though waiting for the concrete to set may slow down your job.

First, dig out enough sod and topsoil to accommodate at least 3 inches of gravel and 3 inches of concrete. Ideally, the pad should sit an inch or so above grade to help with drainage. It's also important to compact soil at the bottom of your small excavation (or leave it undisturbed), and to compact the gravel bed, as well.

One approach is to construct a frame of 2x4s laid on edge, reinforced with 2x4 or 1x4 stakes. This frame can be a permanent part of the pad (using treated lumber) or removed after the concrete has set. Make sure the frame is square and level. (See "Concrete Landing Pad," opposite.)

Place the gravel in the hole, tamping firmly with a 4x4 or a hand tamper. If you will be using reinforcing wire mesh, cut it to fit loosely in the form (so you don't have any wire sticking out after you've poured) and place it in the form, using rocks to hold it up from the gravel.

Pour the concrete, and level it off with a 2x4 that spans across your frame. Finish using a concrete finishing trowel, and use an edging tool where the concrete meets the frame. If you like, give it a final brush stroke with a broom for a skid-free surface.

Brick. Before you install a brick surface, check with your inspector, who may require concrete. (Setting bricks or pavers in a bed of concrete is also an option.) There are two main tricks to getting a nonconcrete landing pad surface that is strong enough. First, tamp the gravel and sand beds (if you're using sand instead of a concrete set). Second, set the landing material so that the load it carries from the stringers is spread over several bricks or pavers. Choose a solid edging to keep the bricks in place, such as pressure-treated landscape timbers or bricks set vertically.

Gravel. The most basic landing pad is a bed of gravel. This is not as stable or as strong as concrete, but it provides excellent drainage and if installed correctly can be surprisingly strong. Check with the building inspector before building a gravel pad.

Dig a hole 10 to 12 inches deep, fill partway with gravel, and install a frame made of treated 2x4s or 2x6s secured with stakes made of 2x4s or 1x4s. Lay 3 to 4 inches of gravel, compact it firm with a hand tamper or a piece of 4x4, then lay the next layer. Don't lay the final 1 ½ inches until the stringers are in place.

When you build your stairs, spread the load so that the stringers will not dig into the gravel, lowering the level of the steps over time. Attach treated 2x4s to the bottom of the stringers, spanning from stringer to stringer. Rest this setup on the gravel, then fill in with the final 1 ½ inches of gravel.

STAIRWAY LAYOUTS

Before you start figuring out the nitty-gritty details, here's the basic idea behind stair layout. To sort out the different possible dimensions and proportions, start by carefully

recording two key measurements. One is the overall drop from the deck surface straight down to the level of the yard or landing. The other is the overall span from the edge of the deck to the end of the stairs.

To work out a preliminary plan, divide the drop into equal segments of *rise* (the vertical distance between tread surfaces), and divide the span into equal segments of *run* (the depth of each tread, including a 1-inch overlap).

If you use precut stringers, the basic proportions are already settled. In that case, you simply make the cuts at the end of the stringer so it rests on the landing pad when the tread support sections of the stringers are dead level.

In stair terminology, the drop is split into increments called *unit rise*, which is the total vertical distance between the top of one tread and the top of the next tread. Horizontal distance is split into increments called *unit run*, which is the horizontal distance traveled by each step. The unit run consists of the width of the tread minus any over-

CONCRETE LANDING PAD

Concrete

Form Board

Welded Wire

Stake

Compacted Gravel

hang or nosing.

Most do-it-yourselfers have to experiment with rise and run ratios to find a design that will provide a safe, comfortable, and code-approved stairway. Here is the sequence you can use to come up with a final plan.

Find the Total Rise. If the ground below your deck is level, you can find the total rise simply by measuring straight down from the top of the deck. But the ground may slope away from the deck. In addition, the ground may slope across the width of the stairs. So you need to determine where the steps will land and calculate the total rise from that point. (See "Stringer Layout," opposite.)

Find the Number of Steps. Let's say you would like a unit run of 11 inches and a unit rise of 7 ½ inches, and your deck is 36 inches off the ground. Divide the total rise of 36 inches by the unit rise of 7 ½ inches to get 4.8. Round up to find that you will need five steps if the ground is level. One of those steps is the deck itself, so subtract it from the equation when figuring total run. Because you are shooting to make each step 11 inches deep, multiply 11 times 4 to find that your landing should be 44 inches from the deck.

Locate the Stair Width. Make two pencil marks on the edge of the deck to indicate the planned width of the stairway. Let's say you want to build steps that are 36 inches wide, including the thickness of the stringers but not including the overhang of the treads on either side of the stringers if you are using notched stringers. You'll probably want to make the landing pad a couple of inches wider on each side, so figure the pad will be 40 inches wide.

Locate the Landing Area. From the marks on the deck, measure out the proposed total run, making sure you are running your measuring tape square to the edge of the deck. Drive a long stake into the ground at these points, making sure the stakes extend above the level of the deck. Plumb the stakes. (If these stakes are more than 60 or 72 inches tall, you will need to have a helper hold a level against them as you proceed, to be sure they are plumb.)

Have a helper hold one end of a string on one of the marks on the deck. Hang a line level on the string, and run the other end to the corresponding stake. When the line is level, mark the position on the stake. Repeat the process to make a mark on the other stake. Measure from the marks on the stake to the ground, or 1 inch above the ground if you want your landing pad to be an inch higher than your yard. If the two measurements differ, use the shorter measurement as the total rise.

Make the landing pad level so that it rises above grade on the low side to compensate for the difference. Let's say, for example, that the mark on the left stake as you face the deck is 40 ½ inches from the ground while the right stake is 42 inches from the ground. The ground slopes away from the deck and down from left to right. Use 40 ½ inches as your total rise.

Figure the Unit Rise and Unit Run. Round the total rise off to the nearest whole number of inches, and divide by 7. If you know you want short rises, you can start by dividing by

STRINGER MARKUP

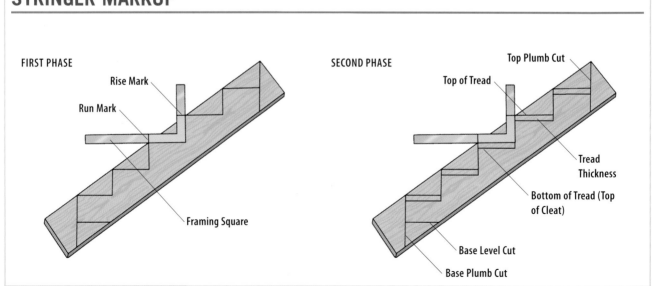

FIRST PHASE

Rise Mark

Run Mark

Framing Square

SECOND PHASE

Top Plumb Cut

Top of Tread

Tread Thickness

Bottom of Tread (Top of Cleat)

Base Level Cut

Base Plumb Cut

6 inches instead of 7. In the example above, 40 divided by 7 equals 5.7. Round again to the nearest whole number. This tells you that to keep the unit rise and unit run you have in mind, you'll need six steps, including the one onto the deck, to cover the total rise.

You can adjust the unit rise or the unit run, or both, to accommodate your true total rise. In most cases, you will not want to change the planned unit run, because it is determined by the lumber you've chosen for stair treads.

The easiest thing to adjust is the unit rise. Divide the total rise (40 ½ inches) by six steps to get a unit rise of 6 ¾ inches. Remember, two times the unit rise plus the unit run should equal between 25 and 27 inches. In our example, two times 6 ¾ inches plus 11 inches equals 24 ½ inches, which is close enough to the general guideline.

Now it's easy to determine exactly where your stairs will land. Again, because one of the steps is the deck surface,

your stringers will have five steps, each traveling 11 inches for a total run of 55 inches. Of course, because you have added a step since figuring the tentative total run, that's 11 inches farther than the original total run of 44 inches.

That's fine, provided the ground is level where the stairs land; simply adjust the position of the landing pad. If the ground continues to slope, you are better off increasing the unit rise so that you can stick with a four-step stringer. To do this, divide the total rise of 40 ½ inches by 5 (the rise includes the fifth step onto the deck). The calculator says that's 8.1, or for practical purposes, a unit rise of 8 inches. Two times 8 inches plus 11 inches equals 27 inches, which is also within the rule of thumb for proper stairway design.

Despite all the figuring, there is no substitute for marking up a stringer, clamping or bracing it in place, and seeing in this full-scale dry run exactly where the treads will fall.

PROJECT: 🐾🐾🐾
STRINGER LAYOUT

You'll use a framing square to lay out stringers by "stepping off" each unit rise and each unit run. This can be done by simply aligning the rise and run measurements on the legs of the square to the edge of the board, but the work will go faster if you use stops as shown here.

TOOLS & MATERIALS
- Measuring tape
- 2x4 framing square
- Stops
- Horses
- Pencil
- 2x12 stringers

1 Extend a level 2x4 from the platform, and measure the distance down to a level landing area.

2 Set stops on a framing square, where numbers on opposite sides match your rise and unit run.

3 Mark the top of the stringer. Slide the stops along the stringer to repeat tread layout lines.

BUILDING THE STAIRS

Here is a look at the basic sequence of building a set of stairs. Of course, you may have to add some construction steps (or skip over a few) if you are building something more complicated or unusual than a relatively short, straight run.

Estimate Stringer Length. To buy the stock for your stringers, you'll need a rough estimate of their length. Here's a quick method. On a framing square, use the stair layout numbers on opposing sides as a guide. The idea is to measure on a diagonal between the number matching your unit rise on one side to the unit run on the other side. This will tell you how far the stringer has to travel per step. Multiply this number by the number of steps you will have, plus one (to be safe), and you will have a good rough estimate of how long your stringer needs to be. For example, a step with a unit rise of 7 inches and a unit run of 11 inches will travel 13 inches per step. If there are five steps, you should buy stringers about 6 feet 6 inches long.

Lay Out the First Stringer. Using a framing square, transfer the rise and run to a 2x12 with the crown side up. It helps to mark your square with tape if you can't find metal stops, sometimes called buttons. The stops are handy because they let you ride the square along the side of a stringer, maintaining the same angle for every tread. Mark the stringers in pencil. Don't be surprised if you get a bit mixed up and have to start over. (See "Stringer Layout," page 181.)

Start at the top of the stringer—the end that will meet the deck. When you come to the bottom step, shorten the rise by the thickness of the stock for the treads.

Make the Stringers. Cut the top and bottom of the stringer—you don't have to cut the notches yet—and hold it up to the deck in the position where it will be attached when you build the stairs. Rest the bottom end of the stringer on the landing pad, or a piece of lumber that simulates the height of your landing pad. Check that the layout lines for the treads are level.

To be safe (as long as you have some extra length in the stringer), you might want to sneak up on the plumb and level cuts at the ends of the stringer. For example, you might leave the mark plus ½ inch or so for the first dry run. You can always trim off the excess and use the margin to correct the angle one way or another.

To make the cuts for a notched stringer, use a circular saw. Because you are entering the board at an angle, you may need to retract the blade guard at the start of each cut to avoid cutting a wavy line. Rest the shoe of the saw

solidly and evenly on the surface of the board as you cut. It's okay to go past your lines a little (¾ inch or so), but only if the board face you are looking at will not be visible once the stairway is completed. But instead of weakening a stringer with overcuts, you can finish circular saw cuts with a handsaw.

It's generally neater to finish the sawtooth-pattern stringer cuts with a handsaw, holding the blade at 90 degrees to the board so you don't get overlapping cut lines on the other side of the board.

Brush on a coat of sealer at all your cuts, and let it sink into all of the end grain. Take care not to bump the projecting teeth of the stringer after they are cut and before treads are attached. The stringer teeth could split off.

After you have cut the first stringer, check it in position to be sure the cuts are correct. Then use it as a template for other stringers. If you are going to have two solid stringers and a notched center carriage, cut the notched piece first and use it to mark the housed stringers.

For a housed stringer, make the top and bottom cuts first. Then position the tread cleats; drill pilots; and fasten the cleats to the stringers with 1 ¼-inch lags or structural wood screws. If you're not sure of the tread layout, you can screw on the hardware after the stringers are installed. This gives you a chance to make corrections. (See "Installing Solid Stringers," opposite.)

(Text continues on page 185.)

POSITIONING STRINGERS

Decking

Header
EXTENDED STRINGER

Joist
Overlap

BUTTED STRINGER

Header

Bracket

Stringer

Blocking

PROJECT: 🐿️🐿️🐿️
INSTALLING SOLID STRINGERS

Clamp a marked stringer in place to check pencil marks for treads before installing the stringer.

TOOLS & MATERIALS

- Level
- Measuring tape
- Combination square
- Stair stringers
- Drill & bits
- Stair brackets
- 1 ¼-in. structural wood screws
- Framing square
- Stair clip
- Lag screws
- Wrenches

1 Make sure the landing pad is level before installing the stringers.

2 Mark the location of each stringer on the platform or deck. The edges of the stringer must be straight.

3 Attach the top edges of the stringers to the platform using corner brackets.

4 Screw galvanized tread brackets to the stringer, following the layout lines.

5 Attach a galvanized clip to the pad. See page 185 for other attachment options.

PROJECT:
SETTING CARRIAGES

On wide stairs, add at least one center carriage for extra support to keep the tread from flexing when someone steps on it. Many building codes require the center carriage.

TOOLS & MATERIALS
- Level
- Drill & bits
- 3-in. lag screws
- Angle brackets
- 1 ¼-in. structural wood screws
- Measuring tape
- Square
- 1x brace

1 Tack the center carriage in place, checking for level at each tread location.

2 Use the access space from inside the platform framing to drive lag screws into the top of the carriage.

3 Reinforce the carriage attachment by installing angle brackets.

4 Measure the stair opening and center the middle carriage.

5 Tack a brace across the bottom of the stringers. This keeps them in alignment as you add fasteners and treads.

(Continued from page 182.)

Locate the Posts. On some designs, you can install the stringers and treads completely, and then attach the main railing post. On stairs that project away from the deck with two railings, of course, you'll need two posts. If your 2x12 stringers are securely bolted into a concrete landing pad, you may gain enough strength for a railing post by bolting it to the pad and the stringer. It will be even stiffer once you add a substantial railing and balusters.

Another option is to set the stringers temporarily, mark the post locations, remove the stringers, and dig postholes. You might set the posts in concrete or build piers with hardware so that the porous post ends stay off the ground.

Attach the Tops of the Stringers. To make a solid connection, you may have to beef up the deck framing. Depending on its size (and the amount of unit rise), you may not have enough joist material to make a solid connection. In that case you will need to add another support, typically fastened between posts.

To attach a stringer to the face of a joist, you may be able to drive nails or screws through the back of the joist into the end of the stringer. In any case, be sure to secure the face of the connection with angled brackets. You may see some parts of this hardware, but most will be concealed by the treads.

Attach the Stringers to the Pad. The stairway will be quite stable once the treads and railings are installed. But to lock the stringers in place, you can install a small galvanized bracket to the concrete pad. (See "Installing Solid Stringers," page 183.) Another option is to set J-bolts in the concrete while it is wet and attach a treated wood cleat to them. Or you can notch the bottom of the stringers and install a 2x4 cleat attached to the pad with masonry nails, or with lag screws and masonry shields. (See below and page 186.)

Install Treads and Risers. If your stair will have three or fewer steps, code allows you the option of omitting a stair rail, which in turn allows you to use open stringers. (See "Building Code for Stairs," page 175). Risers on open stringers are often installed flush to the outside of the stringers, but this design can lead to problems if your cuts are not perfect or if the boards shrink. If you let them overlap the stringers by ¾ inch or so, you will avoid these problems.

On notched stringers, you may like the floating effect that comes from extending the treads 3 or 4 inches beyond the edge of the stringer. If possible, the overlap should be equal on both sides of the tread.

If you're nailing, it's wise to predrill your treads. Driving screws is a better option and provides more holding power. Better yet, use concealed hardware, and drive screws up through brackets into the bottoms of the treads. There won't be any screw or nail heads on the surface of the tread. (See "Tread Options," page 187.)

Driving screws up into treads isn't practical on bottom steps that may be only 6 or 7 inches from the ground. There probably won't be room for a drill. The solution is to attach the L-brackets to the undersides of the treads first, clamp the assembly in place, and then drive screws sideways to fasten the brackets.

RAILINGS: BASIC CHOICES

Whether you are standing on the deck or viewing it from the yard, the railing is the most visible part of the structure. The railing greatly influences the overall appearance of the deck, giving it either vertical or horizontal lines, an open or closed appearance, or a polished or rustic look. But railings must also be designed for safety.

Current codes typically call for a railing that is 36 inches high with balusters spaced so that a 4-inch ball can't fit

(Text continues on page 187.)

STRINGER BASE ATTACHMENT OPTIONS

BRACKET

ANCHORED CLEAT

SPREADER CLEAT

Pad

Bracket

Cleat

Anchor Bolt

Pad

Cleat

Design stairs to complement the overall look of the deck. Note the lights installed in the risers.

⛯ SMART TIP

BOX STEPS

If your deck is only a step up from the yard, you might avoid stringers altogether and build box steps. These are easy-to-build rectangular frames, usually made of 2x6 treated lumber and covered with deck treads. For two or more steps, build a large box, placing progressively smaller ones on top.

ATTACHING CLEATS

An alternative to attaching stringers to a pad with galvanized brackets is to attach a 2x4 cleat. Use lag screws and masonry shields to attach the cleat. After cutting the cleat to size, predrill holes for the screws.

Drill holes for the masonry shields.

Use a ratchet wrench to drive the screws.

Screw stringers to the cleats.

TREAD OPTIONS

On solid stringers, do not rely on nails driven into the treads through the stringers to support the step. This weak detail can cause splits and accidents.

A better way to support treads is to attach a nailing block, or cleat, to the stringer, and nail or screw the tread to the cleat. **Step 1** However, with time the wood may decay.

Galvanized brackets provide durable support for treads. **Step 2** Fasten treads by screwing through the flange into the bracket. On sawtooth stringers, the sawtooth pattern creates a ready-made support for the treads. **Step 3**

If treads extend beyond the stringers, finish treads with curved corners and beveled edges. **Step 4**

1

2

3

4

(Continued from page 185.)

through. If the railing incorporates a bottom rail, the space between rails and deck must also be less than 4 inches. (Be sure to check code requirements with the local building department.) But within these limits, you have lots of options, including building your own railing entirely from wood, incorporating manufactured components into your own railing design, or using a manufactured railing kit.

There's no heavy lifting and no messy digging at this stage. And with a few simple techniques, you can produce a structure that looks professional and handcrafted—something you can point to with pride for years to come.

RAILING MATERIALS

Some lumberyards and home centers carry prefabricated railing systems. They come with all the components ready for assembly, including railings and factory-milled balusters and newels in several different decorative patterns. You can also use cast metal, steel cables, plastic tubing, clear acrylic panels, and so on, as long as you get the approval of the local building department. If your decking is synthetic, you'll almost certainly want to use synthetic railings to match, either building your own of composite material or using a synthetic railing kit.

For wooden decks, the most popular and easiest-to-use

railing materials are stock pieces of dimensional lumber. You can cut and assemble one-by, two-by, and four-by materials in a variety of styles.

Lumber

It is usually best to have the railing materials match the decking and fascia, but this is not a hard-and-fast rule. Sometimes it works best to think in terms of matching the railing with the house, inasmuch as the railing is a vertical line that is seen with the house as a backdrop. For example, on a Colonial or Victorian house, turned spindles and fancy newels may look best, especially if they can mirror elements on the house.

And there's no rule that says you can't stain or paint all or part of the wooden railing to help it blend in. If you have an unpainted deck against a painted house, you already have wood and paint in combination, and there's no harm in continuing that pattern. In any case, paint or stain the top cap to protect it from the weather.

Selecting Lumber

The railing deserves the best lumber you can find. Not only do these pieces get handled, they also provide nooks and crannies through which water can be absorbed. And splinters on a rail can be downright dangerous. You must select railing material carefully. This particular component is important when it comes to appearance, and even more so when it comes to safety.

Cedar and redwood look best and splinter least. However, because they get handled and are exposed to the weather, plan on treating railings made of these materials with a wood preservative at least every other year. Treated lumber of high quality can also work.

Precut Components. You can save time using precut components such as decorative 2x2 balusters. But don't change your railing design just to accommodate their size. With a power miter saw and an easily made jig, you can quickly gang-cut 100 2x2s to the length you need. It can sometimes be a problem to find good-looking 2x2s, be-

This railing works well with the trim on the main part of the house.

cause they often twist if not stacked well. You may want to select a larger stock and rip it into pieces to make balusters.

In some areas you can purchase lumber that has been milled to accept stock components. For example, you should be able to buy a top cap that has a 1 ½-inch-wide groove in the bottom to accommodate 2x2 balusters.

Fasteners

When things come loose on a deck, it is usually at the railing. There's a lot of exposed joinery, and the railing gets leaned on and bumped. So plan for a railing that is as strong as possible at all points.

Unfortunately, there are few specialized railing hardware pieces, and they are not as effective as joist hangers for the framing. In general, the metal connectors for attaching rails to posts are unattractive and provide a place for moisture to collect. And unless they are galvanized, they can rust. There is a post-to-railing clip that is more helpful; it allows you to connect the top cap to the post while concealing the fasteners. Wood cleats that can add an extra nailing surface often look unprofessional and may be susceptible to water damage.

The upshot is the need to make the most of standard fasteners. Start off by attaching the support posts to the outermost joists with either lag screws or through-bolts. Through-bolts offer maximum support. It's also wise to drill pilot holes for all nails or screws that are near the end of a board. Use 3-inch deck screws or 16d galvanized nails for plenty of holding power. Try to avoid driving nails or screws at an angle (toenailing), and driving more than two fasteners at railing connections. For example, where you need to piece a horizontal rail over a 4x4 or 2x4, use a lap joint and one pair of fasteners driven through both boards. This is less likely to cause splitting than driving two pairs.

RAILING BASICS

All railings use some, but not necessarily all, of the following components. *Posts* are structural members, usually made of 4x4s or 2x4s turned on edge for lateral strength. They keep the railing from wobbling and provide the main support that counteracts the weight of someone leaning or falling against the assembly.

Balusters are the numerous vertical pieces, often made of 2x2s, that fill in spaces between the posts and provide a sort of fence. *Bottom rail* and *top rail* pieces run horizontally between the posts, and are either flat or on end. On many designs, the balusters are attached to these rails. Some railings do not have vertical balusters, and use several horizontal rails instead. (Check local codes.)

Other designs use a *top cap,* a horizontal piece of lum-

ber laid flat on top of the post and top rail. It covers the end grain of the post and can provide a flat surface that serves as a shelf.

Complying with Code

The railing is one part of your deck that an inspector will check closely. You'll likely find that any deck more than 30 inches from the ground requires a railing that uses vertical components and must be at least 36 inches high.

If the deck is more than 8 feet high, you may want to build a 42-inch railing for extra security.

When you're planning the railing system, consider one of the most limiting codes: the minimum space between components. Commonly, this dimension must be small enough so that a 4-inch ball can't fit through. This rule is

CAP AND POST OPTIONS

Precut posts are available in many styles and sizes. You can cut them to length and combine them with stock sizes of railing caps and balusters. If you use stock posts, you can dress up the tops with flat or shaped caps. Many have a screw end, so you can drill a pilot hole and easily turn them onto the posts.

designed to prevent children from getting their heads stuck between rails or balusters. Some codes may call for a smaller maximum opening at the bottom of the railing.

There also may be specific requirements about posts and fasteners to ensure that your railing is strong. But there are many design variations that you can use and still comply with code.

RAILING DESIGN CHOICES

One approach to railing design is to work from two lists of dimensions: one that includes stock-size lumber, such as 2x4 and 4x4 posts, and another that includes code require-

ments, such as less than 4-inch spacing between balusters. You'll find there are many ways to put the pieces together.

Here is a quick look at some of the other factors that can affect your choice of materials and the overall design.

Matching Deck Overhangs. The first thing to think about in selecting a design is how you will attach the railings and posts to the deck. There are several possibilities. For example, if you have balusters but no bottom rail so that the balusters are attached to the joists or fascia boards, you may want to cut the decking flush to the joists. Otherwise you would have to make hundreds of little cutouts to make room for the balusters. But if you are using several rails instead of balusters, or if you have a bottom rail to which you'll attach the balusters, then the decking can overhang the joist.

Choosing a Cap Width. If your top cap will butt between the posts, it should be the same width as the post—which usually means it will be a 2x4. If you want a wider cap (handy as a shelf), use a design that places the cap on top of the posts. This style looks best if the cap overhangs the posts by ¼ to 1 ½ inches on each side.

Most railing designs allow you to choose either a 2x6 or a 2x8 for a top cap. The 2x8 may look a little clunky, especially on a small deck, but has a lot of shelf space. Whatever design you choose, select the very best pieces of lumber for your top cap.

Attaching Posts. It once was common to notch 4x4 posts to fit over the rim joist and then bolt the posts to the side of the deck. However doing this reduces the strength of the railing, In general, notched railing posts are no longer allowed by most codes. However, your building inspector may allow shallow notches, such as those in "How to Make Posts," page 194, if the post spacing is close enough. This leaves you two options. One is to bolt full posts to the outside of the rim joists, but this can look clunky.

The best strategy is to attach the posts to the inside of the rim joists and cut decking to fit around them. The first step in doing this is calculating the length of your posts. For example, if your railing will be 36 inches high with a 1 ½-inch-thick cap rail, the post will extend 34 ½ inches above the deck. To this measurement add the thickness of the decking and the width of the joists. With 1-inch-thick decking and 7 ¼-inch-wide joists, the posts need to be 42 ¾ inches long.

Corner Posts. You can install a single corner post or two posts near one another on opposite sides of a corner. Single corner posts should be 4x4s or better.

ATTACHING INTERIOR POSTS

Fastening a post to the inside of rim joists is the easiest and most secure method of attachment. Here a composite 4x4 post is used, but the process is exactly the same for wood posts. Start by temporarily tack-screwing a block of wood under the joist to hold the post up while you install it. Then cut a block of joist material to fit snugly between joists. Plumb the post, and then secure it with 16d galvanized common nails through the joists and the block. Also nail through the joists into the ends of the block.

Position and plumb the post.

Secure the post with 16d galvanized nails.

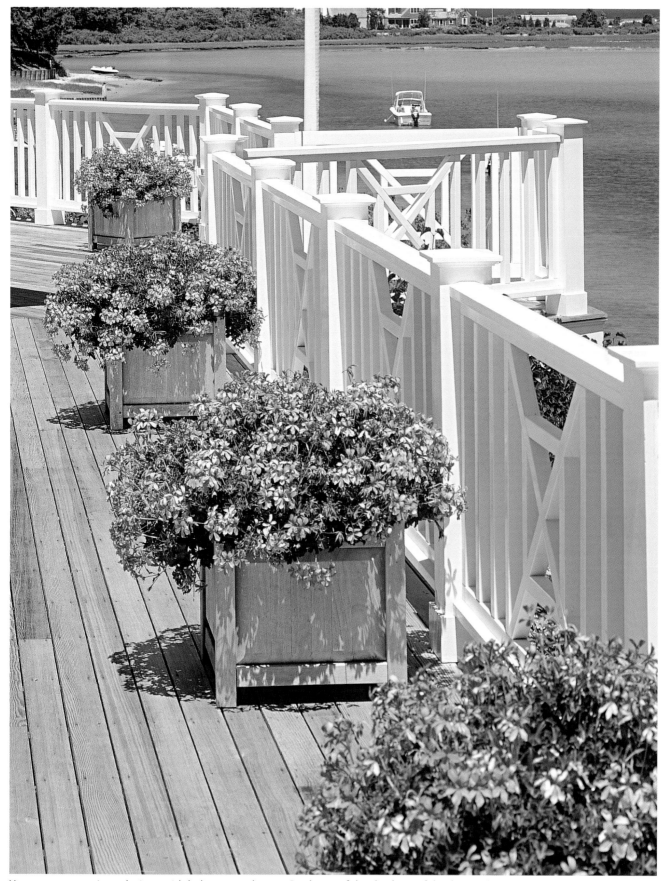

You can create unique designs with balusters and posts. But be careful—this beautiful railing violates most building codes because a 4-inch ball would fit through the space at the top center of each section.

RAILING OPTIONS

Here is a look at several design options. If you want to create your own design, you can mix and match ideas.

Balusters and Top Rail Only. This is the simplest design. But it is suitable only for smaller railings because it lacks posts and a flat-laid top cap, both of which give lateral strength to other designs. Of course, the closer the balusters are to each other, the more strength you gain. On a long deck, this railing can have a monotonous appearance because all the vertical lines are the same width.

To build it, install the balusters for each end of the rail, and attach the rail. Then fill in the middle balusters. Screws work better than nails. The uncompleted railing will wobble a bit if you pound on it.

Cap with No Rails. This has the vertical feel of the first design, with the added strength of posts and the usefulness of a top cap. The easiest way to build this railing is to use a cap with a factory-milled groove to fit the 2x2 balusters. But some outlets offer these caps only in 3 ½-inch widths. If you want to set out some flower boxes, use a 2x6 for the top cap, and attach a 2x2 nailer underneath it. Screw the balusters to the nailer.

Install the posts every 72 inches or so (but within code limits), and lay the top cap on them. Install the nailer between the posts if you're not using the cap with a groove, and attach the balusters.

Two Rails with No Cap. In this system, the horizontal lines are as strong as the vertical lines. The lack of a top cap gives a clean look, but affords no shelf space. You may like the look of a wider, more substantial rail on top, such as a 2x6, and a narrower rail, such as a 2x4, near the deck. Attach the top and bottom rails and then the balusters, or build the baluster-and-rail sections ladder-style.

Horizontal Rails. Horizontal lines dominate in this system. (It may not be allowed locally on decks more than 2 or 3 feet high.) You can butt the ends of the rails where they meet over a post or miter them to create an overlap for a more-finished look. The top rail can be made of 1x6, if you want a large overhang on a 2x6 cap. Unless your posts are no more than 48 inches apart, the other rails should be made of two-by lumber. Remember to place rails below the top rail, spaced closely enough to conform to codes.

POST AND RAILING OPTIONS

FLUSH

DOUBLE CORNER

MILLED BALUSTERS

VERTICAL RAIL

SINGLE CORNER

HORIZONTAL RAIL*

*Only for low decks

ALUMINUM BALUSTERS

An easy way to add elegance to your railing is to use aluminum balusters. Those shown here simply screw to top and bottom rails. Aluminum balusters cost more than wood, but they never warp and they never need painting.

Two Rails with Balusters. This has the look of ladder-style sections between posts, but the rails are continuous, running on the face of the posts (or slightly inset), instead of being butted between posts. This is one of the best approaches because it provides strong horizontal lines and sections of vertical lines with balusters. This helps to give scale and detail to a deck so that it does not look so much like a huge platform stuck onto the side of the house.

First attach posts, which can be 4x4s or 2x4s (spaced and sized according to code); then run the rails and a top cap, if you like, in which case the balusters can butt up against the bottom of the cap.

Sandwiched Panels. This design has several variations, such as using lattice panels, plastic glazing panels, safety glass, or solid panels of siding material. The idea is to build frames for the filler material and attach them to the posts. Another option is to install nailers on the sides of the posts, insert the filler material, and secure it with another set of nailers. A drawback to this design is that water can collect and sit on the bottom rail.

Screen with Lattice Top. This uses a combination of designs and provides a lot of visual interest while increasing privacy and cutting down on wind. The potential weak spot is the slats that can become loose over time. At the bottom they can soak up water that sits on the 2x4 bottom rail. So give the cuts a few coats of preservative, and attach the slats firmly with screws.

Cutting the top of the posts to a point will make them less susceptible to water damage. But a simple angle cut will

also help. The lattice section on top is constructed in much the same way as the sandwiched panels. Install the posts, build the bottom sections ladder-style, and install them between the posts. Add the topmost rail and one side of 1x1 nailer pieces, then the lattice, and the rest of the 1x1.

Top Rail of 4x6 on Balusters. This is an impressive, unusual railing that does not take a lot of extra work and is no more expensive than many other designs. It is vital, however, that you have extremely straight, dry, and split-free 4x6 pieces for the top rail because there is absolutely no way to straighten them as you build.

The decking has to be cut flush to the joists. The bottom of the balusters are sandwiched between the joists, and the fascia is added after the balusters, creating a 1 ½-inch gap between the decking and the fascia. This is a good design for avoiding water damage.

Attach the balusters to the deck with two or three screws or nails. Then measure and cut the 4x6 pieces to fit. (With a helper, you can set them on top of the balusters for measuring.) Next, cut the groove in the 4x6 for the balusters. To do this, draw lines for a 1 ½-inch groove. Be sure you do not cut all the way through to the ends where the groove will be seen in the end grain. Set your circular saw blade to a depth of about 2 inches. First, cut to the lines, then make several passes between the lines, and clean out the groove with a sharp wood chisel. Set the 4x6 pieces in place, and attach balusters with angle-driven screws or nails. Add the fascia board over the face of the balusters.

Crisscross. Making this gridlike pattern will take patience, both to lay it out and to install it. If you want the sections to be squares rather than rectangles, figure how far apart the horizontal pieces will be, and space the vertical balusters in the same way. You can notch the decking for each 2x2 baluster. It's generally easier to install the balusters before the decking. Of course, it would be even easier to cut the decking flush to the joists or fascia. Use screws rather than nails because all those 2x2s will flex if you pound on them.

Figure your grid carefully, laying out the position of all the balusters. You may have to fudge a bit to make the balusters come out evenly spaced. But if you end up with squares that are ¼ inch or so out of square, no one will notice. Install the balusters, the 2x4 top rail, and 2x6 cap. Finish with the 2x2 horizontal rails.

Milled Balusters. Factory-turned balusters, made of treated lumber, vinyl, or composite materials are widely available. These require no cutting (except to length in some cases), which saves you a lot of work. Be sure to inspect each wood baluster carefully for cracks and gouges.

There are many ways you can incorporate these balusters into a railing system. For example, you can build sections of railing ladder style, fastening the balusters to the top and bottom rails with 3-inch screws driven through the rails into the balusters.

INSTALLING RAILINGS AND BALUSTERS

Construction methods vary with different railing designs, but usually you install the posts first, the top and bottom rails next, then the top cap (if you're adding one), and finally the balusters. An alternative approach is to build rail sections ladder-style and install them between the posts. But for most do-it-yourselfers, the piece-by-piece method works best.

PROJECT: 🪶🪶🪶
HOW TO MAKE POSTS

You can square cut the ends of the posts, but angled cuts have a more finished appearance.

TOOLS & MATERIALS
- Measuring tape
- Combination square
- Circular saw
- Clamps
- Mallet and chisel
- Drill and bits
- 4 ½-in. lag screws
- Rachet wrench
- Level

Putting up the Posts

Once you decide on the railing system, you'll know how to continue—for example, by notching the deck edge for posts. Here is a basic sequence, which you may have to adjust somewhat, depending on the railing system you select. (See "How to Make Posts," below.)

Cut and Notch Posts. Determine the length of your posts, taking into account other railing members and the amount of end joist space the post will cover when it is installed.

For instance, if you have 2x8 joists and want a railing that measures 40 inches high, subtract 1 ½ inches for the thickness of the top cap, and add 8 ¾ inches for the thickness of the decking plus the width of the joist, for a post length of 47 ¼ inches. You also may want to subtract ¾ inch or so to leave a reveal between the bottom of the joist and the bot-

1 Use a circular saw to make a 45-deg. angled cut at the top end of the posts.

4 Make another set of cuts for the bottom rail. (See step 2.) Clean the recess with a chisel.

5 Notch the deck overhang so that the post lies flat against the joist.

tom of the post. On decks, this kind of offset generally gives a more finished and professional appearance.

Cut and Notch the Posts for the Railing. The design shown here has a shallow notch and short distances between posts, so it is actually quite strong despite the post notches. **Step 1–Step 4** However, be sure to check with your local building inspector before notching any rail posts. Be particularly careful on corner posts. By the time you make two notches (one for the railing on each side of the corner), the structure of the post may be undermined.

Mark and Notch Decking. On the fascia or joists, mark the positions of all your posts, making them evenly spaced whenever possible. Make square layout lines so that the posts will fit snugly when you plumb them. You can use a

saber saw to make the cutouts or cut the sides for depth with a handsaw, and use a chisel to slice through the back of the notch. **Step 5**

Drill Pilot or Screw Holes. Mark your posts for carriage bolts or lag screws that join the posts to the deck frame. **Step 6** To avoid splits, the fasteners should not go into the deck boards or be driven within 1 ½ inches of the top and the bottom of the joist, if possible. It's better to have bolts only 4 or 5 inches apart than to set them near the edges of the joists underneath. **Step 7**

Once you have the spacing set, clamp the post in place to be sure the fasteners will connect solidly to the frame. Then duplicate the layout on the rest of the posts. For through-bolts, drill a hole that allows the bolt to slide completely through the hole. Its threads don't bite into the wood the

2 Make a series of closely spaced cuts then knock out the waste with a chisel.

3 Make an angled cut at the bottom outside corner of the post. This will create an attractive detail.

6 Drill pilot holes for lag screws where the post will join the deck joist. Countersink to recess bolt heads.

7 Attach the post with lag screws and washers. Check for level and adjust as necessary.

way they do with a lag screw. For lags, you need a pilot hole that's no wider than the central shaft minus the threads.

To make the holes line up, of course, you need to clamp each post in place (and check for plumb) before drilling through the post into the joist. If you are worried about getting the posts exactly plumb, first drill the top hole and temporarily insert the bolt or screw. Then hold the level to the post and drill the second hole.

Attach the Posts. Secure the posts with carriage bolts or lag screws with washers. Some people prefer the appearance of bolt or screw heads that are recessed into countersunk holes. This generally makes a neater, more-finished appearance—and no one will get snagged.

Setting the Rails

Mark and Cut the Rails. When installing rails, it's usually best to hold each piece in place, mark it for cutting, and install it completely before adding another section. Ideally, of course, all of the rails will be single lengths, and you won't have joints except at the corners. (See "How to Install Rails," below.)

But where you must piece the rails, you may want to take the time to make a scarf joint instead of a butt joint, particularly if you have to make the joint over a 2x4 instead of a 4x4 post.

The idea is to cut complementary 45-degree angles where the rails meet, which allows one to slide on top of the other. Clamp the scarf joint in place, predrill, and drive a pair of

PROJECT: 🐾🐾🐾
HOW TO INSTALL RAILS

If you can't create a code-approved post spacing layout that is even, leave the odd space next to the house where it will be the least noticeable.

TOOLS & MATERIALS
- 2x4s
- 2x6s
- Measuring tape
- Circular saw
- Drill and bits
- 2 ½-in. screws
- Router
- Construction adhesive
- Sander

1 On long runs that require more than one piece of lumber, create a scarf joint that falls on a post.

4 Continue attaching the bottom rail to the posts. Brace the top of the posts for stability.

5 This top rail projects past posts on opposite sides of a corner. Cut 45-deg. angles in the rails.

screws to secure this connection. **Step 1–Step 4** Because this joint requires fewer fasteners than a butt joint, it can reduce splitting. And if the wood shrinks, you won't see an obvious gap the way you would between a butted joint.

As you work your way along the deck, double-check your posts for plumb. You can lock up the posts with a top brace or simply check and clamp each post to the top rail as you get ready to drive fasteners. There probably won't be much play near the bottom of the posts where you attach the bottom rail.

If you do not have a corner post so that the rails must meet each other between posts, temporarily attach a rail that is too long. Hold the next rail piece up to it, and mark them both at once. You can make a butt joint here, but a miter looks better. **Step 5–Step 7**

Install Stair Railings. The easiest way to mark for cuts on the stair railing is to tack the top and bottom rails in place and scribe the cuts. Check your posts for plumb; then tack the stair rail pieces so that they are parallel with the stringer. Mark the upper ends for cuts in two directions, flush to the top and to the inside of the deck railing. Use a level to mark the lower ends for a cut that is plumb with the end of the stairway. Mark the lower post to be cut off flush with the top edge of the top rail.

Cut the lower post and rail with a circular saw, and attach the rail to the post with decking screws or galvanized nails, drilling pilot holes for all fasteners.

2 To make a scarf joint, cut 45-deg. angles in opposing ends of the rails that meet at the post.

3 Tap the rails into the post notches, and drill pilot holes for the screws. Install two screws per joint.

6 Apply adhesive to the mitered ends, clamp in place, and drive screws to secure the joint.

7 For an added detail, round over and smooth the top of the rail using a router or sander.

Installing the Top Cap

Measure and Cut. Hold and mark the pieces in place whenever possible. The corners require precise, splinter-free cuts, so use a power miter saw or a guide for your circular saw. It's wise to leave boards long until you get a perfect miter at the corner. Then you can cut the caps to length.

Bevel-Cut the Splices. Avoid butt-end splices if you can, because if the wood shrinks they will look bad and invite moisture into end grain. When splices are necessary, place them on top of posts, and scarf-joint the boards with 45-degree cuts.

Install the Stair Railing Cap. You can use a bevel gauge (or sliding T-bevel) to mark the angle of the upper plumb cut on the stair railing. It's best to mark the cuts with the cap in place. Set your circular saw or power miter saw to cut both ends of the stair railing cap at this angle. Prevent waste by cutting the cap a bit long at first, so you can test fit the top end and adjust the angle if you need to. Some end grain will be exposed on both ends, so treat them with some preservative. Get the joint as tight as possible, and smooth the angle transition by sanding.

Setting Balusters

Estimate Materials and Spacing. You should be able to get a good lumber estimate based on how many balusters you will use per linear foot of deck. If you will be installing a lot of balusters in a long, uninterrupted run, pay attention to the spacing between each one, and try to let the odd-size spacing fall next to the house wall.

It is easier to plan spacing in units of balusters between posts. You can figure out the spacing mathematically, but it pays to clamp or tack a set of balusters in place to check your work.

Cut the Balusters. If you have a power miter saw, you can build a jig with a stop block so that you can mass-produce balusters. If you will be cutting with a circular saw, cut one baluster to the correct length, make the angle cuts on the ends if including that detail, and use it as a template for the other balusters. You'll probably cut the stair railing balusters at a different angle than the rest of the balusters, so don't cut them yet. (See "How to Install Balusters," opposite.)

Drill Pilot Holes. You can get away without predrilling on intermediate connections but not near the ends of boards. There you need pilot holes to ensure against splits and to make the joints stronger. And by laying the balusters side by side and drilling straight lines of holes (with a string line to guide you, if need be), you will add a touch of professionalism to your deck. Of course, you need to use a framing square to square-up your balusters before drilling.

Install the Balusters. Figure out the baluster spacing, and cut a spacer block as a guide so that you won't have to measure each installation. (See the "Smart Tip," below.) Use the spacer next to one of the posts and move on down the line of balusters. But double-check for plumb periodically. On long runs, you can make very small adjustments at each baluster (on the scale of 1/16 inch) to adjust the spacing as needed.

Install Stair Railing Balusters. If you will have stair railing balusters that butt up against a rail cap, find the angle for the top cut by holding a baluster in a plumb position against the top rail and the top cap. Hold a 2x2 spacer on the baluster, and mark the angle. Then check an angle-cut piece in place.

If you are not using a top cap, you can simply attach balusters to the sides of the top and bottom rails. But you will have to increase the offset where the rails run at an angle, or duplicate the angle on the top and bottom cuts of the balusters so that they appear to step down the stairs.

💡 **SMART TIP**

USING SPACERS

No matter how careful you are at measuring, there is the chance of making an error. When you measure the same dimension dozens of times, as you do installing balusters, the chances increase. Beat the odds by confirming the margin between two balusters and cutting a block of wood to use as a spacer. Rather than measuring, just hold the block in place. **Step 1** Also use a spacer block beneath balusters to make sure that each one is the same distance up from the bottom edge of the rail. **Step 2**

PROJECT: 🪵🪵🪵
HOW TO INSTALL BALUSTERS

If you cut angled tops and bottoms on the main support posts, follow up with the same type treatment on the balusters

TOOLS & MATERIALS
- 2x4s
- Table saw
- Circular saw
- Sliding T-bevel
- Clamps and horses
- Drill-driver and bits
- 2-in. screws
- Belt sander

1 Mark a sound 2x4 for cutting, and rip the balusters using a table saw.

2 Using the T-bevel, copy the angle on the support posts and transfer it to the balusters.

3 Clamp a group of balusters together, and remove imperfections using a belt sander.

4 Drill pilot holes for the screws in the balusters to avoid splitting the wood.

5 Work your way around the perimeter of the deck, fastening the balusters with screws.

BUILDING BALUSTRADES

An alternative method for building railings is to construct balustrades, which are complete sections of railings with balusters. You can assemble them flat on the deck as though you were making a ladder. Once these sections are built, you install them between the posts. This system does not have the margin of error provided when you install railings and balusters piece by piece.

Install balusters.

Attach the sections to posts.

DRAINAGE DETAILS

RAIL CAPS

Angled Cap Sheds Water

Flat Cap Collects Water

POST TOPS

Angled Cut Sheds Water

Square Cut Collects Water

BALUSTER BASES

Face-Mounted Sheds Water

End-Mounted Collects Water

BUILDING A COMPOSITE RAILING

If you are using synthetic decking, you'll most likely want synthetic railing to match. In this case, the deck was made of 1-inch-thick composite boards, so the railing is made of the same material. This railing could just as easily be made of ⁵⁄₄ lumber decking for a wooden deck. Essentially the railing consists of 1-inch by 1-inch balusters sandwiched between two bottom rails and two top rails with a 5½- inch-wide cap rail. The top and bottom rails are made by ripping 5 ½-inch pieces exactly in half. Doubled rails makes the railing stronger—a good idea because composite is not as stiff as wood. It also allows water to drain through between the rails. This railing is simple to build, but it will help to have a table saw to rip the composite boards to the widths you need. You could also accomplish the task with a rip guide on a circular saw.

The railing is attached to 4x4 cleats that are attached to the inside of the joists. See "Attaching Interior Posts," page 190.

(Text continues on page 203.)

💡 SMART TIP

GANG CUTTING & PREDRILLING

If you are cutting balusters on a miter saw, you can save time by measuring and cutting four balusters at a time (below left). And when you are predrilling for screws, it's always handy to have two drills—one fitted with the drill bit and one fitted with a driver bit. To speed the work even more, predrill all the balusters at once so you can just grab the drill with the driver bit and install all the balusters (below right).

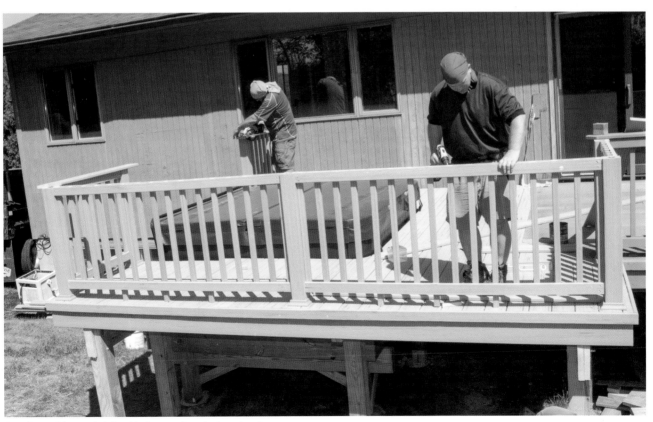

A railing with sandwiched balusters is a design that is easy to execute with composite boards.

PROJECT: 🦫🦫🦫
MAKING A SANDWICH RAILING

Although composite material is not as strong as wood, this system creates a strong railing that won't sag.

TOOLS & MATERIALS
- Composite decking boards
- Measuring tape
- Pencil
- Drill/driver
- Countersink bit
- Two-foot level
- Circular saw

1 Center the cleats across the width of the posts, make sure they are flush to the top of the post, then screw them in place.

2 Put the top and bottom rails in position against the posts, and scribe the layout line for the final length cut.

3 Toe-screw the outside top and bottom rails through the cleats into the posts.

4 About every 3 feet, install a baluster that extends to the decking. This will prevent the rail from sagging.

5 Screw the remaining balusters in place using one screw at top and one at bottom.

6 Scribe and cut the top and bottom inside rails and toe-screw them through the cleats into the posts. Then screw them to the top and bottom of every fourth baluster.

7 Use a circular saw to trim the protruding balusters flush to the top rails.

(Continued from page 201.)

Installing Rails and Balusters

Attach the Outside Rails. The rails will be attached to 1x1 cleats screwed to the sides of the posts. Cut the cleats to reach from the top of the post to the bottom of the bottom rail. Predrill and countersink holes for three 2½-inch composite screws. Center the cleat across the width of the post and insert the screws. **Step 1**

Cut the rails to approximate length, then scribe the outside rails in position to fit between the posts. **Step 2** Cut these rails to final length, then predrill and toe-screw into the outside rails at an angle that will send the screws through the cleat and the post. **Step 3** Use two screws per connection.

Attach the Balusters. To prevent the railing from sagging, one baluster about every 3 feet will extend to the deck. Cut these balusters to reach from the deck to a couple of inches above the top rail—you'll cut them off in place later. Predrill, make sure they are plumb, then screw them to the rails with one screw at top and one at bottom. **Step 4** Secure them with one screw driven up the through the decking into the bottom of the baluster.

Cut the rest of the balusters to ½ inch less than the distance from the top of the top rail to the bottom of the bottom rail. Predrill, plumb and screw them in place flush to the top of the top rail. **Step 5**

Attach the Inside Rails. Put each of the inside rails in position against the posts to scribe and cut them to length as you did the outside rails. Put the bottom inside rail in place and make sure it is in the same plane as the outside bottom rail. Predrill and screw the bottom rail to every fourth

baluster. Then install the inside top rail in the same way making sure it is flush to top of the balusters. **Step 6**

Trim the Protruding Balusters. You can use a handsaw or a reciprocating saw to trim the protruding balusters flush to the top rails, but the quickest and easiest way is to use a circular saw. **Step 7**

💡 **SMART TIP**

A DIGITAL GAUGE

You can use your fingers as a gauge to make sure you are predrilling through the cap rail into the middle of the top rail below. Put your index finger under the cap, touching the side of the top rail, and then slide your thumb against the side of the cap. Keep your hand in this position as you place it on the cap with your thumb aligned to the edge of the cap. Drill a hole about ½ inch in from your index finger.

PROJECT: 🐾🐾🐾

INSTALLING A MITERED CAP RAIL

By laying out miters in place, you'll ensure a professional-looking cap rail.

TOOLS & MATERIALS
- Composite deck boards
- 2 ½-inch composite deck screws
- Pencil
- Angle square
- Circular saw
- Drill/driller
- #7 predrill/countersink bit

1 With the meeting cap rails tacked in place, you can accurately mark where they meet before cutting a 45-degree miter on one board.

4 Retack the cap rails. Check the fit of the miter and that the overhangs are equal before permanently installing the cap.

5 Predrill and countersink for pairs of screws into the outside and inside rails, inserting screws in preparation for driving them in.

Installing the Cap Rail

In the sandwiched rail design, the cap rail is made of 1-inch-thick by 5 ½-inch-wide composite decking. The caps are mitered at the corners for a clean, professional look.

Miter the Corners. The key to creating a tight professional-looking mitered cap rail is to do the cutting in place so you can scribe the board lengths rather than measuring. Start by cutting the boards to a length that will overhang the corner posts by at least 7 inches. Then put a cap in place with approximately equal overhangs at each corner post and equal overhangs at the outside and inside

of the top rails. Then temporarily secure the board with a couple of screws driven just far enough to keep the board from moving. In the same way, position and tack-screw the cap that will meet the first board, letting the boards overlap at the corner.

Now mark the point where the two boards meet at the inside of the railing. Extend the mark to the surface of the top board and use an angle square to lay out a 45-degree cut. Set your circular saw to cut about 1¼ inch deep. Place a block under the marked board to raise it up (unlike wood, the composite will flex enough to do this while still tacked in place). Make the cut. **Step 1**

2 After mitering one cap rail, you can use it to scribe the cut on the cap that will meet it.

3 Untack the second board to make its miter cut.

6 Drive in pairs of screws, spaced about four balusters apart.

INSTALLING A PLASTIC RAIL KIT

Plastic railings can actually have a more refined look than the typical homemade railing of composite or wood. The rails have molded profiles and there are no fasteners visible when installed. They blend beautifully with capped composite or PVC decking boards and can be purchased in matching or contrasting colors. There are various systems from different manufacturers, so be sure to read the instructions that come with your kit. This kit has sleeves that fit over 4x4 wooden posts. It employs round aluminum balusters with a powder-coated finish. In this kit all the fasteners are provided.

(Text continues on page 207.)

Remove the block and use the cut on the top cap to scribe the miter cut on the cap it will meet. **Step 2** Remove the tack screws from the cap you just marked and make the miter cut. **Step 3**

Predrill and Fasten the Caps. Put the cap back in place and re-insert the tack screws, then check several places along both caps to make sure the overhang is equal on both sides. **Step 4** Predrill and countersink the caps for composite screws, spacing pairs of screws about four balusters apart. For each pair of screws, drive one into the outside top rail and one into the inside top rail. **Step 5– Step 6**

💡 SMART TIP

COUNTERSINKING

Composite screws are self-tapping, and in general you can drive them without pre-drilling. But in prominent spots, such as on a railing—especially when driving screws through the cap rail—it's a good idea to pre-drill and countersink screws for a neater appearance. Do this with a bit that combines a drill bit with a countersink. A #7 bit creates the perfect countersink for composite screws. However, #7 bits are not widely available. Every hardware store or home center carries #8 bits, which will work just fine.

PROJECT: 🔧🖐🖐

HOW TO PREPARE THE POSTS AND RAILS

With the supplied template it's easy to get the rail support brackets in the right spots.

TOOLS & MATERIALS
- Post sleeves
- Post bases
- Rail brackets
- Rails
- Adapter strips
- Foot block
- Baluster spacers
- Balusters
- Post caps
- Provided screws
- Drill/driver
- ⅛-inch drill bit
- Measuring tape
- Miter saw
- PVC adhesive or silicone

1 Drop post sleeves over the 4x4 railing posts.

2 Slip the post base over the sleeve down to the deck.

3 Fold the supplied template around the post sleeve and secure it with a short bungee cord, rubber band, or tape.

4 Position the top and bottom rail brackets in the appropriate template holes and secure with screws provided.

5 Put one end of the bottom rail against the inside of one post and scribe a cut line against the inside of the other post.

6 Use a miter saw to cut the bottom rail to length, then use the bottom rail as a template to lay out a cut for the top rail.

7 Drill a ³⁄₁₆-inch hole for the foot block centered on the bottom rail. Screw the foot to the bottom of the bottom rail.

8 Cut the adapter strips to 2 ½ inches shorter than the rails and center them so they won't interfere with the support brackets.

9 Measure and mark both ends of the baluster spacers so that balusters on each end will be equidistant from the posts.

(Continued from page 205.)

Preparing the Posts and Rails

Install the Sleeves. When you install the wooden 4x4 posts, plan them to be about an inch or so shorter than the plastic sleeves that come with the kit. The exception is posts at bottom of stair rails—it's a good idea to let those run longer than the sleeves in case you need to adjust the post lengths after the stairs are constructed. Slide the sleeves over the posts, **Step 1** then slip the post bases over the sleeves and slide them to the deck. **Step 2**

Install the Rail Support Brackets. The kit comes with a cardboard template to make it easy to locate the brackets that will be used to attach the rails. Secure the template to the post with a short bungee cord, a rubber band or tape. **Step 3** Two of the four holes in the template are marked Horizontal top and Horizontal bottom. Put a supplied bracket in these holes, being sure to orient it as shown on the template. Then secure the brackets with two screws each, using the screws provided for the purpose. **Step 4**

Cut the Rails. Place a bottom rail against the inside of one post and scribe for a cut where it meets the other post. **Step 5** Use a miter saw to cut the railing to length—bring the arm down slowly for a smooth cut. Then use the bottom rail as a template to mark and cut the top rail to

length. **Step 6**

Install the Foot. The kit comes with an adjustable foot block to support the railing midway along its length. Find the center of the bottom rail and drill a ³⁄₁₆-in. hole at that point. Attach the block to the bottom of the bottom rail with the screw provided. **Step 7**

Install the Adapter Strips. This same railing system can be used with square balusters, in which case no adapter strips are necessary. For the round balusters used here, cut the strips to 2 ½ inches shorter than the rails and then center them in the top and bottom rails. **Step 8**

Cut the Baluster Spacers. The baluster spacers are strips with holes in them that snap into the rails. They hold the balusters in place at the proper spacing. Position each strip in on its rail and measure so that the distance between each end of the rail and the closest baluster will be the same. **Step 9**. Mark and cut both ends of the spacer strips.

Install the Rails and Balusters. Now that all the cutting is done, the rest of the job is easy. You just need to insert a few screws to connect the rails to the posts, put the spacers in place, and insert the balusters and install post caps.

(Text continues on page 209.)

PROJECT:
HOW TO INSTALL RAILS AND BALUSTERS

With all the parts cut to length, assembling the rails and balusters to the posts is a simple job.

TOOLS & MATERIALS
- Bottom and top rails
- Supplied screws
- Bottom and top spacers
- Support foot with cover
- Balusters
- Post caps
- Drill/driver
- ⅛-in. drill bit
- PVC adhesive

1 Attach the bottom rail to the posts with one provided screw driven down through the rail brackets.

4 Lower the foot cover.

5 Put the top baluster spacer over the lower spacer and fit the top rail over the top brackets.

8 Pull the top baluster spacer up over the balusters and snap it in place under the top rail.

9 Put PVC adhesive or silicone around the inside perimeter of the post cap.

2 Snap the bottom spacer into place.

3 Rotate the foot down to support the rail, predrill, and insert a provided screw.

6 Screw the top brackets to the bottom of the top rails.

7 Put the balusters in place through the holes in both spacers.

10 Press the post cap in place on the post sleeve.

(Continued from page 207.)

Attach the Bottom Rail and Set the Foot. Fit the adapter strips into both rails. Put the bottom rail in place under the bottom rail bracket and secure each end with one screw that's provided with the kit. **Step 1** Snap the bottom spacer into place over the bottom rail. **Step 2** Raise the foot block cover to reveal the adjustable foot. Rotate the foot down until it is supporting the bottom rail, then put a ⅛-in. drill bit into the hole in the foot and predrill down into the deck. Secure the block with the screw provided and lower the cover. **Step 3– Step 4**

Attach the Top Rail. After you install the top rail, you'll be putting the balusters through the holes in the bottom and top spacers, then pulling the bottom spacer up the balusters to snap it into the bottom of the top rail. For now, lay the spacer strip for the top rail atop the bottom rail. Put the top rail in place over the top rail brackets and secure it by screwing through the brackets up into the rail. **Step 5– Step 6**

Install the Balusters and Caps. Put each baluster in place through both spacers. **Step 7** Work the top spacer up over the balusters and snap it in place under the top rail. **Step 8** Put a bead of silicone adhesive along the perimeter of the post caps and press them down onto the top of the post sleeves. **Step 9– Step 10**

INSTALLING THE STAIR RAILS

The system for installing plastic stair rails is similar to installing guardrails on the deck. There are a few minor differences because the rails meet the posts at an angle.

Cut the Parts. Slip the post sleeve over the post. Rest a bottom rail on the stair-tread nosings and mark the angled cut where it will meet the bottom post. **Step 1** Use the layout line to set the angle on a power miter saw and cut the rail. **Step 2** Keep this setting on the saw—you'll use it to make all the other cuts. But the cut you just made against the bottom post and scribe the cut to meet the upper post. **Step 3**. Test fit the bottom rail. If it fits properly, cut the top rail to the same length at the same angle.

PROJECT: 🐾🐾🐾
HOW TO INSTALL STAIR RAILS

Mark the rail cuts in place for a perfect fit.

TOOLS & MATERIALS
- Top and bottom rails
- Rail brackets
- Stair baluster spacer strips
- Baluster adapter
- strips
- Supplied screws
- Pencil
- Power miter saw
- Drill/driver

1 Put a bottom rail along tread nosing and mark the angled cut.

4 Cut the top rail to the same length and angle as the bottom rail, then cut the baluster adapters and spacers to fit.

5 Install bracket pieces flat side up on the bottom posts as shown here. For the top posts, install the bracket pieces flat side down.

The baluster spacers work in the same way as they do for the guardrails. However, they have oval holes because the balusters come through them at an angle. Cut the baluster spacers to fit the rails. As you did for the guardrails, cut both ends of the spacers so the end holes will be equidistant from the ends of the rails. Cut the baluster adapters to 2 ½ inches shorter than the inside of the rails to leave room for the brackets. **Step 4** The foot for stair rails is angled at the top to meet the bottom of the bottom rail. Center and install the foot as you did for deck guardrails.

Install the Rails. The stair rail uses the same bracket pieces as the guardrails. However, to follow the angle of the rails, two bracket pieces are used at each connection instead of one. Put the cardboard template in place as you did for the guardrails and attach one bracket piece at each of the two holes designated for stair brackets. For the posts at the bottom of the stairs, orient these pieces with the flat slide up. For the posts at the top of the stairs, orient these pieces with the flat side down. **Step 5** Then snap a second bracket piece onto each attached piece—For the bottom-of-stair posts it'll be beneath the attached bracket piece, **Step 6** while for the top-of stair posts it will be on top of the attached piece.

Screw the rails in place through the brackets using one screw that goes through both bracket pieces into the rail. **Step 7**

2 Use a miter saw to cut the marked end of the first rail.

3 Put the cut end of the rail in position against the post and mark to cut the other end.

6 Clip another bracket piece to the installed one—the configuration shown here is on a top post.

7 Place the rails on the brackets as shown, and then drive a single screw through both bracket parts into the rail.

THE DESIGNERS' WORK

Creative Homeowner selected six of the country's premier deck designer-builders and asked them to present some of their best designs to our readers. They represent a broad regional sampling: George Drummond lives in Virginia; Bob Kiefer and Gus de la Cruz in New Jersey; Gary Marsh in California; Barry Streett in Colorado and Rick Parish in Texas. Their decks, many of them design award-winners, appear on the following pages.

These professionals don't just design decks—they build them as well. They recognize that a superior design addresses questions of engineering and craftsmanship as well as aesthetics. They know that a structurally sound deck requires good footings and strong framing, and careful joinery and attention to detail.

For each of the designer-builders, you'll find a section called "Techniques to Use," which summarizes specific tips and tricks that each has learned through years of practice and experience. Even if you choose not to build one of their decks, you'll find ideas here that you can use.

We hope you enjoy leafing through this impressive collection of designs and ideas. We also wish you luck in achieving your dream deck. The designer-builders welcome consultation by telephone, should you want to purchase plans for one of their designs.

Samples of the builders' work show their high degree of craftsmanship.

Bob Kiefer

Gary Marsh

George Drummond

Gus de la Cruz

Rick Parish

Barry Streett

DECKS BY KIEFER

Bob Kiefer, owner of Decks by Kiefer in Martinsville, New Jersey, designs and builds custom decks for a demanding clientele. He begins each design by interviewing his clients about their likes and dislikes, and how they plan on using the outdoor living area.

DECKS BY KIEFER

Martinsville, New Jersey

(908) 339-2124

www.decksbykiefer.com

TECHNIQUES TO USE

For his well-to-do clients, Kiefer usually spares no expense to ensure that a deck will withstand warping and cracking for decades. Although economy may factor into your project, you can still use Kiefer's ideas and techniques to add strength and elegance to your deck.

• Kiefer prefers 2x4 redwood (or 1x4 ipé) for decking, whereas most builders use (nominal) 6-inch-wide stock. The narrow boards account in part for the distinctive appearance of his decks. However, if you use a grade of lumber that contains knots, 2x4s can present a problem. If you end up with a large knot in a location that requires a nail, you won't have room to work around it as you would with 2x6 decking. By using lumber that has virtually no knots, you can eliminate this problem.

• Wherever possible, Kiefer avoids miter cuts in decking and rail caps. He's found that any slight imperfection or shrinkage will mar the appearance of a mitered joint. Instead he uses square cuts, staggering them in the decking to create a pleasing herringbone pattern.

• Kiefer steers clear of end-to-end butt joints along the length of the decking. These joints often crack because the boards must be nailed so close to their ends. If shrinkage occurs, unsightly gaps can result. Where feasible, he uses 20-foot-long decking runs (or 18-foot if 20-footers

are not available). To avoid overly long decking on larger areas, he usually chooses to install boards in a herringbone pattern.

• To install structural posts, Kiefer uses an unconventional approach. By waiting until the deck is nearly completed before pouring concrete, he avoids errors in footings that can make building the rest of the deck a nightmare.

• For structural support, he uses lumber no larger than 2x10. Larger pieces tend to shrink and crack. Kiefer's beam design is simplicity itself: he gang-nails three 2x10s to form a support that is considerably stronger and much less likely to crack than a 4x10.

• He usually builds rail posts out of 2x4s and 1x4s. They assemble easily, resist cracking, and look more elegant than a 4x4. (See photo oppposite.)

• To achieve the distinctive banded appearance of his fascias, Kiefer stacks several 2x4s rather than using a single 1x8 as most builders would. The 2x4s don't crack as readily as the wider, thinner boards, and the round milled edges on the 2x4s accent the horizontal lines between the boards. To economize, you can use 1x4s and round the edges with a sanding block or a router equipped with a roundover bit.

• Kiefer makes curved fascia under the decking using a technique that is feasible for anyone who owns a decent table saw. (See page 228.) However, his laminated curved benches and railings may prove too difficult for the average do-it-yourselfer. (See page 223.)

To avoid butt joints and miter cuts, Kiefer often uses shorter decking boards and herringbone patterns, left. Also note the distinctive banded design of the fascia, repeated on many of his decks.

By fastening 2x4s and 1x4s together, Kiefer crafts handsome, unusual-looking posts.

SLEEK RETREAT

With its sinuous curves, this handsome deck may remind you of an appliance or car from the 1950s. The natural softness of the wood makes it a relaxing place to withdraw from the world, however briefly.

DESIGN CONSIDERATIONS

The deck's smooth lines emphasize the curved, banded fascia. The overall effect contrasts markedly with most (rectangular) houses in style and materials, yet the horizontal lines harmonize well with the siding found commonly on today's homes.

From the house, you step onto an upper level designed as a barbecue area that will accommodate a table and chairs. This 13 x 20-foot space provides generously for traffic flow. An overhead trellis offers support for hanging flower baskets or climbing vines and provides shade for a table and chairs that you might set up for dining.

A wide, curved step leads to the lower level, which projects farther into the yard. Here there is no railing to obstruct the view, and the ample space allows for plenty of general seating and entertaining. Three large planters bring foliage onto the deck. Curved benches tie into the planters and follow the deck's contours. This stunning element presents a challenging project to the amateur carpenter, so it may be worth the expense to hire a professional.

Instead of simply stepping the deck down to the yard, Kiefer includes a small landing as part of the stairway. This extends the deck farther outward, making a smoother transition from deck to yard. The elevated landing makes a pleasant place to sit and sip a drink. A second, standard-size stairway next to the house allows more convenient daily traffic flow to and from the yard.

Ground View

SLEEK RETREAT, PLAN VIEW

MATERIALS USED FOR THIS DECK

Framing	Tripled 2x8s for beams	**Benches**	2x4s for supports
	2x8 joists		2x4 seat pieces, ripped to 5⁄16″ and
	2x8 ledger pieces and headers		laminated
Decking	2x4s	**Planters**	2x6 framing pieces
Fascia	2x4s; curved pieces ripped to 5⁄16″		2x6 floor pieces
	and laminated		1x6 tongue-and-groove sides
Railing	2x4 post pieces		2x4 top trim
	1x4 post pieces	**Hardware**	Concrete-filled metal posts
	2x12s for curved top and bottom rails		Lag screws and washers for installing
	Doubled 1x12s for curved railing cap		ledgers
	1x6s for curved nailers		Joist hangers for 2x10s
	2x4 straight top and bottom rails		Angle brackets
	1x2 nailers		Fasteners for joist hangers
	2x6s for straight railing cap		3″ deck screws or 10d galvanized nails
	2x2 balusters		½″ x 3 ½″ lag screws with washers,
	2x2 handrails		for posts
Overhead	(posts shared with railing)	**Masonry**	Concrete
structure	2x6 double beams		Concrete tube forms
(Pergola)	2x6 rafters		
	1x2 top pieces		

CONSTRUCTION TECHNIQUES

Install pocket beams and Lally columns as described on page 164. To frame the curved section, see page 174. Other techniques used are more specific to this deck.

Building a Curved Railing

The straight sections of railing are built ladder-style as described on page 165.

Mark for the post locations on the curve, but do not install them. To make the top and bottom rails, lay pieces of 2x12 on the deck, and use the round decking edge to mark them for curved rip cuts, keeping the width of the pieces at a uniform 3 ½ inches. Cut each section a little longer than needed. Use these pieces to mark for the curved nailers, which you'll cut to a consistent 1 ½-inch width. Use the same technique to make curved one-by pieces for the top rail. These should measure 5 ½ inches wide and as long as you can make them.

Install the posts, and then cut the rails and nailers to fit between them.

Install pocket beams and Lally columns as described on page 164. To frame the curved section, see page 174.

Install the rails, assemble the nailers and balusters, and then attach the baluster subassemblies to the rails. The nailers make it easier to position the balusters centered on the top and bottom rails and add a bit of strength. Note: you can't build these sections ladder-style on the ground, because they won't lie flat.

For the railing cap, cut the bottom one-by pieces so that they center on the posts, and attach them with screws. Cut the top pieces so that the joints fall at least 12 inches from those in the bottom pieces. To attach them, apply exterior woodworking glue and drive 1 ¼-inch screws up through the bottom pieces.

Handrail

In many areas of the country, handrails are required on stairways of three or more steps. Handrails should measure between 1 ½ and 2 inches in diameter. In this case Kiefer used 2x2s, which fill the bill nicely. Make sure that there is enough clearance to really grasp the handrail, and then anchor it securely by driving screws through the 2x6. The design is straightforward. Choose clear lumber, and sand it smooth. Drill pilot holes for all screws to prevent the small pieces from splitting.

Bench with Laminated Curved Seat Members

Make no mistake, as handsome as it is, this bench is difficult to build. You'll have to resaw a number of pieces from 2x4s, preferably using a table saw, to produce strips that measure 5/16 to 3/8 inch thick and 3 ½ inches wide. Then you'll laminate five or six of these strips to form each bench slat. (Laminate the curved portions of the fascia in the same way.) Note: cut the 2x4s longer than you'll need so that the assembled bench slats won't end up short.

To make a gluing form, cut pieces of plywood that match the curve of the deck. Then laminate the strips together using epoxy, clamping them to the curved form every 6 inches. You'll need to use lots of clamps—in all likelihood more than 100. Take care that you cover every strip thoroughly with epoxy, or the slats may delaminate. Allow the assembly to dry for 24 hours; then belt-sand the edge.

Each bench seat consists of eight slats spaced about ⅜ inch apart. Nine 12 ½-inch-long laminated 2x4s form the seven vertical supports, four on one bench and three on the other. These are spaced equidistant from one another and approximately 12 inches from (and perpendicular to) the planters/tables on each end.

PERGOLA

1x2s

2x6s

2x6s

Post Made from 2x4s and 1x4s

HANDRAIL

Plugs

Screws

2x2

2x6

2x2 spacer

RAISED DECK WITH SWEEPING OVERLOOK

Ground View

The backyard of this house slopes steeply down to a lovely pond. The homeowners needed a stairway down to the pool in the side yard and wanted a clear view of the pond. To accommodate them, Kiefer built a set of stairs off to the side and a round balcony that overlooks the pond.

DESIGN CONSIDERATIONS

When the homeowners met with Kiefer, they requested a generously sized deck but not a particularly expansive one. For large parties, they intended to entertain below by the pool. The deck design had to provide room for a standard patio table with four chairs as well as a barbecue area, without impeding the traffic down to the poolside. The central, offset semicircular area measures about 8 feet in diameter—room enough for the out-of-the-way dining area. It also makes a nice vantage point from which to lean on the rail and admire the pond below.

At 12 steps down, a simple, straight stairway would have jutted far out into the yard. Even a stairway with one landing would have protruded too far to suit the homeowners' tastes. Building two upper landings took extra work but proved well worth the effort, keeping the steps close to the deck. The third landing at the bottom provides a small conversation area or a space for potted plants.

One small vertical area just above the middle landing is covered with skirting, while the rest of the deck's underside is left exposed. Although it may seem desirable to have concealed some of the framing, a skirt that large would have made the deck appear box-like and would have added considerably to the expense.

A curved balcony like this one creates a dramatic effect, especially when elevated high in the air. The combination of circles and rectangles looks almost Victorian.

The high elevation makes the framing go slowly and involves some danger as well. If you are not accustomed to this type of construction, consider hiring a contractor to at least build the framing. Holding the beams temporarily in place while you install the rest of the framing is difficult work.

RAISED DECK WITH SWEEPING OVERLOOK, PLAN VIEW

2x10 Ledger

Down →

4' x 4' Landing

4' x 5' Landings

Beam Pocket

2x4 Decking

Beams (3) 2x10s

2x10 Joists (16" O.C.)

Extra Nailing
Surface
Made with Extra
2x4 Material

Laminated Header

17

15'6"

28'

MATERIALS USED FOR THIS DECK

Framing	Tripled 2x10s for beams		2x6 railing cap
	2x10 joists		2x2 balusters
	2x10 ledger pieces and headers		2x2 handrails
	2x4 redwood for curved header/fascia	**Hardware**	Concrete-filled metal columns, primed,
	2x6 stairway joists		with screws for attaching to beams
	2x12 stringers		Lag screws and washers for installing
Decking	2x4s		ledgers
Fascia,	1x6 skirting		Joist hangers for 2x10s
skirting,	1x4 fascia pieces		Angle brackets
step risers	1x4 riser pieces		Fasteners for joist hangers
Railing	2x4 post pieces		3" deck screws or 10d spiral-shank
	1x4 post pieces		galvanized nails
	2x12s for curved top and bottom rails		½" x 3 ½" lag screws with washers
	Doubled 1x12s for curved railing cap		for posts
	1x6s for curved nailers	**Masonry**	Concrete
	2x4 straight top and bottom rails		Concrete tube forms
	1x2 nailers		

CONSTRUCTION TECHNIQUES

Installing Beams High in the Air

Anchor the ledger pieces for the main deck to the house 2 ¼ inches or so below the level of the interior floor at the threshold. Mark for the end joist that butts the house, and determine the beam pocket's location. Using a circular or reciprocating saw (or both), cut the pocket 4 ⅝ inches wide and 9 ¼ inches long. Then install the end joist, but don't install the ledgers for the top landing yet.

Now comes the tricky part. (Have at least two strong-backed helpers on hand, and use stable stepladders or sturdy scaffolding.) Build the long beam from three 2x10s, using stock that measures a foot or so longer than it needs to be. On a 16-foot 2x10, make a mark showing the distance the beam should be from the house; you will use this piece as a temporary brace. (See the drawing "Bracing and Supporting the Beams," below.) Insert the beam into the beam pocket; then raise the other end to make it level.
Install plenty of bracing, using more than shown if necessary.

Once you've securely anchored the long beam, build the other three, cutting them to exact length and bracing them together to form a single U-shaped piece. Raise the assembly into place, and support it.

Use plumb bobs to position the concrete footings. Dig the holes, insert tube forms if you'll be using them, and attach the columns to the undersides of the beams so that they extend at least 8 inches into the holes, with at least 12 inches of concrete under the column. (See "Hanging the Columns," page 164.) Recheck for level, pour the footings, and allow the concrete to set. Do not remove the temporary bracing until the deck is finished.

BRACING AND SUPPORTING THE BEAMS

Ledgers

16' 2x10 Temporary Brace

Beam Pocket

2x6 Temporary Brace

Temporary Bracing

Temporary Bracing

FRONT PORCH/DECK FOR A CORNER LOT

These homeowners wanted a deck with a spa, but they had a corner lot with no true backyard. Kiefer designed a structure that serves as an entry porch on one side and a deck on the other. A striking curved overhead structure adds elegance.

DESIGN CONSIDERATIONS

Those who own corner lots can feel like second-class citizens because they often have little or no private yard space to call their own. One solution is to build a tall fence, but that can seem unfriendly to the neighbors and make the owners feel claustrophobic. A deck with a substantial railing or trellis can provide some privacy without making it look as though you're trying to shut out the world.

As part of his solution for these homeowners, Kiefer simply treated the rear of the house as a backyard by placing a spa there. A railing with an attention-grabbing overhead structure provides a subtle barrier. The wide expanse of deck space, with its lawn furniture and potted plants, further screens off the spa area and makes it feel more like a deck than a front porch.

Part of the deck serves as an entryway. Just outside the sliding glass doors, a curved landing one step up from the main surface mirrors the larger curve of the deck. A short section of railing, two planters, and an angled bench form an ensemble that nicely frames the entrance into the house.

Two sets of steps that provide access to the lawn incorporate substantial landings. These set off the deck as a private space belonging to the house much more effectively than simple stairways would.

The overhead structure, made of laminated curved pieces and winglike rafters, is a stunning achievement. It contributes more visual appeal than it does shade, and it looks even more inviting with clematis or wisteria climbing up it.

Ground View

FRONT PORCH/DECK FOR A CORNER LOT, PLAN VIEW

10'

12'

28'

3' 6" Radius

Overhead Structure

HOT TUB AREA, PERSPECTIVE VIEW

2x8 Joists 16" O.C.

3' 6" Radius

Short Railing

3 2x8s

2x8 Joists 16" O.C.

18"x18" Bench

2x4 Decking

8'

34'

PLANTER, PERSPECTIVE VIEW

2x6s

1x6 T&G

ELEVATION

Laminated Beam

Curved Railing Made from 2x12s

Laminated Fascia

Posts

Rafter

Doubled Beam

Planter (2x6s & 1x6s)

Bench (2x4s)

37"

18"

2x4 Fascia

Concrete Tube Form

CONSTRUCTION TECHNIQUES

Use Lally columns set in concrete to support beams made from three 2x8s. (See page 164 for a description of this technique. For framing curves, see page 174.) To support the spa, Kiefer pours a steel-reinforced concrete pad. However, check with your local building department for code requirements.

Planters. To build the bench, see page 169. The planters, though simple in design, must be built carefully using dry, straight lumber.

First, build a simple box from pressure-treated 2x6s laid on edge. For the floor, use 2x6s as well, but lay them flat, and allow ³⁄₁₆-inch gaps between the boards for drainage. Cover the box with 1x6 tongue-and-groove redwood, and cap it off with 2x6 pieces. Kiefer butt-joins these rather than mitering them. (See drawing, opposite.)

Fill the planter with 6 inches of gravel and a couple of inches of sand to ensure that it will drain easily and that the inside boards will have a chance to dry out.

Curved Overhead. This structure resembles an elevated train track. Make winglike end cuts on both the beams and rafters, using the same pattern for each. For the curved beam sections and top pieces, use the laminating technique described on page 169.

CURVED OVERHEAD

2x3 Top Pieces
2x8 Rafters
Doubled 2x8 Beam
Posts
2x4 Top & Bottom Rails
2x2 Baluster
2x4 Fascia

MATERIALS USED FOR THIS DECK

Framing	Tripled 2x8s for beams		**Planters**	2x4 seat pieces
	2x8 joists			2x6 framing pieces
	2x8 ledger pieces and headers			2x6 floor pieces
Decking	2x4s			1x6 tongue-and-groove sides
Fascia	2x4s; curved pieces are resawn			2x6 top trim
	to ⁵⁄₁₆" thickness and laminated		**Hardware**	Concrete-filled metal columns
Railing	2x4 post pieces			Lag screws and washers for ledgers
	1x4 post pieces			Joist hangers for 2x10s
	2x12s for curved top and bottom rails			Angle brackets
	2x4 straight top and bottom rails			Fasteners for joist hangers
	1x2 nailers			3" deck screws or 10d spiral-shank
	2x2 balusters			galvanized nails
Overhead	(Posts shared with railing)			½" x 3 ½" lag screws with washers,
	2x8 doubled beams; resawn as above			for posts
	2x8 rafters		**Masonry**	Concrete
	2x3 top pieces; resawn as above			Concrete tube forms
Benches	2x4s for posts			

VERANDA WITH TURNED BALUSTERS

The homeowners needed a front porch, but they wanted more than just a structure for entering and exiting the house. By making the porch fairly large and adding a couple of distinctive flourishes, they ended up with a cheery yet classic-looking veranda.

DESIGN CONSIDERATIONS

A backyard makes a good place for a showy deck with interesting curves, angles, and levels, but a complicated structure on the front of the house looks out of place. This more public area calls for a more subdued design.

On the other hand, the standard front porch, with its small landing and set of stairs, can look pretty drab. And though you probably wouldn't want to sunbathe, dine, or lounge on a front porch, you might want to sit in a chair and read the paper, pausing to wave to the neighbors from time to time.

This combination porch-deck recalls verandas of the Old South. It can make your neighborhood a slightly friendlier place without putting you entirely on display. The railing partially screens a person sitting in a chair.

Constructed of cedar, the veranda has a slightly less formal look than redwood. Unfortunately, most of the cedar sold today is light-colored sapwood, which doesn't offer a great deal of rot resistance. To compensate for this, apply an annual coat of preservative-sealer.

The design, which could hardly be simpler, consists of a rectangle with a set of stairs. Several details, however, give it a distinctive look. Kiefer designed and built one-of-a-kind newels for the post tops, but the store-bought turned balusters add classic elegance without requiring custom work. The fascia, made from two 2x4s and one 1x4, adds depth to Kiefer's usual banded look.

Ground View

MULTI-RETREATS ON MULTI-LEVELS

The owners of this deck wanted to be able to reach the deck from different rooms of the house. They also specified clear sight lines from the house to the swimming pool in the yard.

Ground View

ELEVATED DECK WITH A SWEEPING STAIRCASE

The owners wanted a grand outdoor living space, but they also wanted a deck that looked as if it was conceived as an integral part of the house—not an afterthought.

Ground View

ELEVATED DECK WITH A SWEEPING STAIRCASE, PLAN VIEW

40'

24'

Permacast
Columns

2x8s 16" O.C.

(3)
2x10s

MATERIALS USED FOR THIS DECK

Framing	Tripled 2x10s for beams	**Stairs**	2x12s for stringers
	2x8s for ledgers	**Hardware**	Metal lally columns
	2x8s for joists		Permacast columns
Decking	1x4 Ipé		Copper flashing
Fascia	1x12 Koma trim		Joist hangers
Railing	2x4 posts		Lag screws and washers
	2x4 rails	**Masonry**	Concrete
	2x2 balusters		Concrete tube forms
	1x12s for curved portions of railing		
Oversized	2x4s		
Posts	1x4s		
	⁵⁄₄x8		

DESIGN CONSIDERATIONS

People whose only knowledge of New Jersey is of the flat southern part of the state are often surprised to learn how hilly the northern end can be. And it is in the central and north areas that Bob Kiefer designs and builds decks. Yards that slope toward the rear of the property line, such as the yard that holds the deck shown here, are quite common in Kiefer's area, and it's evident in his portfolio.

As is the case with most of his clients who own swimming pools, these homeowners wanted a large dining and entertaining area, but they did not want the deck or its railing to block the view of the pool from the house. Kiefer met this objective by building a landing one step down from the sliders that lead into the

interior of the house. The landing is connected to the main part of the deck by a short flight of stairs. This drops the main area of the deck enough to allow a clear sight line from the house to the pool.

The lines of the deck follow the contour of the house. There is a rectangular area that serves as a dining space and a large circular area for entertaining, sun bathing, and other outdoor activities.

Sites like this require the designer to think of how the bottom of the deck will look from the ground, especially when there is a pool or patio area in the yard. Kiefer answers this challenge in a couple of ways. Rather than install the typical deck stairs, Kiefer likes to add on curving staircases. These dramatic features are often focal points in their own right. For this deck, he encased steel columns in decorative columns to add design interest.

CONSTRUCTION TECHNIQUES

To add to the stability of elevated decks, Kiefer likes to place beams for the decks into beam pockets cut out of the foundation walls. Use a diamond blade in a circular saw to cut out the pockets. On this deck, the center beam that bisects the radius of the deck is set in a beam pocket. (For more information see page 164.)

One of Kiefer's goals was to make sure the deck looked good to someone standing on the ground. The exposed beam is trimmed with 1x12 Koma, a PVC-based trim board the looks like wood. The material can be cut and nailed like real wood, but it will never rot and is insect proof. The column and beam design helps make the deck appear as if it was always part of the house and not added on as an afterthought.

Post Design. The oversized posts at the top and bottom of the stairs and in the corners of the deck have a unique panel design. Attach three pressure-treated 2x4s to one another, and fasten

this assembly to the deck framing. The decorative panels will fit over the treated lumber like a sleeve; you'll need a router with rail and stile bits to create them. Make the panel pieces by cutting ⅝x8 clear redwood to 3 inches to form the rails and ripping the same size lumber to 1 ½ inches for the stiles. Cut 1x4

clear redwood to 24 inches long for the center panel. Make the cap from a 2x10 cut to size, and trim it using 1x2s with edges routed to match the base.

PANELED POST

Chamfered 2x10

Routed 1x2

Pressure-Treated 2x4

1x4

⅝x8 Ripped to 1½" and Rabbeted to Accept the 1x4 Panel

⅝x8 Cut to 3" (Turned on Its Side)

2x4 with Routed Edge

Gus de la Cruz operates Barrett Outdoors in New Jersey, a fairly large business that keeps three or four crews busy much of the time. The company—named after Syd Barrett of Pink Floyd, a favorite of de la Cruz's—has won numerous building and designing awards.

BARRETT OUTDOORS

Millstone Township, New Jersey

866-418-1891

www.barrettoutdoors.com

RELAXATION STATION, PLAN VIEW

POST DETAIL

DESIGN CONSIDERATIONS

The owners were not interested in heavy-duty grilling or formal outdoor dining, and they already had a good-size paver patio for gatherings. They pretty much just wanted a place that felt like a comfortable seating area.

Shape and Size. Sometimes a small, simple change can make all the difference. The existing, narrow rectangular deck lacked "flow" in two ways: moving around on it was often awkward because of a bottleneck when people sat on chairs; and it just felt boxy. Gus de la Cruz solved these problems by bumping it out an additional 5 feet (1.5m) away from the house at one end, and he did this with a 45-degree angle.

The change eliminated traffic flow problems and gave the deck a spacious, open feel with plenty of legroom for people in lounge chairs and plenty of space for potted plants. The bumped-out area is also just wide enough for a six-person dining table, should they choose to add one in the future.

In some ways this deck feels like a larger-than-average front porch. It has a narrow section that functions simply as a walkway to the driveway. But because it is 6 feet (1.8m) wide rather than the more common 4 feet (1.2m), it feels like a usable space; the grill comfortably resides here, or it can be wheeled out to the wider area when needed.

Materials. The decking and the railing are similar in color, forming a soothing monochromatic palette agreeable with the landscape. Lighter tones in the lattice skirting, which is only about 2 feet (61cm) tall, perk up the view from the yard or patio.

All visible parts of the deck and rail are made of high-quality composite for easy maintenance. This is especially welcome in a woodsy setting; organic matter like seeds and leaves accumulate and would be a cleaning headache for other surfaces.

MATERIALS USED FOR THIS DECK

Framing (all treated)	6x6 (15cmx15cm) posts
	Metal 2x8 (5cmx20cm) joists, header, and ledger, with fastening hardware
	4x8 (10cmx20cm) metal beams
	2x12 (5cmx30cm) pressure-treated stair stringers
Footings	Plastic footing pads
Decking and fascia	5/4x6 (3cmx15cm) composite decking
	Hidden fasteners
	1x8 (2.5cmx20cm) fascia board
	Composite lattice sheets for skirting
Railing	4x4 (10cmx10cm) railing posts
	Composite railing system

CONSTRUCTION TECHNIQUES

Framing

Install the ledger 2 ½ inches (6.5cm) below the house's threshold, which will put the finished deck surface 1 ½ inches (4cm) below the threshold. A metal ledger is a channel rather than a solid piece. Metal joists attach to the ledger via special angle brackets.

Dig straight lines of postholes to support the beams. If codes allow, attach plastic footing pads to the bottoms of the posts, and set them in the holes. Otherwise, pour in-ground or aboveground concrete footings, depending on local codes. Use your leveling system to mark all of the posts for cutting a beam's width below the bottom of the ledger. Cut the posts, and attach the beams on top.

Install the joist framing. At the angled bump-out, install joists that are longer than needed; brace them in position; and use a straightedge or chalk line to mark them for cutting to length. Add header joists.

Attach the railing posts to the inside of the framing. Add blocking to make the posts firm.

Decking, Fascia, and Railing

Install the decking, starting at the house and moving outward. Once the decking is installed, use a chalk line to mark for cutting straight lines that are 4 inches (10cm) from the edges of the framing. Cut the lines. Cut perimeter decking pieces to frame the deck, and install them. Add fascia pieces beneath the overhanging decking (opposite).

Railing like this is in kit form, with the balusters precut. Slip the sleeves over the 4x4 (10cmx10cm) posts. Cut the railing pieces to fit between the posts, and test the fit. Assemble each rail-and-baluster section, and attach it to the posts using the hardware provided (right).

Stairs

Measure to determine how many steps you will need; estimate where the stringers will end; and pour or lay a concrete or paver landing pad. Cut and install the stringers. Dig postholes for the bottom railing posts, and set the posts in concrete for firmness. Add the treads and risers, then slip the post sleeves over the posts, and install the railings (top).

11 CASA DECKS

George Drummond of Casa Decks in Virginia Beach, Virginia, has a knack for building modestly priced decks that have plenty of flair and tailored features. Though the majority of Drummond's decks are on the small side, they never seem to feel cramped. He manages to use space efficiently and eliminate traffic bottlenecks by allotting just the right amount of room for all the things people usually do on a deck.

CASA DECKS

Virginia Beach, Virginia

(757) 523-4505

TECHNIQUES TO USE

Whenever a deck calls for steps, Drummond likes to make them at least 14 inches deep. Although 11 to 12 inches is considered the standard tread depth for a stairway, this dimension, in his view, doesn't "feel right" on a deck. Drummond believes that standard-depth treads pose a tripping hazard because people expect deck dimensions to be more relaxed and expansive than those on a regular stairway.

• Although pressure-treated pine is generally held to be of lower quality than redwood or cedar, it offers superior resistance to rot, dents, and scratches. And, of course, it costs less. As Drummond's decks show, if you choose the boards carefully and stain them, treated lumber can rival redwood for comfort and appearance.

• For the decking, railing, and other visible elements, Drummond pays extra to get No. 1 lumber. This grade is less likely to shrink and crack, which ensures a better-looking deck over the long term and fewer splinters. It also has fewer knots and tends to be straighter.

• Drummond's approach—planning for functional areas and traffic paths—makes it easier to maximize your possibilities with limited resources. But even if you're building a large deck with expensive materials, make sure you allot space carefully for each functional area, or you may end up with lots of unusable space.

• For the structural members, Drummond pays less but still chooses carefully. He uses "No. 2 or better," which most building departments require, but he selects old-growth lumber. In most parts of the country, pine will offer better quality than "hem-fir," a general designation that includes wood that sometimes shrinks and warps severely. (In some regions, hem-fir may perform well, but check with people who have used it.)

• Drummond allows his lumber more ground contact than most builders—many of his skirts extend below lawn level—but he takes precautions to ensure that it can handle the moisture. He is very careful about the treated lumber he chooses for these applications, going with the highest preservative retention levels possible. Lumberyards don't generally carry the products he wants, but they can be special ordered.

• New composite decking and railing materials have gained some acceptance in Drummond's area, and he uses them quite often.

• Note the counter design on page 271. Instead of mitering the corners of the countertop and bench pieces on the deck, Drummond carries them through, giving the structures a great deal more strength as well as a more interesting appearance. And as most experienced deck builders have discovered, mitered joints tend to pull apart as wood shrinks, leaving unsightly gaps.

• When building low to the ground, Drummond places landscape fabric on top of the joists before installing the decking. If you live in an area with lush vegetation as he does, the fabric ensures that you won't have grass growing up through the cracks in the decking.

• When building a deck that sits less than 5 feet off the ground, Drummond usually does not attach it to the house with a ledger board. This may add a bit to the up-front materials and labor cost because it requires more footings and posts. But on most decks, Drummond believes that even a flashed ledger may allow moisture to collect, which over the long term can damage both the deck and the house.

• Most of Drummond's decks have "solid" skirts that hide the framing and concrete footings. (Actually, there are ⅛- to 1-inch gaps between the vertical or herringbone-patterned skirt pieces.) Although a skirt gives a deck a finished look, some people are reluctant to install one, either because it adds labor and expense or because they worry about cutting off air circulation beneath the deck. However, Drummond has found that a skirt adds little to the overall cost and effort, and that the gaps between the skirt and decking pieces allow adequate circulation, even during the hot, humid summers in Virginia.

Drummond creates decks that contain defined activity areas—note the ground-level seating area off of the main part of the deck.

FLOATING OCTAGONS WITH WALKWAYS

Ground View

Rather than build a small rectangular deck just off the house for barbecuing and lounging, Drummond and the homeowners came up with this solution, which extends the outdoor living areas farther into the yard. Wooden pathways lead to octagonal platforms that sit among flower beds and overhanging trees. One octagon serves as a small dining area, and the other contains a bar and refrigerator.

FLOATING OCTAGONS WITH WALKWAYS, PLAN VIEW

ELEVATION WITH FLOWER BOX

2x4 Top Trim

Box Made of 1x6s

2x6 Shelf (3 2x6s)

2x2 Cleat

2x6 Decking

2x6 Joist

4x6 Beam

Dirt Filled Back In

Concrete Tube Form

2x6 Decking

Planters
17" x 17"

Counter

2x6 Joists
16" O.C.

4'2"

Bench

2x6 Joists
16" O.C.

6'8"

DESIGN CONSIDERATIONS

The surface of this treated-pine complex rises only slightly above ground level, making it more a part of the surroundings than a promontory from which to view the yard. In fact, the octagons and walkways seem almost to "float" in the yard.

That sensation is modified, however, by the built-in bench and counter, which emphasize that this structure is a dining and entertaining center. The smaller octagon offers just enough space for preparing and barbecuing food. The larger octagon easily accommodates a large table and chairs for dining.

Planter Boxes. The benches and counter both incorporate generously sized planter boxes. The boxes contain large pots rather than loose dirt, which allows the homeowners to change plants as they flower. The planters that adjoin the counter house small

cabinets underneath. Drummond routed wiring to one of these to provide power for a small refrigerator. This keeps food and drinks cool for when the clients entertain on hot summer days.

Building a deck this close to the ground (especially one with no ledger) requires a lot of digging, so recruit plenty of strong-backed help if you can. A high-school kid or two hired for an afternoon may save your body some serious wear and tear. If the soil in your yard is difficult to excavate, you may want to choose a design that doesn't protrude so far into the ground—for instance, one that calls for 2x8 or even 2x10 joists and flush beams rather than under-joist beams.

MATERIALS USED FOR THIS DECK

Framing	4x4 posts	**Cabinets**	2x4 top trim pieces
	4x6 beams (2 2x6s)		2x6 shelves
	2x6 joists		2x2 cleats
Decking	2x6s		15-lb. roofing felt (planter lining)
(approx.		**Hardware**	3" lag screws with washers for
460 sq. ft.)			bench posts
Benches	4x4 posts		Joist hangers for 2x6s
	2x4 framing pieces		Angled joist hangers for 2x6s
	2x6 seat braces		Angle brackets
	2x6 seat pieces and edging		Fasteners for joist hangers
Counter	4x4 posts		2" deck screws
	2x4 angle braces		3" deck screws
	2x4 bottom braces		Self-closing hinges for cabinet doors
	2x4 countertop pieces and edging	**Masonry**	Concrete
	2x2 braces for countertop		Concrete tube forms
Planters and	1x6 side pieces		

CONSTRUCTION TECHNIQUES

Supporting a Deck Nearly Flush to the Ground

Drummond uses pressure-treated Southern yellow pine. This grade is so saturated with treating agent that Drummond feels comfortable sinking the beams into the ground. Although 0.40 lumber is rated suitable for ground contact, you may want to special-order the higher-rated lumber.

Lay out the corners of the decks and walkways using stakes. Based on the highest point in your yard, establish the desired heights of the decks. String level lines on the stakes, and then excavate to a depth of 7 ½ inches below the string lines for the entire deck and 5 ½ inches deeper for the beams. Allow yourself plenty of room to work.

Footings. Lay out and dig the footing holes. The smaller deck requires four beam footings (two for each beam) and four perimeter footings. The dining deck has six beam footings (three for each beam) and four perimeter footings.

For the beam footings, position a concrete tube form in each footing hole so that its bottom end measures 12 ½ inches below the future surface of your deck. Use a water level, line level, or carpenter's level laid on top of a long, straight board to level the tube

forms with one another. Anchor the tube forms firmly with scrap 2x4s and screws, as shown in the detail drawing. For the footings that do not support beams, set the tube forms 5 ½ inches higher than those for the beam footings. Note: before you do this, check the actual width of your 4x6s. If they don't measure exactly 5 ½ inches wide, adjust the height of the non-beam footings accordingly.

The local building department may require the use of anchoring hardware for beams that rest on footings. However, such hardware is not really necessary because the 4x6 beams will not wander off the footings once you build the framing. Pour the concrete, and allow it to set.

Framing for Freestanding Octagons

Set the beams in place, but do not cut them to exact length yet. Adjust the baseplate on your circular saw for a 22 ½-degree cut (to yield a 67 ½-degree bevel on your good piece). Then cut eight 2x6 joists to a length of 80 inches (on the long side) and eight more to 50 inches (also on the long side). Screw together these two sets of outside joists on top of their respective beams. The beam structures will be a bit flimsy and

not yet perfectly square, but they will firm up as you add the joists. The two octagons will measure about 3 inches shy of 10 and 16 feet in diameter, which will allow for the 1 ½-inch decking overhang.

On each octagon, measure for the interior joists; then square-cut them to fit. Make sure that all interior joists for each octagon measure exactly the same length. Now, check for squareness. Add the remaining joists, and then build the frames for the pathways. Lay the decking, allowing it to overhang the framing 1 ½ inches on all sides.

Planters, Cabinets, and Counter

The flower boxes and storage cabinets should have a simple, rustic appearance, so don't attempt to make them look like fine cabinetry. However, select good-looking wood that is not likely to shrink, warp, or crack. No. 1 pressure-treated lumber that is labeled KDAT (kiln-dried after treatment) makes a good choice.

Planters. For each flower box, cut five pieces of tongue-and-groove 1x6 lumber to a length of 22 ½ inches, five pieces to 22 ½ inches plus the distance you want the front to travel downward to the ground, and two pieces that are notched as shown.

Assemble each side, attaching 2x2 braces at the top and bottom with 2 ½-inch deck screws. Check each side for squareness. Notch out the decking overhang for each box. Join the sides together, check the box for squareness, and then cut 2x6 shelf pieces to fit. Attach the shelf and the 2x4 top trim pieces with 3-inch decking screws. Build the benches as described on page 219, but assemble the seat lum-

ESTABLISHING FOOTINGS THAT ARE LEVEL WITH EACH OTHER

12½" Below the Surface of the Deck

2x4

Tube Form

Resting on Excavated Ground

BUILDING THE COUNTER

2x4s

2x4s

2x2 Braces

4x4 Post

34½"

8¾"

1¾"

FLOWER BOXES

2x4 Top Trim

2x6s (Shelf)

2x2s

1x6s

22½"

Depth Determined by Grade

Depth Determined by Height of Flowerpots

ber as shown with this deck for a more interesting effect. (See pages 202–204.)

Cabinets. Construct the cabinets in much the same way you did the flower boxes, but make the sides taller. Also, add a second 2x6 shelf at the bottom. Build the side with the door as shown; then make a door that measures 2 inches larger than the opening in both directions. Install self-closing hinges so you won't have to worry about latches.

If, like Drummond's clients, you would like to have a refrigerator, hire an electrician to run an underground cable in conduit that is approved by the local building department. You may need to have a new circuit installed as well.

Counter. Lay the pieces for the counter on the deck, and measure them for cutting. Assemble the counter upside down so that you won't end up with screwheads on the working surface. Lay three 2x4 countertop pieces flat, and then sandwich them between two 2x4 edging pieces laid on edge. At-

tach 2x2 braces at both ends and every 2 feet or so to keep the top flush with the edging. Then attach the edging to the countertop.

Cut the posts to 34 ½ inches long. On the bottom ends, cut out a notch that measures 1 ¾ inches deep and 8 ¾ inches long. Install them as you would rail posts. Set the counter on top of the posts and cabinets, level it, and attach it to the cabinets using 2-inch screws. Drive the screws from the inside of the cabinet into the 2x2 braces. Lastly, cut angle braces, and screw them to the posts and the counter from underneath.

CABINET WITH DOOR

2x6s (Shelf)

40"

ABOVEGROUND POOL SURROUND

As Drummond's clients discovered, this is a handsome way to dress up an inexpensive aboveground swimming pool. However, be aware that materials and labor for a structure like this can run up some serious expense. If you don't already own an aboveground model, you may find that a standard in-ground pool wouldn't cost appreciably more.

Ground View

ABOVEGROUND POOL SURROUND, PLAN VIEW

(2) 2x6s

2x6 Railing Cap

17" Wide Bench

4x6 Beams

2x6 Decking

Divider Strip

2x6 Joists

Step

20'

6'

11'

40'

10'

13'

7'

8'

20'

20'

DESIGN CONSIDERATIONS

The homeowners primarily wanted a smooth transition to the pool. The house occupies a corner lot, which means that setback requirements limited the area that they could use. Still, they wanted something of a rambling feel. Drummond's design allows them to step from a breakfast nook onto a lower deck that provides ample room for dining and lounging, and to move easily from there up to pool level.

Pool Surround. A 4-foot-wide walkway runs around two-thirds of the pool, allowing enough room for swimmers to pull themselves out of the water and sit with their feet dangling in it. This also provides enough width for a lounge chair, provided there isn't much traffic. (If you prefer a full-scale lounging area next to the pool, allow at least 6 feet.) Because there are two walkways leading to this area, traffic rarely poses a problem.

Along the other one-third of the pool, a fixed bench on the lower deck provides a place for buffet eating. The skirting that covers the pool serves as the back for the bench. Around the perimeter of the pool, solid skirting alternates with lattice panels, some of which are hinged to allow access to pool machinery and to provide usable storage space.

ELEVATION

2x6 Railing Cap

2x2 Balusters

2x4 Rails

2x6 Decking

2x6 Joists

2x12 Stringer

2x4 Nailer

1x6 Skirting

Rail Posts Set in 42" of Concrete

MATERIALS USED FOR THIS DECK

Framing	4x4 posts		2x6 seat pieces and edging
	4x6s (or doubled 2x6s) for beams	**Planters**	2x4 top cap pieces
	2x6 joists		2x4 framing pieces
Stairs	2x6s for treads		1x6 tongue-and-groove for sides
	2x12 stringers		15-lb. roofing felt for lining
	1x8 risers	**Hardware**	Joist hangers for 2x6s
Decking	2x6s		Angled joist hangers for 2x6s
Skirt	1x6 verticals		Angle brackets
	2x4 edging		Fasteners for joist hangers
Railing	4x4 posts (also used as structural posts)		3" deck screws or 10d galvanizednails
	2x6 railing cap		3" lag screws with washers for rail and
	2x4 top and bottom rails		bench posts
	2x2 balusters		2 ½" deck screws for attaching
Benches	4x4 posts		balusters
	2x4 framing pieces	**Masonry**	Concrete
	2x6 seat braces		Concrete tube forms

CONSTRUCTION TECHNIQUES

The lower deck calls for standard techniques, but constructing symmetrical, firm framing around the pool for the upper deck poses more of a challenge. In Drummond's design, the posts for this framing carry through upward, so they can double as rail posts.

Building around a Raised Pool

Pools of this type can be fairly strong, but don't use the pool to support the deck in any way. It isn't built to take this kind of strain. This means that you must build and support the deck so that it doesn't touch the pool or end up bearing on the pool in the future. To ensure this, use spacers that keep all joists and posts at least ¾ inch away from the pool edge, and hold the decking off the pool edge by ½ inch or so. Also, install solid footings, and set them well below the frost line for your area.

Footings. The pool surround, a nearly freestanding structure that measures about 6 feet high, needs more lateral support than most decks. The solution is to sink numerous posts deep in the ground and fill each hole with plenty of concrete. This requires lots of deep footing holes, so consider hiring a landscaping company to dig them for you. At the very least, recruit some help and rent a power auger. For the posts, select lumber that has a rating of 0.40 or higher that can withstand ground contact. If you cut off the end that goes into the ground, soak it in preservative for a while before installing it.

The pool surround does not require beams. Your inspector may insist that you double the outside joists, but positioning the posts every 5 to 6 feet gives the structure plenty of support. The solid skirting adds rigidity. Along the bench-side edge of the pool, joists attached to both sides of the posts

provide adequate support for a narrow ledge.

Post Locations. Lay out the post locations next to the pool first. Check your pool sides for plumb; if they aren't, vary your measurements accordingly. At each end of the pool, locate the exact center of the curve, and dig a posthole at this point, centering it 4 inches from the edge of the pool. Next, dig holes at the points on both sides where the curve begins. Then locate two in-between holes as shown. Center all holes 4 inches from the pool edge.

Lay out and dig the remaining post-

holes. Make the holes that will hold structural rail posts at least 42 inches deep to provide stiffness. The other holes need only follow local codes for footings. Build the framing before you pour concrete. (See the Plan View, Elevation, and Framing Detail for additional information.)

POOL POST LOCATIONS

Postholes Dug 4" O.C. from Edge of Pool

Equal Distances

Centerline

Post at Point Where Curve Begins

FRAMING DETAIL

Rail Post at Least 36" above Joists

Note: Posts Set in Holes—No Concrete Yet

Extra 2x4 as Backing

ACCESS PANEL

Joists ¾" Above Pool

Cut Off Post Top

3" Deck Screws

2x12 Stringer

2x6s

Bottom Stair-Rail Post

Main Deck Area

Beam

2x6 Joists

Lattice

3" Deck Screws

2x4s

2x4 Nailer

Laying the Decking

Around the curved ends of the pool, you can install the decking so that it overhangs the pool; then cut a curved line so the overhang is 1 inch or so. To do this, use the pool itself as a reference for establishing the line. As an alternative, cap the edges of the decking with 2x6 trim, as shown in the rendering and plan view (pages 209 and 210).

To support the narrow section of pool surround trim, use short pieces of 2x6. For the butt joints on the pool surround trim, angle-cut the decking pieces to 15 degrees, laying them as you go. If necessary, adjust the angle on your last cuts to make it come out all right.

Build the benches as described on page 219. For the bench that runs alongside the pool, build a simple frame out of 2x4s, making it 17 inches high.

To provide access to the pool mechanism, Drummond constructed a removable decking section. To maintain a seamless look, install the decking before you cut this opening, keeping track of where you need to locate the "trap door." Using a circular saw and then a handsaw or reciprocating saw, cut the decking flush to the inside edges of the joists below. Screw the cutout pieces to lengths of 2x2 to make a simple panel. Attach nailers to the joists, setting them at a proper height to ensure a smooth decking surface once the panel is in place. Drill a fingerhole or two into the trap door using a 1 ½-inch spade or Forstener bit.

Providing Access to the Area Beneath

For the skirting, make sure you have top and bottom nailing surfaces that are plumb with each other. Cut lengths of 1x6 to fit so that they come within about 1 inch of the ground. Attach them to the outside joists and bottom nailers.

You'll need to get under the deck from time to time to maintain your pool, and you may want some storage space as well. To build simple but sturdy access panels, sandwich factory-made lattice panels between two 2x4s as shown. Attach them to the joist and nailer with screws. If you think you'll need to remove the panels more than once a month, hang the panels using strap hinges, eyescrews, and hooks.

TWIN DECKS SURROUNDING A PORCH

The homeowners' house had a rectangular screened back porch with a simple set of steps leading down to the yard. Because traffic flowed right through the middle of the porch, there was no good place to dine or lounge. The homeowners do a lot of entertaining, so they wanted more usable space as well as clearly defined areas. Drummond's solution called for rebuilding the porch as well as installing twin decks.

DESIGN CONSIDERATIONS

A screened porch provides welcome refuge during those nights when the mosquitoes are swarming, but it doesn't offer the outdoor feel of a genuine deck. The ideal situation for many people is to have both.

The existing screened porch was one of the "stick-'em-on" types often added by home builders as an after-thought. A simple rectangle, it had little visual appeal. Worse than that, it had a major design flaw: the locations of the entry door and the screened door leading outside created the traffic problem mentioned in the introduction at left, which rendered the porch useless for entertaining.

Drummond thus decided to reroute traffic through the porch. He tore out the existing screening and installed two doors, one on each side and close to the house. This freed up most of the porch for dining and lounging.

Deck Wings. Each of the doors leads to a separate deck area: a sun deck with benches to the right and a dining/cooking deck to the left. Although smaller, the sun deck has a more spacious and relaxed feel because it usually contains less furniture. The dining/cooking deck has ample room for a table with chairs as well as a barbecue.

This house has vinyl siding, which can easily be damaged by heat. Drummond cautioned the owners about

Ground View

this, so they located their grill 6 feet away from the house. Keep this in mind if your siding is made of vinyl or other flammable material.

Like many homes in warm climates, this one has heat-pump units (which also provide air conditioning) that are situated outdoors. Homes in other areas may have air-conditioning units located outside. A walkway leads around the outdoor units and into the house via a utility room that is near a bathroom. This allows guests who are on the deck easy access to the bath-

room; it also leaves the pump units accessible but not visually exposed.

To the east of the house, a park provides a fine view, and the owners wanted to give guests ample opportunity to gaze in that direction. They also wanted to connect the two decks. Drummond addressed both problems gracefully by adding a small deck to the east of the porch with three spacious stairs that lead down to the lawn. The two larger deck areas remain clearly separate, but the steps allow

easy movement between them and provide a perfect place from which to admire the view.

TWIN DECKS SURROUNDING A PORCH, PLAN VIEW

Steps

14'

31'

19'6"

Landing

16'6"

Steps

Landings

Screened Porch

2x6 Decking

Bench

Steps

Carriages

(2) 2x6s

2x6 Joists
16" O.C.

Steps

2x6 Railing Cap

MATERIALS USED FOR THIS DECK

Framing	4x4 posts	
	Doubled 2x8s for beams	
	2x6 joists	
	2x12 carriages for stairways	
Decking	2x6s	
(approx.	1x4 edging	
260 sq. ft.)		
Skirting	1x6 vertical pieces	
Railing	4x4 posts	
	2x6 railing cap	
	2x4 top and bottom rails	
	2x2 balusters	
Bench	4x4 posts	
	2x4 framing pieces	
	2x4 banding pieces	
	2x6 seat braces	

	2x6 seat pieces and edging
Hardware	Joist hangers for 2x6s
	Angled joist hangers for 2x6s
	Angle brackets
	Fasteners for joist hangers
	3" deck screws
	3" lag screws with washers for rail and bench posts
	2 ½" deck screws
	3 ½" screws with concrete shields
Masonry	Concrete
	Concrete tube forms or lumber for building forms
	Solid concrete blocks for footings

CONSTRUCTION TECHNIQUES

This deck rambles a bit and has several different levels. When laying it out, make sure that the levels will be oriented correctly in relation to each of the doors. Also, take into account the slope of the yard, if any, and carefully determine where the stairway will end. If you miscalculate, you may have to add another step, which could cause the deck to protrude farther into the yard than you want.

Screening in a Porch

Though a screened porch has a relaxed feel, it requires careful planning and construction: mosquitoes have a way of finding even tiny openings. For this reason, it's best to stick with a simple rectangle. More complicated shapes require numerous screened sections. If you'll be screening in a previously open porch, plan the job carefully to minimize the number of small sections you'll have to cover.

In addition, consider whether it makes more sense to install the screens permanently or make them removable. If you go with the latter option, you may find it more practical to purchase screened window units from a specialty shop. If you'd rather build them yourself, consider using metal or plastic stock that is designed for the purpose, rather than building them out of wood.

Framing for Widening Stairs

To provide adequate backing for the stair carriages, attach a 2x8 below the 2x6 outside joist. Cut and install standard carriages every 2 to 3 feet, and support their bottoms with concrete footings or a slab. Make sure that all the standard carriages are square to the 2x8 backing piece. At the 45-degree corners, leave room for a middle carriage.

The tricky part is to support the two sets of side treads at the points where they meet the middle steps at a 45-degree angle (forming a supplementary 135-degree angle). Here, a regular-size carriage would be too short, so it's best to cut the treads to fit after you've installed the standard carriages. Using a power miter saw, make 22 ½-degree cuts on the ends where they meet (to yield complementary 67 ½-degree angles). Set them in place, and then measure for a double carriage that will run through the middle of the miter joint. This carriage need not fit precisely, but it should provide support for all the tread pieces.

Stair Detail

Elevation

Set treads temporarily in place to measure for middle stringer.

2x6

2x8

Ripped 2x4

2x6s

Concrete Footing

Doubled Carriage

Bench

2x4s

1x4 Deck Edging

1x6 Solid Skirt

4x4 Post

COZY DECK WITH BENCHES AND PLANTERS

DESIGN CONSIDERATIONS

Perfect symmetry generally makes for an uninteresting deck, but the design should have balance. This one illustrates that principle well. The bench/planter, which is fairly massive, anchors one end of the deck, but it faces toward the homeowners' pool, helping to establish it as the focal point of the yard. The other two smaller planters on the yard side of the deck balance the barbecue area on the house side.

Bench/Planter. With its 3-foot height (plus the height of the flowers) the bench/planter helps to enclose the deck. Guests can easily ignore the neighbors and focus on the deck area and pool just beyond. The two other planters step down one level toward the pool, contributing to the sense of privacy without imposing a walled-in effect.

The homeowners wanted a deck that would provide a smooth transition from the house to the pool and help to focus attention on the pool. They wanted plenty of planter space for flowers as well. Drummond came up with an unusual bench/planter to take care of these latter two requirements. He positioned it so that people sitting on it would face the pool.

Ground View

MAKING A SQUARE DECK LIVELIER

Years ago, a previous owner had added a stodgy, rectangular deck onto the homeowners' house. When the homeowners called in Drummond, they had no complaints about the deck's usefulness, and it provided ample room for everything they needed to do. But they still felt that they had outgrown it: their yard had developed into a thing of beauty, which left the deck looking like a poor relation. The homeowners' purpose in modifying the deck was strictly to spruce up its appearance. Drummond proposed that they cut off two corners and add a large circular section.

Ground View

MAKING A SQUARE DECK LIVELIER, PLAN VIEW

PREEXISTING DECK, PLAN VIEW

6'

2x8 Joists

Bench

12'6" Radius

1x6 Fascia

2x6 Decking

7

Step

Bench

6

(2) 2x8s Beams

2x8 Header Joist

DESIGN CONSIDERATIONS

This design departs from Drummond's usual precepts about functional areas. He calls it an "impact deck," intended as a visual statement that would make a dull deck exciting. It provides room for a table with chairs, but a great deal of space could be considered wasted because it has no clearly assigned use. Sometimes, however, "wasted" space can lend an air of expansiveness and luxury.

The circular addition provides a graceful transition to the yard. Because this area sprawls expansively, a person walking on it does not feel funneled in a particular direction. The wooden surface fans out and seems more a part of the lawn and landscape than a stairway toward it.

Adding On. If you have a squarish deck that lacks style, resist the temptation to tear it down and start over from scratch. You can probably save some money as well as labor by adding on to the structure instead. A solution that works for a lot of homeowners is to cut out a triangular area and attach a new

section of decking that runs at an angle to the existing deck. If you then add a distinctive curve or some unusual angles and put in a bench or a new style of railing, you'll hardly remember the ho-hum structure that stood there before.

Chances are that you won't be able to match the existing decking exactly. The old surface will have weathered or may have been built from material that is now hard to find at the local lumberyard or mill. However, most of Drummond's add-on clients find that a difference in color or texture is not displeasing to the eye, especially if the new surface begins one step up or down, as with this deck. For extremely different wood colors, a deck stain—either semitransparent or solid-color depending on the severity of the problem—will hide any discrepancy.

MATERIALS USED FOR THIS DECK

Framing	4x4 posts	Fasteners for joist hangers
	Doubled 2x8s for beams	3" deck screws
	2x8 joists	3" lag screws with washers for bench
	2x6 joists for step	posts
Decking	2x6s	2 ½" deck screws
Benches	2x4s for seat pieces	3 ½" screws with concrete shields
	1x4 spacers between seat pieces	**Masonry** Concrete
	2x4 braces	Concrete tube forms or lumber for
	4x4 posts	building forms
Hardware	Joist hangers for 2x6s & 2x8s	Solid concrete blocks for footings
	Angled joist hangers for 2x6s & 2x8s	
	Angle brackets	

CONSTRUCTION TECHNIQUES

This deck is less complicated than it appears, but you'll need to work carefully and pay attention to details. Before you begin cutting, make sure the old deck has adequate support. Also, avoid shortcuts when marking and cutting the curve.

Cutting an Old Deck to Prepare for an Addition

Preparing for the addition will probably take less time than you imagine. Using a circular saw and a reciprocating saw, you can cut away the old decking in a couple of hours. But again, support the deck properly before you start, and plan your cuts carefully to avoid any unpleasant surprises.

Temporary Support. If possible, remove fascia pieces and header joists so that you can climb under the existing deck and assess the situation. If there isn't enough clearance for this, then cut the decking to create access from above. Wherever there's a post or foot-

ing that you'll bypass with your cut, check to see that the existing joists will be well supported after you've made your cuts.

The temporary supports needn't be anything elaborate. Lay a short scrap of 2x6 on the ground, and then cut another piece of 2x6 long enough that it will wedge in tightly beneath the joist or joists. Attach the two pieces using toenails or angled screws to keep them from sliding out of position. If you have a number of joists to support, use a 4x4 as a header as shown (opposite).

Removing the Existing Structure. Chalk a line, and then cut away the decking. Next, use a circular saw and a reciprocating saw to cut the joists from underneath. You may have to cut them back by as much as 3 ¾ inches: 1 ½ inches to accommodate a new header joist, ¾ inch for the fascia piece, and 1 ½ inches to allow for decking overhang.

Building a Large Curved Section

Install the beams so that they meet in the center of the curve, as shown in the Plan View on page 230. Install the double center joist first, and then run the angled joists wild. (You'll cut them to size after you've installed them all.) Tack a nail at the reference point, and then attach a string and pencil to it. Mark the radius on top of the joists to indicate where you want the framing to end—probably 2 ¼ inches short of the decking to allow for a ¾-inch fascia and a 1 ½-inch overhang. Hold straight boards in position to establish the header joist locations, and then mark each joist for cutting. Cut the joists using a circular saw, and install the header joists.

For the fascia board, Drummond finds that a regular 1x6 or 1x8 is flexible enough to bend into position. Hold it (or them) in position, and mark for cutting. Install the decking, allowing it to

ELEVATION

2x6 Decking

Original Deck Area (with Spa)

1x6 Curved Fascia

4x4 Post

4x4

2x4 Seat Pieces

run wild so that each piece overhangs the fascia by at least 1 ½ inches.

To cut the decking, Drummond uses a router equipped with a straight bit. It takes four passes to cut through 1 ½-inch-thick lumber. He makes a simple trammel beam from a length of 1x4, drilling a hole for the router bit and then mounting the router on it. He attaches the board to the radius point using a nail driven through a drilled hole so that it will swing freely. Note: this will require using a heavy-duty router equipped with a long, straight bit with a ½-inch shank.

Slotted Benches

Because the benches do not have angles, they need to be anchored securely. One is attached to the house with masonry screws, and the other is screwed into the old deck. If possible, use posts that run up from the footings for extra strength. Otherwise, anchor them securely to the deck.

Cut the long seat pieces and the spacers. Join them together using 3-inch screws, and check the assembly for squareness as you work. Next, add the end pieces. Cut the posts, attach two braces to the top of each, and check these to be sure they're square. Attach the posts to the deck and the seat to the posts and braces.

TEMPORARY JOIST SUPPORT

4x4

2x6s

Toenails

SLOTTED BENCHES

8 2x4 Seat Pieces

21 1x4 Spacers

16¼"

16"

2 2x4 End Pieces

2x4 Braces

45°-Angle Cut

Notched 4x4 Post

1¾"x8¾" Notch

A DECK BUILT FOR ENTERTAINING

The owners wanted a large deck, but they also wanted style, and they didn't want to disturb the large, stately trees growing in the yard.

Ground View

POOLSIDE DECK

This deck has two distinct areas. The upper portion is used for dining and relaxing, while the lower section serves as a continuation of the pool deck.

Ground View

POOLSIDE DECK, PLAN VIEW

2x8

45'

12'

15'

2x6 12" O.C.

Composite 2x6 for Seats

(2) 2x6

Composite Decking

4x4 Covered with
Composite Sleeve

MATERIALS USED FOR THIS DECK

Framing	4x6 post	**Bench**	4x4 post
	2x8s for beams on upper deck		Vinyl sleeves
	Doubled 2x6 for internal beams on lower deck		2x6 bench braces
			2x4 framing
	2x6 joists		2x6s for seats
Decking	Composite decking pre-grooved to accept hidden fasteners	**Hardware**	Joist hangers
			Angle brackets
	Composite decking without grooves for fascia/edging		Joist hanger nails
			Eb-ty hidden fasteners with stainless-steel #7 screws
Skirting	Composite decking installed vertical with ⅜" gap for ventilation		FastenMaster ledger locks for rail and bench posts
Railing	4x4 post	**Masonry**	Concrete
	Composite sleeves for post		Tube forms
	Composite railing sections, post caps, and trim base		

DESIGN CONSIDERATIONS

The 550 square feet of this deck are divided between two levels—each with a specific function. The top level contains enough space for a table, chairs, and a cooking center. It is where the family does most of its outdoor dining and relaxing. The deck extends out beyond the edge of the lower level to provide some design interest. And it is enclosed within a distinctive railing system.

The lower level is located four steps below the upper area. It is part of the same structure as the upper portion, but it has a closer relationship to the in-ground pool than it does to the elevated dining area. This ground-hugging platform is only 7 inches off of the concrete pool deck. Swimmers use this part of the deck as a staging space for the pool and pool activities. Built-in benches at the far end of the deck are used for seating and to hold towels for swimmers. It is also a good spot for adults to supervise small children in the pool. The benches also serve the design function of balancing the weight of the elevated portion of the deck. Benches closest to the house shield an air-conditioning unit located near the deck.

The steps between the two areas span the entire depth of the deck. This opens up the space, facilitates traffic flow, and does not block the views from the upper deck. The steps serve as emergency seating when needed.

CONSTRUCTION TECHNIQUES

A composite decking material with a hidden fastener system covers this deck. In many cases, the manufacturer of the composite decking is not the manufacturer of the fastening system. It is important that you make sure both are compatible with one another before starting work. Because composite materials are man-made, the joist span tables printed for pressure-treated pine, cedar, or redwood may not be applicable to the composite material you have chosen. Check with the manufacturer for appropriate spans, especially if you plan to install the decking at an angle. Angled installations often require shorter spans between joists.

The classic white balustrade on this deck is really a composite railing system. The composite has a textured feel to it. Pressure-treated 4x4 posts bolted to the rim joist provide structural support for the railing. The connections for this assembly are then covered with blocking and trim boards. A composite sleeve fits over the wood post. Use a carbide-tipped blade to trim the sleeve to size.

Lighting. Composite railing systems often have another advantage: it is easy to hide wiring for low-voltage lighting systems. Drummond installed lights on some of the posts. There are also lights inset in the steps and along the front edge of the lower portion of the deck for safety.

For built-in seating, Casa Decks uses 2x6 braces for support. But to hide the bracing under the trim boards, the company bevels the edges of the 2x6. This still provides the necessary holding power. To finish the seating, let the seating boards run wild and then trim them to fit. Cover the edges with a trim board for a neat, finished appearance.

BENCH BRACE

12"

3½"

22½ °

2x6 Brace

3½"

Composite Fascia

A SHADED AREA TO ENJOY THE VIEWS

Space was tight for this deck, and the homeowners wanted a combination sitting/eating area that would not interfere with the views of a nearby golf course.

Ground View

A SHADED AREA TO ENJOY THE VIEWS, PLAN VIEW

22'6"

12'

2x6 Shade Element

4x6

2x6 12" O.C.

Decking
⁵⁄₄x6 Composite

2x10   6x6 Posts

MATERIALS USED FOR THIS DECK

Framing	4x6 posts		**Hardware**	Joist hangers
	4x6 beam (girder)			Angle brackets
Decking	⁵⁄₄x6 decking			Joist hanger nails
	⁵⁄₄x6 fascia			2 ½" stainless-steel screws
	⁵⁄₄x6 undertrim			FastenMaster ledger locks for rail and
Railing	4x4 posts			bench posts
	2x4 framing			3" stainless-steel framing nails
	2x2 balusters		**Masonry**	Concrete
	⁵⁄₄x6 railing cap			Tube forms
Pergola	6x6 posts			Solid block for footing base
	2x10 double header			
	2x10 ledger			
	2x6 shade elements			

DESIGN CONSIDERATIONS

At first, the design parameters spelled out by the homeowners seemed a little daunting. They wanted a combination sitting, dining, cooking area; a shaded retreat; and an unobstructed view of a nearby golf course.

They also wanted the deck to be level with the main living area of the house so that the new deck would function as an outdoor extension of the interior living area. However, local covenants concerning limits on the size of decks and other structures limited Casa Decks in the design approach it could take.

The limits on space did not prevent Drummond from coming up with an interesting design that projects only about 12 feet from the house at its widest point—well within the established space limitations. This area is covered by a wood pergola system that matches the trim of the house. The railing is a standard wood railing system that is topped with a gray composite material.

This design shows how plans can change during construction or after the homeowners gain some experience living with their new deck. In their original discussion, the homeowners wanted room for a cooking area on the deck just outside the kitchen. The final design provided enough room for a grill and cooking area, but the homeowners decided to move the grill off of the deck. This provided more room for dining, and it opened up the views from the deck and interior of the house.

CONSTRUCTION TECHNIQUES

The pergola is supported by 6x6 posts. Drummond could have used smaller posts—4x4s or 4x6s—to carry the load, but he felt that the larger posts were more in proportion to the mass of the house. The shade elements in the pergola are made of 2x6s, a good size board to use due to the span of the pergola.

Because the pergola is attached to the house, it is necessary to create a watertight seal between the pergola's ledger board and the house. This seal is just as important as the seal on the ledger that connects the main deck area to the house. (See page 249 for more information.)

The pergola shade elements have decorative end cuts to provide design interest and to impart a light and airy look to the design. Drummond varies the size of the cuts based on the size of the lumber used. This helps keep all of the design elements in proportion.

(See the drawing, right.)

Even on a small deck such as this one, Drummond likes to provide a set of utility stairs that lead to a garage or utility area of the yard. This helps with overall traffic flow on the deck, providing direct access to two areas of the yard. If a deck divides a yard in two, having only one set of stairs often leads to part of the yard receiving little use.

Drummond likes to provide solid skirting around the base of the decks he builds. It provides a different look from the lattice skirts often found on decks. In this case, the skirting matches the composite decking used on other portions of the deck. To facilitate under-deck ventilation, be sure to provide a ⅜-inch space between the skirt boards.

DECORATIVE END CUTS

2x4 — 1" — 6"

2x6 — 1½" — 7"

2x8 — 2" — 8"

SMALL DETAILS ENHANCE GREAT VIEWS

The homeowners wanted a large outdoor living area, but they also wanted a deck that would not obstruct the view from the house. The result was a multilevel design with distinctive details.

Ground View

DESIGN CONSIDERATIONS

The owners of this deck had definite requirements in mind when they began discussion with Drummond. They wanted the deck to fit with the overall design of the house; they wanted defined areas within the design; and they wanted to preserve the view.

Drummond's first goal was to create a design where the leading edge of the deck was no more than 30 inches high. Anything above that height would have required a railing system that would obstruct the view. He was able to meet the height requirement by building a 7-foot-wide level off of the back door of the house. This level steps down to a middle area whose height is within local building code height limits.

The top platform extends to the end of the house where it serves as a cooking center. The far edge is covered by a small vinyl arbor. The arbor is wired for lighting, making it possible to cook and serve food into the evening hours.

The cooking area can be reached directly from the yard by a set of utility stairs on that side of the deck. The stairs consist of a step-down platform with steps running from the front and back of the platform. Drummond always tries to manage traffic flow in his designs. These stairs provide access to the deck and the back door of the house from both the driveway and the yard without the need of crossing the main deck areas. Such an arrangement helps ease congestion on the deck when the owners are entertaining. Children playing in the yard can reach the house without disturbing adults on the deck.

The lower level of the deck not only provides a large eating or entertaining area, it also connects the kitchen to a screened room at that end of the deck, tying together the main outdoor living areas.

SMALL DETAILS ENHANCE GREAT VIEWS, PLAN VIEW

42'

5/4x6 Composite Decking

Pergola

20'

2x6 12" O.C.

Steps with 14" Run

MATERIALS USED FOR THIS DECK

Framing	4x6 post	
	Doubled 2x8s for beams	
	2x6 joists	
	2x12s for step stringers	
Decking	Composite 5/4x6 decking	
	Composite 1x12 fascia	
Skirting	1x6 cedar spaced 3/8 inch for ventilation	
	2x4 framing	
Bench	4x4 post	
	White vinyl post sleeve	
	2x6 bench braces	
	2x4 framing	
	Composite decking for bench seats and fascia	
Pergola	4x4 posts	
	White vinyl post sleeve	

Post base and cap (vinyl)
2x6 lumber or vinyl with aluminum inserts and end caps
2x2 lumber or vinyl with end caps for shade elements
Copper and vinyl flashing

Hardware
Joist hangers
Angle brackets
Joist hanger nails
2 ½" stainless steel screws
FastenMaster ledger locks for rail and bench posts
3" stainless-steel framing nails

Masonry
Concrete
Tube forms

CONSTRUCTION TECHNIQUES

Although there is no need for a railing system on the middle level, Drummond added built-in benches for extra seating and to help give the area a sense of enclosure.

The steps down to the lower level are constructed with a 7-inch rise and a 14-inch run. Normal stair construction calls for a 11 or 12-inch run, but Drummond feels that outdoor stairs should have a slightly deeper tread than those found inside. He believes deeper treads are easier to maneuver and safer when used on a deck. The flow of the steps provides stadium seating for large gatherings. Low-voltage lights installed in the risers provide illumination.

The lower deck area is one step up from the yard. It has a rounded edge to match the radius of a bow window on the house. Casa's crews usually simply let the decking on a radius edge run wild, trimming them to size when they all are in place.

All of the decking is a cedar-colored composite material, a trend that is growing in Drummond's area. Redwood-colored composite trim boards provide contrast.

Ledger Details. One area that Casa Decks pays particular attention to is the ledger connection between the house and deck. It is also necessary to ensure a watertight seal between the house and any overhead structure attached to the house, such as the pergola in this project. Drummond says that building inspectors examine these areas closely because of publicity of deck failures.

For ledger attachments—the pergola detail is shown below—Drummond uses a two-piece flashing system. After removing the siding, insert a section of copper flashing up under the siding. The flashing should

be long enough to tuck under the undisturbed siding below the pergola. Attach a 2x8 ledger through the flashing and into the house framing. Then take a second section of flashing that is preformed to cover the top of the ledger. This should extend up under the house wrap on the wall and cap the entire top of the ledger, creating a watertight seal. Make sure the building paper covers both pieces of flashing under the siding. Use copper or vinyl flashing as these should meet the corrosion requirements of the newer preservatives used in pressure-treated wood.

For the shade elements, use 2x6 and 2x2 lumber. In larger structures, you

will need to install blocking between the pergola joists for stability. Stagger the blocking to give the entire overhead structure a more finished look. You can also attach a 2x2 to the ledger under the pergola arms for a more finished look.

Pergola Ledger

Building Paper

Preformed Vinyl Flashing

2x2

Copper Flashing

2x6

2x8

2x2

CHAPTER 12

ROLLING RIDGE DECK AND OUTDOOR LIVING

Barry Streett has been building decks for about 25 years, starting in Maryland and then moving to Colorado in 1995. Many homes in his part of Colorado are on steep sites, which means that they do not have usable backyards. So his decks often effectively take the place of a backyard. Streett long ago decided to work at the high end of the design and skill scale. He prides himself in doing work that other builders cannot do, and feels that he can meet the needs and fulfill the desires of the most exacting customers.

ROLLING RIDGE DECK AND OUTDOOR LIVING COMPANY

Evergreen, Colorado

303-670-4919

www.rollingridgedeck.com

TECHNIQUES TO USE

Streett enjoys difficult engineering challenges—feats like building on severe slopes, creating elaborate curves, and building decks elevated more than 20 feet (6.1m).

• To create custom metal railings, he first designs them himself and then has a metalworking partner make the railings to fit. A strong powder coating is applied for great protection against rust. It is important to use a reputable and experienced fabricator and powder-coater to ensure that the rails are solid and last a very long time.

• Streett often uses large engineered beams—cedar exterior glue-laminated beams, for instance—which span longer distances because they are stronger than the usual doubled 2-bys (5cm-bys). This enables him to be a minimalist below the deck. The fewer the posts, the more pristine the deck looks from the outside. (Cedar glue-laminated beams might not be approved in wetter climates; there, pressure-treated beams are often required.)

• For joists and beams, he uses the best lumber: No. 1 southern yellow pine kiln-dried after treatment (KDAT). It is worth the extra cost because it is so stable and straight.

• He also sometimes builds with steel framing, which produces perfectly flat deck surfaces with fewer beams. He prefers to use "G90" galvanized joists rather than the usual "G60" because they are stronger. In his dry climate, powder-coating the joists is not needed.

• Streett's footings are often extra heavy duty, especially when supporting high decks with few posts. This means digging to below the frost line or, better yet, to bedrock and pouring steel-reinforced concrete columns that rise 8 inches (20.3cm) or so above grade. In his dry climate, he can install non-treated Douglas fir posts. In looser soil, he often installs massive helical piers, which are actually screwed into the ground with special equipment.

• Streett does not like the look of exposed decking ends; he prefers a cleaner appearance. So he usually cuts decking flush with outside joists, then installs the fascia so that its top edge is flush with the top of the decking. This method works well for high-quality composite materials but is not recommended for wood decking or lesser-quality composites, which may warp, leading to unsightly gaps between decking and fascia.

• Although Streett's decks are by no means inexpensive, he is opposed to wasteful spending. He tends to "value engineer" when designing, meaning that he may change the size or shape of a deck to save a significant amount of money. A 16-foot (4.9m) framing expanse may cost a great deal more than a 14-foot (4.3m) one, for example, so he may encourage the customer to go with a slightly narrower deck.

(Above) Sun shining through a pergola creates partial shade with a playful pattern of light for this spa and lounging area.

(Opposite bottom) Many of Streett's decks include covered porch areas. Here, a vaulting bead-board-and-timber ceiling provides cover for a full-service outdoor kitchen.

LOG CABIN CHIC

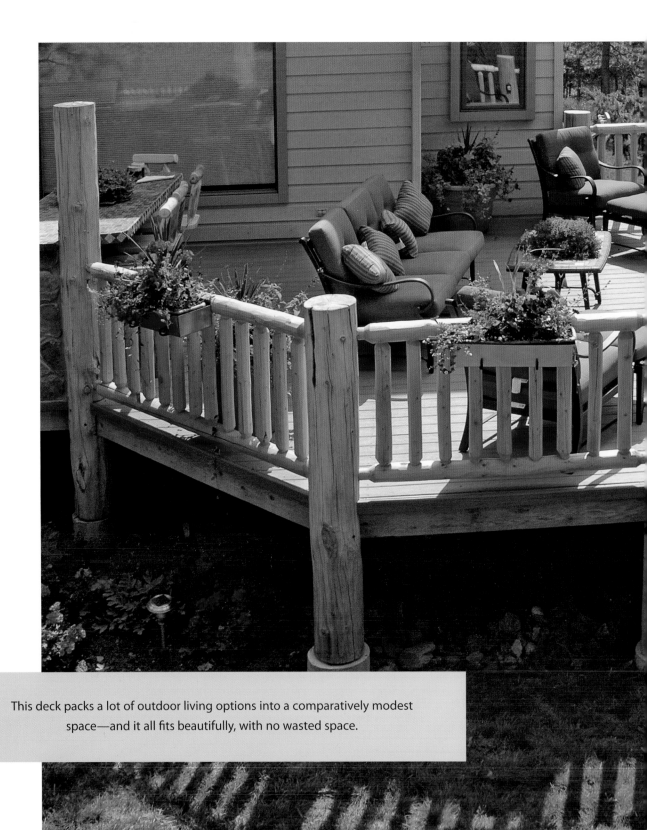

This deck packs a lot of outdoor living options into a comparatively modest space—and it all fits beautifully, with no wasted space.

LOG CABIN CHIC, PLAN VIEW

ELEVATION

MATERIALS USED FOR THIS DECK

Framing	6x6 (15cmx15cm) posts
(all treated)	2x8 (5cmx20cm) and 2x10 (5cmx25cm) joists, headers, and ledgers
	2x10s (5cmx25cm), tripled for beams
	Joist hangers
	2x8 (5cmx20cm) blocking pieces
	2x12 (5cmx30cm) stair stringers
Footings	Concrete and forms
	Anchoring hardware for bottom of log posts
Decking and fascia	5/4x6 (3cmx15cm) composite decking
	Hidden fasteners
	1x10 (2.5cmx25cm) cedar fascia
Railing	10 inch (25.4cm) log posts
	Log rails and balusters
	Stainable chinking
	Long screws for attaching to framing

DESIGN CONSIDERATIONS

The owners had a long wish list: an outdoor kitchen with lots of features, a dining area, and a fireplace with wide-open seating facing it. A larger deck could have been built, but it would have looked out of scale with the medium-size house. So Streett designed carefully.

The outdoor kitchen is just out the door from the house's kitchen. The dining area, off to the side on its own lower level (barely visible at left in the photo on page 312), has room for a round table for four or six plus some potted plants.

Logs

The log railing system, produced by a local fabricator, is a sentimental favorite in Colorado. It is made of lodgepole pine, which has a natural honey color and is prone to rustic cracks and splits. Less-expensive log structures have the bark peeled by machine, resulting in a mostly smooth surface that has been called "semi-rustic." The more expensive method, used here, removes the bark by hand with an old-fashioned draw-knife. The result is a more authentic pioneer look. Rails and balusters are hand-cut to fit into holes, and the resulting imperfections are all part of the charm.

Streett normally discourages buyers from purchasing log railings because they typically last only about 10 years and then need to be replaced. He builds in such a way that replacement can be done without dismantling the whole deck, but it is still an expensive proposition. Some homeowners love the logs so much, though, that they are willing to pay for replacement down the line.

Fitting In

The house itself is standard horizontal siding with plain trim and no rustic features. To help tie things together so that the new rough-hewn railings would fit with the house, Streett made a couple of alterations. He framed the house's door with poles in a simple post-and-lintel arrangement. This framing is simply ornamental; the door's original trim is left in place and simply covered by logs. And when building the deck, he applied cedar trim to match the color of the house trim; it can be seen on the deck's fascia and the fireplace roof. Small complements like this go a long way toward pulling together two different styles.

Fireplace and Outdoor Kitchen

The outdoor living room faces the fireplace, which is the deck's focal point. Because the fireplace is gas-fired, it does not need a chimney, stays clean looking, and does not produce smoke. It is housed in a structure that is covered with natural "thin stone."

The spacious L-shape kitchen features a large high-end grill, together with a refrigerator and matching stainless-steel doors for access to storage underneath. The counter siding incorporates the same stone as the fireplace. The two-level countertop, made of small slate tiles, has a decorative diamond pattern along the edging. The work surface is 36 inches (91cm) tall, while a snacking/bar surface is 42 inches (1.1m) tall with an overhang to accommodate bar stools.

CONSTRUCTION TECHNIQUES

The log railing posts are part of the structure, supporting the outer flush beam.

There is a center drop beam for the larger deck. Build the framing on temporary supports; then install the footings, posts, and interior drop beam.

Framing

Install the ledgers with flashing at the house for the two deck levels. [The lower level uses 2x10 (5cmx25cm) framing because it has no center beam.] Where the center beam will be, dig a straight row of footing holes, pour concrete into forms, and install the support posts with temporary bracing. Use a level or transit to mark the post heights, and cut them one beam's width lower than the bottom of the ledger. Assemble the beam of three 2x10s (5cmx25cm), and set the beam on top of the posts.

Attach the joists to the ledger using joist hangers, and rest them on the beam or a temporary support. On the wider deck area, the joists split on the beam. Install blocking as required. Use a chalk line and square to mark the joists for cutting at the ends, and cut them using a circular saw. Attach two or three layers of 2x10s (5cmx25cm) to the joist ends to make a flush beam.

Railing

Dig postholes for the combination railing and structural posts, and pour concrete footings with code-approved hardware for securing the post bottoms. Use a small chain saw to notch the posts so they will fit flat against the flush beam. Check with a string line to be sure that the posts form straight lines.

Assemble the balustrades, and attach them to the posts. Slip the posts onto the mounting hardware; press the posts against the flush beam; and drive long screws through the beam and into the posts. Cut a channel in the back of each post where post lights will go; run the wiring; and then fill the channel with chinking.

Fireplace and Outdoor Kitchen

The fireplace is a metal gas-fired unit. Follow instructions for running natural gas and electrical lines to it. Install the unit, and surround it with framed plywood. Cover the plywood with roofing felt, wire lath, and mortar; then apply the stone facing. Fill the joints between the stones with mortar. Build the roof with plywood, roofing felt, and shingles, and add a simple log structure to hold up its ends.

Make the outdoor kitchen counter using wood or metal studs, cement-based backer board, and stone facing. For the countertop, make the substrate out of two layers of backer board. Tiled outdoor countertop surfaces often fail, but yours can last if you use the right products: set the tiles in high-quality polymer-reinforced thin-set mortar or epoxy resin mortar. Fill the joints with epoxy grout. (For more instructions on building an outdoor kitchen counter, see Creative Homeowner's *Building Outdoor Kitchens for Every Budget*.)

SCALLOPS AND CURVES

This soaring deck nimbly wraps around the house on three sides, with nary a straight line on its outer perimeter, and no curve like another.

SCALLOPS AND CURVES, PLAN VIEW

PLYWOOD-STRINGER DETAIL

DESIGN CONSIDERATIONS

The owners were tired and bored with their existing quadrilateral deck and wanted something special. Streett came through with flying colors, crafting a one-of-a-kind deck with unique crescent contours.

High Deck

The deck is about 12 feet (3.7m) aboveground. Streett installed an under-deck drainage system, with a gutter and downspout tucked away behind the beam. This keeps the space below dry, so it can be used as a sheltered porch/patio.

The tall structural posts are made of treated Douglas fir, a material that is extremely stable but exhibits a pattern of incisions required for the treatment process. To make the space below more attractive, Streett stained the posts. He also clad the beams with fascia boards and covered the undersides of the joists with plywood panels to create a ceiling. After the patio was

installed, he clad the bottom 4 feet (1.2m) of the support posts with stonework.

The Curves

The deck is made with multiple curves. Looking from right to left (as you view the deck from the outside), there are two scallops reminiscent of the top of a

heart shape. Continuing on, the curve becomes progressively flatter, until it forms an S-shape and turns the other way at the house's corner.

A bench snugs up to the railing at the second scallop. Recent code changes in some areas no longer allow you to put a bench next to a railing because children might stand on the

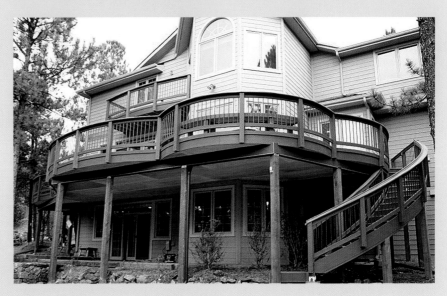

MATERIALS USED FOR THIS DECK

Framing	6x6 (15cmx15cm) posts	**Ceiling for**	Under-deck drainage system,
(all treated)	2x10 (5cmx25cm) joists and ledgers	**patio**	with gutters
	2x10s (5cmx25cm), doubled		"Breckenridge Panel" plywood
	or tripled for beams		for ceiling, plus trim
	Joist hangers	**Railing**	4x4 (10cmx10cm) treated posts
	½ inch (1.3cm) plywood for curved headers		Long screws and washers for
	2x10 (5cmx25cm) blocking pieces		attaching posts
	Plywood strips for stair stringers		Composite post sleeves
Footings	Concrete and forms		2x4 (5cmx10cm) composite top
Decking and	5 /4x6 (3cmx15cm)		and bottom rails
fascia	composite decking		Decking pieces for top cap
	Hidden fasteners		and graspable stair rail
	Composite fascia		Metal balusters
Stone facing	Thin stones		
	Roofing felt and metal lath		
	Mortar		

bench and climb over the rail; check your local building codes to be sure.

Curved railings like this, which follow the contours of the deck precisely, call for first-rate workmanship and professional-level tools.

The Stairway

It is common for an upper deck to have an all-metal spiral stairway, which can be purchased as a kit. This stairway is much more ambitious because it is made of decking material and follows the curve of the deck. Streett had to build the stair stringers in place, a painstaking process (left).

Layout

The homeowners can get access to the deck from inside the house via two sliding doors. The grill area is near the kitchen door in the first scallop, for convenience. A fire-pit area (bottom), suitable for buffet dining or just creating a convivial atmosphere, occupies the second scallop, and the dining table fits nicely in the large area to the left. There is room for a lounge chair near the dining table. Tucked away at the end of the deck, around the corner, is a private area for relaxing or sunning, big enough to accommodate several recliners and a small table (top right).

CONSTRUCTION TECHNIQUES

Building a second-story deck is a challenging project that requires the skills of experienced builders. Take plenty of safety precautions when working high.

Framing with Curves

Install the ledger against the house using code-approved flashing and strong fasteners. Dig rows of postholes to nearly follow the contours of the deck; pour code-approved footings; and install support posts taller than they will be, temporarily bracing them in position. (Alternatively, build the joist framing on temporary supports, and install the beam, posts, and footings later.) Use a transit to mark the posts for cutting to height, one beam's width below the bottom of the ledger. Build the beams, and attach them to the tops of the support posts using code-approved hardware. [On this deck, most of the beams are double 2x10s (5cmx25cm), but for the beam with longer runs between supports posts, triple 2x10s (5cmx25cm) were required.]

Temporarily but firmly brace the posts and beams, using 2x6 (5cmx15cm) braces and long stakes. Attach the joists to the ledger using joist hangers. Allow them to run past the beams. Attach them to the beams, correctly spaced, and use bracing as needed to hold them firmly in place. To mark the tops of the joists for cutting on a curve, use a string-and-pencil compass to get a general idea; then use ⅜-inch (1cm) flexible copper tubing or a piece of composite fascia to lay out the final curves. Take your time, and stand back to examine the curves until you are satisfied. Cut the joists to length; you will need to adjust your circular saw's bevel slightly for each cut. Install curved headers made out of plywood.

If you will build a curved bench, install simple framing of paired 4x4 (10cmx10cm) posts that follow the deck's curve. Install blocking as needed to keep the posts firm.

Install an under-deck drainage system, with gutters and downspouts as needed.

Decking and Fascia

You may choose to install the decking and railing first, then the curved stairs, or build the curved stairs first. Here, we show the decking first. Attach 4x4 (10cmx10cm) posts to the outsides of the headers. Install composite decking using hidden fasteners. At the curves, install the decking so that it overhangs; then carefully curve-cut it flush to the outside of the headers. Add fascia boards so that their tops are flush with the decking surface.

Notch post sleeves as needed, and slip them over the 4x4 (10cmx10cm) posts. Use a heating system to bend the top and bottom rails, as well as the top cap, so they follow the deck's contours. Cut the pieces so they fit between the posts. Build sections of rails and balusters, and attach them between the posts. Add the top cap, made of bent decking.

Stairway

Build the stringers for the curved stairway in place. Install the outside posts, consistently spaced away from the inside posts, and anchor them with temporary braces. Attach strips of plywood to the posts on each side, level with each other. Because the plywood is only 8 feet (2.5m) long, you will need to use several pieces, with butt joints landing on the posts. Check that the plywood strips are level with each other as you attach them (right).

Use a level and framing square to mark and cut notches in the plywood so that you end up with stringers that are level with each other. Install three more layers of plywood, notched to match, for each stringer. Each piece will be slightly different from the underlying one, so hold them in place as you mark them.

Build a landing at the bottom of the stairway. Install the treads; the front tread is full width, and the back tread is rip-cut at an angle. Add fascia and other trim. Bend railing pieces, and install them as you did for the deck railing.

PRIVATE FAMILY ROOM

Like a large fresh-air great room, this space serves several functions: it includes a spa, a luxury outdoor kitchen, and a cozy area for buffet dining and campfires.

PRIVATE FAMILY ROOM, PLAN VIEW

MATERIALS USED FOR THIS DECK

Framing
(all treated)

Footings

Decking and
fascia

Framing	6x6 (15cmx15cm) posts
(all treated)	2x10 (5cmx25cm) joists, ledgers, and straight headers
	2x10s (5cmx25cm), tripled for beams
	Joist hangers
	½ inch (1.3cm) plywood for curved headers
	2x10 (5cmx25cm) blocking pieces
	2x12 (5cmx30cm) for stair stringers
Footings	Concrete and forms
	Hardware for posts and beams
Decking and fascia	5/4x6 (3cmx15cm) composite decking
	Hidden fasteners
	Composite fascia

Stone facing	Thin stones
	Roofing felt and metal lath
	Mortar
Roof	Glue-laminated beams
	6x6 (15cmx15cm) cedar posts
	2x10 (5cmx25cm) rafters
	Skylights
	Lights, fan, and wiring
	Plywood sheathing
	Roofing felt, shingles, and flashing
	Tongue-and-groove siding for the ceiling

DESIGN CONSIDERATIONS

Though they had only a small space with which to work, the family wanted an outdoor kitchen with plenty of amenities, room for a fire pit and living room, and a roof to cover about two-thirds the deck, so they would be able to enjoy it when weather was bad. A spa was also on the wish list; a dining table was less important. Streett built a beautiful deck that suits their lifestyle to a T.

Size and Shape

The space for the deck is a 27-foot-long (8.2m) alcove at the back of the house. The family did not want the deck to protrude outward too far into the yard, and Streett agreed; a larger deck would overpower the house and seem out of place.

The deck design features his signature curves. On a deck this small there was no need to throw in an S-curve for visual interest. A single standard-radius bump-out, with straight lines on each side, looks complex enough. An added patio made of stamped and stained concrete offers its own curves and creates a fun transition to the yard.

Instead of a dining room there is a sort of all-purpose area that includes stuffed chairs, a fire pit, and occasional tables. Food can be brought directly from the indoor kitchen to this area, or it can be served buffet style in the outdoor kitchen on the other end.

Spas are often placed in a destination area well away from dining and cooking areas, but this deck design integrates it for a cozy effect. Placed just in front of the deck and unsheltered by a roof, spa bathers are safely out of range of grilling smoke and can enjoy the starlight once the sun goes down. Given the size of the deck, the spa feels remarkably like its own space.

The deck is about 28 inches (71cm) above grade—just under the 30-inch

(76cm) height where a railing would be required by code. With no railing, the deck has an open, spacious feel.

Outdoor Kitchen

The outdoor kitchen is on the far side of the deck from the kitchen door. Because of the overhead, it was necessary to put the grill on the periphery with open space on three sides so that cooking smoke can dissipate. (If a grill is placed near walls and is covered by a roof, you would need to install a commercial-grade exhaust fan, or diners would find themselves choking from the smoke.) A spacious traffic path makes the indoor kitchen easily accessible.

The outdoor kitchen counter is faced with thin stone and topped by a granite counter with colors to match the hues in the facing stones. It includes a large gas grill, a refrigerator, storage doors and drawers, and a double side-burner. (Like many builders in areas with freezing winters, Streett tries to talk homeowners out of a sink with running water because if they forget to shut off and drain the supply and drain lines prior to winter (easily done!), the pipes will freeze—with disastrous results.)

The Roof

A roof overhead was high on the list of priorities, but a number of builders had said it could not be done. Sometimes you have to keep looking for the right builder: Streett carefully installed a watertight roof that blends well with the house.

He built the roofline at an angle that fits naturally with the house's architecture—and with no visible sections of unsightly metal flashing. For the front roof beam, Streett used a glue-laminated lumber, which can span a long distance. That means that there is only

one post near the middle of the span; a second post would have made the deck feel more constrained.

A pair of skylights brings in natural light while sealing out rain, and recessed canister lights brighten the space at night.

To make the deck usable most of the year, a ceiling fan provides a pleasant breeze during the summer, and electric infrared heating units keep things comfortable on frosty nights. These heating units are popular because they provide ample directed heat for a small energy cost. Homeowners claim that they extend the outdoor season by as much as two or three months.

CONSTRUCTION TECHNIQUES

Because the spa will rest on concrete rather than framing, have the patio poured first; then build the deck. In this case, the concrete was formed and poured one stair-step higher, where the spa goes.

Framing

Use high-quality lumber for all of the framing. This deck is enclosed on three sides by the house and the steps, so there is little ventilation. That is not a problem in a dry climate like Colorado's, but in your area you may need to ventilate the underside of the deck using lattice sections.

Pour the concrete patio and the raised concrete section for the spa. Dig straight rows of postholes, and pour concrete footings according to local codes. Install the ledger against the house using code-approved fasteners and flashing.

Build the framing on temporary supports: most codes require joists to be installed 12 inches (30.5cm) apart where composite decking will run at an angle. Attach joists to the ledger using joist hangers, and let them run long. Install blocking, and check that the joists are correctly positioned at the ends away from the house. Use a chalk line to mark the tops of the joists for straight cuts on each side. Mark for the cuts with a square, and cut using a circular saw.

For the arced section, mark the tops of the joist for cutting using a string-and-pencil compass. Cut the joist ends, adjusting the circular saw's bevel slightly for each cut. Attach the two straight header joists; they can run a bit long on the inside of the deck. Make a header for the curved section using three layers of ½-inch (1.3cm) plywood strips. (See page 128 for more instructions.)

Run electrical and plumbing lines for the lights and spa.

Stairs, Decking, and Fascia

For the wide stairs you will need to cut quite a few 2x12 (5cmx30cm) stringers. Attach them to the header at the top and to the concrete at the bottom.

Install the decking using hidden fasteners. Cut decking ends at 45 degrees, and allow the pieces to overhang. Use a chalk line to mark the ends for straight cuts; use a string-and-pencil compass to mark for the curved cut. Make cuts using a circular saw. Cut and install fascia to cover the cut decking ends.

Use a deck oven or blanket heater to warm up decking pieces to be used as curved stair treads, and press them against jigs, as shown on pages 254–255. Install the fascia; then install the riser lights and then the treads.

Outdoor Kitchen

Build the outdoor kitchen by framing it with metal or wood studs and cladding with concrete backer board. Have the appliances, doors, and drawers on hand to make sure your openings are correct. Run electrical lines, and install receptacles and lights. Cover the backer board with roofing felt, metal lath, and thin facing stones. Install the granite countertop, then the appliances and doors. (For full instructions, see Creative Homeowner's *Building Outdoor Kitchens for Every Budget*.)

The Roof

Only experienced roofers should tackle this job, but here is an overview: Attach the cedar roof posts to the decking

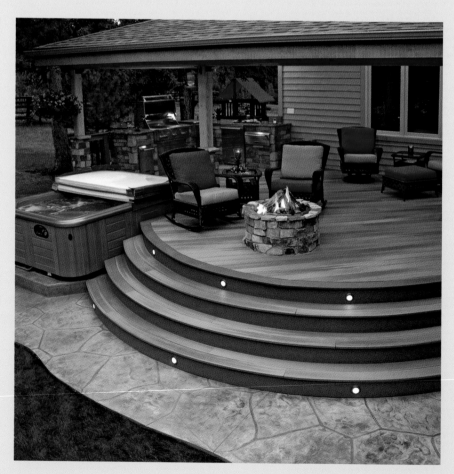

using approved hardware. They should rest directly above a joist and a beam. Brace them temporarily in place, making sure they are plumb. Order glue-laminated beams to fit, and install them; where they meet the house you may support them with a post against the house or by cutting a pocket hole and inserting them. Install the rafters, and frame for the skylights. Run electrical lines, and install boxes for the lights and fan.

Cut away the house's siding where the roof will meet it. Cut and attach plywood sheathing, and add roofing felt. Install flashing at the top. Install the skylights, and flash them as needed. Install flashing at the outer edges of the roof, and apply shingles. At the sloped end where the roof meets the siding, install individual pieces of step flashing as you go, and tuck them under the siding pieces so they will not be visible.

Cover the underside of the rafters with tongue-and-groove siding. Make cutouts for the electrical boxes, and trim around the skylight. Add the light fixtures and trim, and install the fan.

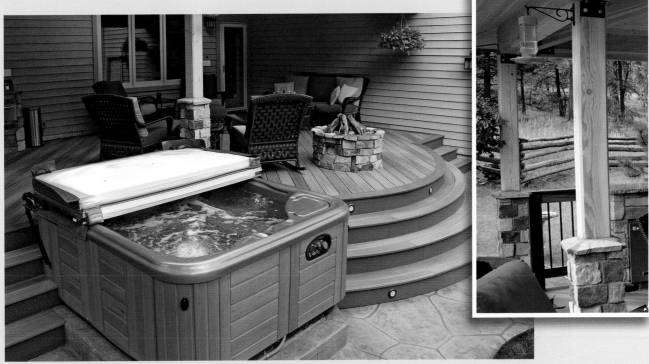

ROCKY MOUNTAIN HIGH LIFE

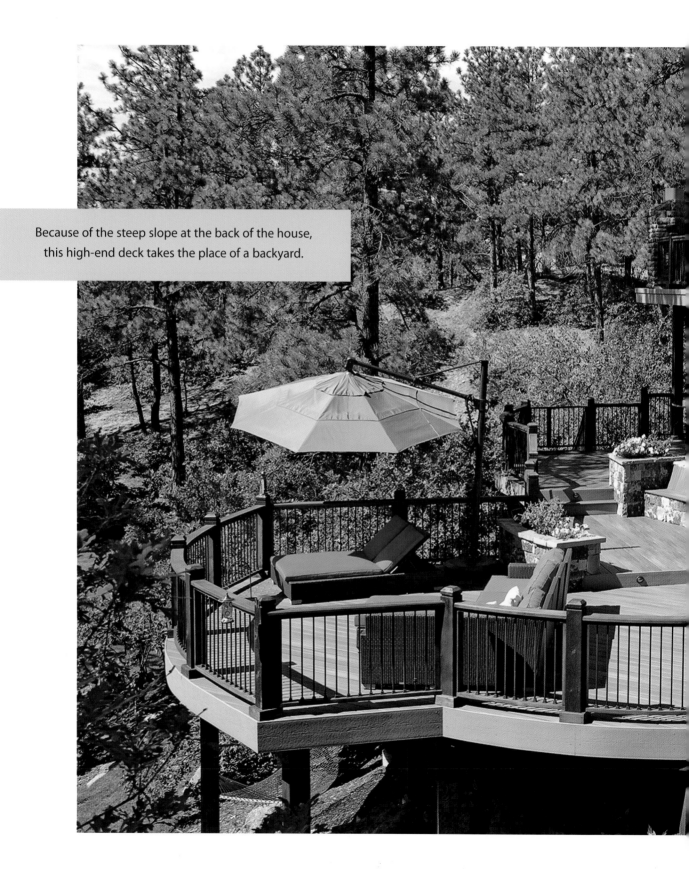

Because of the steep slope at the back of the house, this high-end deck takes the place of a backyard.

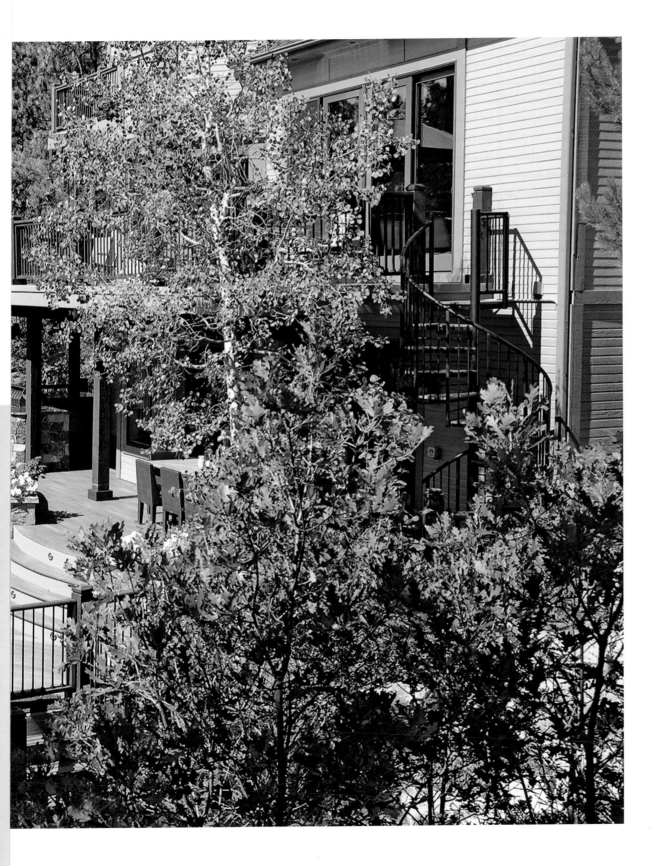

Bench, Planters, and Railing

An unusual curved bench, located in the middle of the deck on the house side, provides couch-like seating. The back and seat are made of decking with capstones topping off the bench and thin stones providing stylish cover for the area under the seating. Built-in planters covered with the same thin stones flank the bench on each side.

Several large wooden planters covered with thin stones help tie the design together while adding splashes of color. The planters are made of treated plywood and have galvanized liners, which prevent rust and lengthen the life of the wood.

The railing, made of natural cedar with a dark stain, follows the curved and straight lines of the deck. Massive 6x6 (15cmx15cm) posts suit the character of the spacious setting, and thin, dark metal balusters barely inhibit the view.

Bar-Style Outdoor Kitchen

This outdoor kitchen is not very close to the indoor kitchen, which is the usual arrangement, and has enough amenities to function on its own. The large gas grill can handle just about any barbecue challenge. Most of the time, however, the homeowners use the kitchen like a bar in a finished basement. For that reason, it has a sink with running water, an ice-filled cooler, a refrigerator, and an overhanging counter where you can pull up bar stools.

Materials

The decking is a composite material that looks and feels a lot like natural wood. This is partly because it has a matte rather than shiny finish and partly because there is greater-than-usual variation in color and pattern. Materials like this cost more but make a deck feel more natural while retaining the low-maintenance advantage of composites. The decking runs in several directions, helping to define various areas.

The thin stone used for the outdoor kitchen, planters, and bench siding is "chopped," meaning it is hand cut. It is installed dry stacked, without mortar in the joints. This is a more challenging installation because the pieces have to fit together tightly, but the results look more like solid stone.

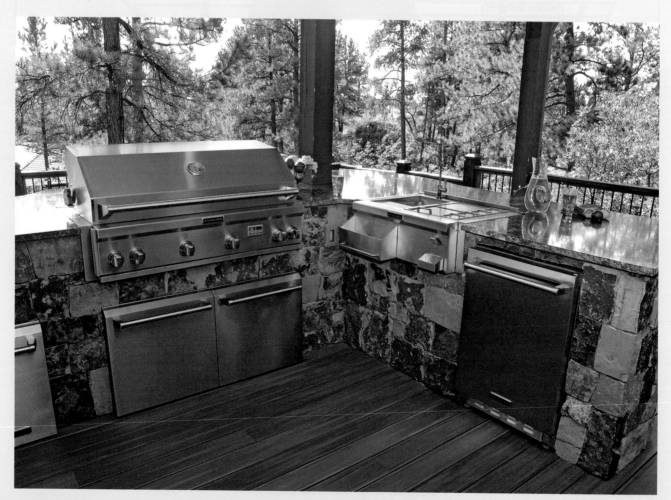

CONSTRUCTION TECHNIQUES

A massive elevated structure like this is a major undertaking, calling for the expertise of experienced professionals. Because of the height, extra-large posts are required. Choose massive lumber pieces carefully. They should be rated No. 1 or select and kiln dried, so they will not warp or crack.

Framing

The framing is complicated because different levels share beams. Make sure various levels are multiples of 7 ½ inches (19.1cm) higher or lower than each other. Install the ledger; then build the joist sections on temporary supports. Install curved headers where needed. (See page 128.) Build and attach beams to the undersides of the joists. Dig postholes, pour footings according to code, and install posts to support the beams.

Railing and Decking

Install the railing posts inside the framing, and attach blocking to keep the posts firm. Run wiring for the riser lights.

Install decking at various angles, using hidden fasteners. Cut the decking flush to the headers and outside joists, and install fascia that covers the cut ends of decking pieces.

Build railing sections that fit between the posts. Build the straight sections using 2x4 (5cmx10cm) top and bottom rails with evenly spaced balusters. Attach the sections, and add 1x4 (2.5cmx10cm) pieces on the sides of the posts. Make curved sections using 2x10s (5cmx25cm) or 2x12s (5cmx30cm), as needed. Cut them so that they follow the deck's curve and are 3 ½ inches (8.9cm) wide.

Bench and Planter

Build the bench using 2x4s (5cmx10cm) and 2x12s (5cmx30cm) for framing, as shown in the illustration on page 181. Cover the front and top with treated ½-inch (1.3cm) plywood, and install stone facing and cap pieces. Use a heating pad or oven to bend the decking pieces for the seat.

Make planters out of simple 2x4 (5cmx10cm) frames and treated plywood sheathing. Cover the plywood with thin stone, and hire a fabricator to make galvanized linings to fit. Set the liners in, and add capstones.

When not visiting with clients or designing and building decks, Gary Marsh, owner of All Decked Out in Novato, California, spends a good part of his time sculpting in a variety of media. Auto-body putty and clay are two of his favorites. He keeps his workshop surprisingly tidy and organized, despite a profusion of objects that tell of his interests: four or five sculptures in various stages of completion, a professional drafting table, and a serious collection of woodworking tools.

ALL DECKED OUT

Novato, California

(415) 897-7623

www.garymarshdesign.com

TECHNIQUES TO USE

As long as you're not building on a steep incline, you won't have to take the sometimes extreme steps that Marsh does to support his decks. Use standard footings and posts. The upper portions of most of Marsh's designs contain a number of stylish features and finishing touches that you can incorporate into your deck if you work with care.

• Marsh approaches each job with an open mind. Rather than limit himself to conventional formulas, he spends some time dreaming about the possibilities. As you plan your deck, you'll naturally think in terms of mimicking those you see in your area. But compared with house building, it's usually (but not always—especially in Marsh's unique situations) fairly easy and inexpensive to build a deck that incorporates unusual twists and turns. Don't be afraid to use your imagination.

• Because of the tremendous views that many of his clients enjoy, Marsh thinks hard about which way people will face. Whenever possible, he orients a bench so that a person sitting on it won't have to twist around to take in the scenery. This sometimes requires altering the shape of the deck so that occupants won't be forced to stare at the house.

• Though Marsh speaks jokingly of being "at one with the wood," he takes lumber selection very seriously. He spends plenty of time both choosing material at the lumberyard and deciding at the job site which pieces will go where. For every part that will be touched when the deck is finished, such as handrails, he reserves the best-quality stock. For pieces that need to remain stable—railing caps, for instance—he uses only certified kiln-dried material. Pieces that will be bent into curves, on the other hand, call for green lumber with a vertical grain. If you're unsure about selecting the right lumber for a particular application, ask for help at the lumberyard.

• Although you probably won't need to resort to Marsh's more serious engineering efforts, note how he reinforces some portions of his decks for specific purposes. For example, he avoids the conventional approach of screwing or bolting rail posts to the side of the deck. These will fail over time, especially in situations where extra strength is needed. In almost every deck that Marsh designs and builds, he uses posts that are bolted within the framing for a strong connection. (For a detail on an alternative way to reinforce rail posts, see "Sheltered but Open," page 325.)

• Marsh uses a variation of an unusual technique for making caps on a curved railing. He cuts the curves out of a piece of 2x12 (or two 1x12s) but doesn't throw away the waste. Instead, he uses the offcuts from one section as parts for others. This requires serious laminating: you must use glue that will stand up to the weather and join the pieces tightly to avoid ending up with a sloppy-looking cap. This will save you a good deal of expensive material.

• To enhance the appearance of moldings, Marsh often finishes them using a router equipped with a roundover or chamfer bit. He'll often stop the roundover or chamfer short of the edge of the board to add a distinctive look. (See "Soaking and Dining Areas with Shingled Siding," page 335.)

• To bend curved horizontal rail members and fascia pieces, Marsh uses another unconventional technique. Because some boards, for one reason or another, bend more readily than others and some curves are tighter than others, he treats each piece individually. He starts with a green piece of one-by lumber and planes it down until it bends enough for the curve in question. This means that some pieces will be a bit thicker than others, but because several pieces will be joined to make laminated rail or fascia members, the total thicknesses of the members end up identical.

• Marsh's planter design is more elaborate than most. It calls for a galvanized metal liner with a downspout. He orders the liners from a sheet-metal shop and builds simple boxes around them. He then positions them carefully so that no structural members will be regularly soaked by the runoff from rainfall or overwatering.

Well-thought-out design and attention to detail are hallmarks of Marsh's decks.

SWEEPING ELEGANCE IN A SMALL SPACE

A stunning pool with a waterfall was located only 10 feet from the house. But in this setting, the beauty of the surroundings called for a deck that conveyed a sense of spaciousness. By using curved lines throughout and incorporating a stairway that appears much grander than its actual size, Marsh created a sense of open-ended luxury in a limited space.

Ground View

SWEEPING ELEGANCE IN A SMALL SPACE, PLAN VIEW

Storage Below —

MATERIALS USED FOR THIS DECK

Framing	4x8 and 4x6s for beams		curved edging
(pressure-	2x8 joists		2x6 seat pieces
treated pine)	2x8 ledgers and headers	**Hardware**	3 ½" deck screws
	2x12 stair stringers		Joist hanger nails
Decking	2x6s		Post anchors for anchoring posts
Fascia	1x8s, planed and laminated, for		to concrete
	fascia and skirting		T-straps for tying beams to posts
	1x6s, planed and laminated, for		Joist hangers for 2x8s
	banded skirting		Angled joist hangers for 2x8s
Railings and	4x4 posts		Angle brackets
bench backs	2x12 and 2x6 pieces for railing caps		Lag screws with washers for anchoring
	1x4s, planed and laminated, for		the ledger
	curved horizontal rails		Machine bolts for railing posts
Benches	4x4 posts	**Masonry**	Concrete
	2x4 framing pieces		Precast concrete piers
	1x6s, planed and laminated, for		

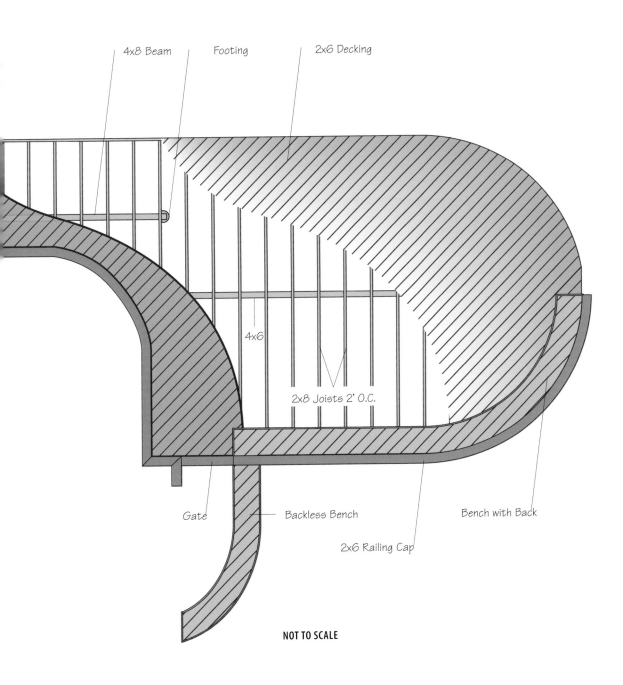

4x8 Beam

Footing

2x6 Decking

4x6

2x8 Joists 2' O.C.

Gate

Backless Bench

Bench with Back

2x6 Railing Cap

NOT TO SCALE

DESIGN CONSIDERATIONS

The homeowners wanted a convenient means of descending to the pool (outside the sliding doors of the house) that wouldn't obstruct the expanse of the deck. In addition, they requested separate areas for sunning and dining.

Marsh met both challenges by incorporating an unusually shaped stairway near one end. It helps to define the circular sunning area next to it without taking up much space. Yet despite the stairway's small footprint, its sides curve away from each other, creating a sense of grandeur. You hardly notice that its steps have only 7 ½-inch risers and 11-inch treads—dimensions that are usually found only on standard porch or interior stairways.

Aside from the point where the deck meets the house, there's hardly a straight line to be found. The deck jogs and snakes around, partly to follow the contours of the pool, spa, and gardening areas below and partly for aesthetic reasons. Looking out onto a steep backyard filled with a wild profusion of foliage, an angular deck would seem out of place. This one blends

nicely with the yard's natural curves and slopes.

Functionality with Style

The deck was planned to be functional as well as aesthetically pleasing. The curved walls that enhance the stairway also hide pool equipment. The center walkway measures only 5 feet wide to accommodate the plantings below. This leaves enough room for guests to lean on the railing and gaze out while traffic flows through comfortably behind them. Between the walkway and the stairway is a barbecue area just large enough for a small charcoal grill and a food-preparation cart. (You could also build a wide shelf into the straight section of railing in this part of the deck as a permanent food-preparation area.)

The main deck provides ample room for dining. A bench with a back follows the circular contours of its perimeter partway around, giving those who sit facing the house a sense of enclosure. For those who'd rather look outward over the lawn, a backless

bench extends out into the decorative rockwork area that surrounds the spa.

The elegant railing features a curved cap and three horizontal rails. (The local building codes may not permit such a railing. Check with the building department in your area.) Marsh routed a detail into the caps that gives them a furniture-like appearance.

For the skirting that covers the rounded sections on each side of the steps, he used horizontal bands that mimic the railings above. From ground level, this gives the whole ensemble—steps, skirt, and railing—the appearance of a unified structure rather than that of a basic deck with a few features tacked on.

FRONT ELEVATION: STAIRS AND RAILINGS

2x6 Railing Cap

4x4 Posts

1x6s

1x8 Fascia

CONSTRUCTION TECHNIQUES

Marsh attaches a 2x8 ledger to the house. He supports the 4x8 and 4x6 beams with 4x4 posts that rest on concrete piers set in a bed of poured concrete. Because this is earthquake territory, he uses plenty of T-straps to anchor the beams to the posts.

Installing Curved Horizontal Fascia and Skirting Pieces. Marsh doesn't soak redwood pieces in water to make them more flexible. He's found that soaked boards often check or twist. (Checking develops when the surface dries faster than the core, causing the grain to separate.)

At the lumberyard, Marsh looks for one-by boards that bend more easily than others. These contain more moisture, but as they dry out they'll grow stiff. To prevent premature drying, keep them out of the sun and covered until you use them. Even an hour in the sun can dramatically change a one-by board's moisture content.

Planing Boards to Bendable Thickness. Rent or buy a large power planer or jointer that will quickly shave down the boards. With a soft material like redwood or cedar, the work will go quickly, provided the jointer's blades are sharp. Plane each piece individually until you think it will bend sufficiently. Then, try carefully bending it into position with the help of an assistant. If it feels likely to break, plane it down a little more. However, don't make the board any thinner than necessary. The stiffer the piece is, the better it will hold an even curve.

In most cases, a single thickness of fascia or skirting will be strong enough, especially if it is fastened to a framing member every 16 to 24 inches. If you need the additional strength of a second piece, laminate the two pieces

using an exterior glue recommended for your area. You will need to clamp the piece frequently, nailing or screwing the second piece tight to the first.

Curved Horizontal Railing Pieces

To choose and plane boards for the curved railings, use the method described previously. However, you'll probably need to laminate two pieces together to create a strong, safe railing if you do much planing.

Measuring for curved sections in advance is almost impossible, so avoid cutting the lumber to length until after you've attached it. With one or two helpers, check carefully to see that the curve follows the contour of the deck. Then, fasten the rail to the posts using nails or screws.

Laminating the Railing Pieces. To add a second board, you'll need lots of clamps. Allow one for every 4 to 6 inches. Use pads to ensure that your clamps won't mar the wood. Apply adhesive to the new piece, press it into place, and clamp it, making sure that

all edges are flush. Allow the assembly to set overnight.

Making the Cap. To make the cap for this railing, cut pieces out of 2x12 or other appropriate width. Lay a 2x12 in place between posts, bend a piece of ¼-inch molding to approximate the curve, and mark the curve.

Don't throw away all the scrap lumber you produce. Use the cutout sections to fill in other parts of the curved piece as shown. Glue on slightly oversize pieces using a urethane glue, clamp them, and allow the glue to set completely. Then trim the glued-up piece to size.

To support the railing cap, install 3 ½-inch wide spacers as shown in the illustration "Curved Railing."

CURVED RAILING

3½" Spacers

4x4 Post

1x4s

1x8 Fascia

CREATING CURVED CAPS

2x12

Cutout from Bottom of Board

SHELTERED BUT OPEN

The homeowners already had a simple deck in place when they called Marsh. What it needed most urgently was shelter from the elements. The deck sat above the treetops near the rim of a valley, which left it exposed to gusty winds that often made eating or lounging unpleasant. They also wanted some relief from the sun, as well as a few design strokes that would relieve the deck's rectangular plainness.

On the other hand, the homeowners didn't want to give up their spectacular views. Marsh responded with a tempered-glass windbreak that surrounds about half of the deck's perimeter, a pergola that covers a third of its area, and some generously sized planters that bring color on board. Here, Marsh uses a basic shape to create a deck that feels not the least bit squarish yet still satisfies the eye with its clean, uncluttered lines.

Note: Sway bracing and earthquake bracing are not shown. Verify any similar design with a structural engineer.

Ground View

SHELTERED BUT OPEN, PLAN VIEW

4x6s

4x6 Plus 2x12s

Pergola

2x4s

4x4 Post Beneath Rafters

4x4 Posts

MATERIALS USED FOR THIS DECK

Framing	4x6s for beams		**Pergola**	4x4 posts
(pressure-	2x8 joists			2x12s and 2x4s for beams
treated pine)	2x8 ledgers and headers			4x6s for top rafters
Decking	2x6s			2x4s for top pieces
Fascia	1x8s		**Hardware**	3 ½" deck screws
Railing and	4x4 posts			Joist hanger nails
windscreen	2x6s for angled post braces			Post anchors for anchoring posts
	1x2 nailers to hold glass			to concrete
	Sheets of ½"-thick tempered glass			T-straps for tying beams to posts
	(check with local codes for required			Joist hangers for 2x8s
	thickness)			Angled joist hangers for 2x8s
	8" beveled cedar siding			Angle brackets
	Rough-sawn 1x4s for trim pieces			Lag screws with washers for
Planters	Galvanized sheet-metal liners,			anchoring the ledger and for
and bench	ordered to fit			angled post braces
	2x4s for framing		**Masonry**	Concrete
	8" beveled cedar siding			Precast concrete piers
	Rough-sawn 1x4s for side and			
	top trim pieces			
	2x6 seat pieces			

Planter

2x6 Decking

Bench

Planters

PERGOLA ELEVATION

2x4 Top Pieces

4x6 Rafter

2 2x12s

4x4

Cedar Siding

1x4

1x4

2x6 Decking

DESIGN CONSIDERATIONS

The existing deck on this site provided more than ample space for lounging and dining. In fact, it felt too roomy, and the lack of interesting angles or curves heightened the sense of bare expanse. A quick and obvious solution would have been to buy a large collection of patio furniture and add a few flowerpots. However, it's much easier to achieve a sense of harmony if you can build in elements that express themes and variations.

Blending Design

The house was covered with painted, rough-textured siding, and Marsh decided to continue that look throughout the deck. He covered the railings and planters with rough beveled siding and used rough-sawn material for the posts and beams of the pergola.

In keeping with the straightforward design, Marsh used simple squares for the post caps. The closest thing to a flourish is the routed detail he added to the pergola's rafters.

Coping with Wind and Sun

As for the wind problem mentioned earlier, a simple solution proved best. On part of the deck, large panels of tempered glass span the distance from post to post. During times of high wind, this area provides comfort as well as unobstructed views. To enclose the entire deck with glass, however, would have transformed it into a room. This way, when the wind settles down, the rest of the deck still has the wide-open feel of an outdoor space.

With no tree cover, the deck some-

times got so hot that it radiated heat into the house itself, making it uncomfortably warm as well. The pergola covers the section of the deck that gets the most sun. By spacing 2x4s across the top at 7 inches on center (resulting in an interval that equals their width), Marsh achieved a pleasing symmetry as well as the right amount of shade.

The rough-hewn look of the planters complements that of the railings. Marsh equips the planters with galvanized sheet-metal liners and drain spouts that eliminate the possibility of overwatering.

CONSTRUCTION TECHNIQUES

If the site on which you're planning to build slopes severely, as this one does, hire a professional to install the footings.

The framing is straightforward. However, a heavy wind gust can exert a great deal of force on a large expanse of glass, so Marsh reinforced the posts for the windscreen with some sturdy bracing.

Cladding a Railing. A standard railing already existed, but Marsh encased it with siding and a top cap. With most railings, this is a simple enough job, but make sure you have adequate nailing surface for the siding at all points. For horizontal siding like this, you can simply nail directly to the posts and 2x4s that make up the railing. You may be able to butt the siding up against

the cap; if not, you'll need to remove it. If the railing has balusters or rails that protrude beyond the plane of the posts, remove them as well.

Building the Overhead. As with most overheads, the pergola design looks more complicated than it actually is. The tricky part is to lift all those pieces before you've firmed up the structure. To do this, cut the posts to length and temporarily brace them in position. Construct the lower beams by sandwiching a 4x6 between two 2x12s.

Set the beams in place, and anchor them with bolts. To cut the grooves along both bottom edges and the ends of the 4x6 rafters, use a router with your choice of bit.

You might want to experiment with the top 2x4 pieces to determine how

much shade a particular spacing will provide. For this design, Marsh used 2x4 scraps as spacers. To install the pieces, drive two deck screws at each intersecting joint.

Constructing the Windscreen

If your area sustains high winds, consult the local building department for advice on how much bracing the windscreen will need. The angle brace shown is simple, but its triangular configuration is extremely strong. If the deck joists run parallel with the braces, align each post with one of the joists. Then, simply angle-cut 2x6s at 45 degrees on both ends; make the braces about one-fourth again as long as the vertical drop of the post. If the joists

PERGOLA DETAIL

2x4 Top Pieces 7" O.C.

2x4s 16" O.C.

4x6 Rafter

2x12

2x4s

4x4 Post

2x12

Flashing Covers Edges of 2x12s

END-WALL ELEVATION (LOOKING OUT)

2x6 Cap

1x2s

4x4

½" Tempered Glass

END-WALL ELEVATION (LOOKING IN)

36"

2x8 Blocking Between Joists

2x6

8" Beveled Cedar Siding, 5½" Reveal

run perpendicular to the braces, install pieces of blocking that will provide solid anchor points for the braces. (See illustration.)

When you install the posts, double-check them to be sure they're plumb and to ensure that the openings will be square. The glass panes must fit securely.

Glass panes of this thickness cost a lot, so it's best to have the dealer install them. If they break a pane, you won't lose any money.

To install the glass yourself, nail the first set of 1x2s in place, and then test-fit the glass. Next, run a bead of silicone caulking along the 1x2, and set the glass in place. Run another bead of caulking along the edges of the glass;

then immediately fasten the other 1x2s so that they firmly sandwich the pane.

SHADY GARDEN SPOT

Besides an unobstructed view, the homeowners wanted a cozy getaway that would surround them with foliage. Oversize planters and an extensive overhead structure help make this deck a snug nest from which to view the world.

DESIGN CONSIDERATIONS

Although the overhead structure shelters much of this deck, plenty of sunshine still gets through to keep plantings healthy. Because the deck faces south, its perimeter receives full sun for most of the day, making it a good location for flowerpots. Two gigantic planters are set back a bit, which gives them partial shade. Other areas get various amounts of sun, allowing the owners to choose a range of shade- and sun-loving plants.

A Gardener's Deck and More. This makes an ideal deck for a serious gardener who still enjoys comfort. A simple potting table located beneath the pergola features a sink with faucet and plenty of counter space. You can work in the heat of the day without breaking a sweat. If gardening is not your forte, the counter can be put to other uses or omitted.

The planters sit 2 feet above the deck surface, which saves the home-

Outside View

owners a good deal of back strain. At 4 feet square, they resemble small gardens that allow easy access from several sides.

Because dining usually takes place after the sun has sunk low, the eating area remains uncovered. The deck's only curved line helps to set this space apart, and the wide arc encourages diners to give the view a sweeping gaze.

From the eating area, you pass between large planters and down wide steps. One stairway descends toward the view, and a second, smaller set of steps leads to the work area and potting table. Benches set against the house also make this a pleasant place for a rest or chat.

2x6 Decking

Planter

Steps Down

2x6 Railing Cap

2x8 Top Trim

SHADY GARDEN
SPOT, PLAN VIEW

MATERIALS USED FOR THIS DECK

Framing	4x6 posts			1x8s for trim and siding
(pressure-	4x12 beams			2x8s for countertop
treated pine)	2x8s for joists, ledger, and blocking			2x6s to frame around plumbing
Decking	2x6s			Plumbing materials for the faucet
Fascia	1x10s, planed as needed for the curve			and small sink
Railings	4x4 posts		**Bench**	4x4 posts
	2x4 rails			2x4 framing
	2x2 balusters			1x6 edging
	1x4s (2 pieces) for the top rail, planed			2x6 seat pieces
	for the curve		**Trellis**	One-by stock, ripped to ¾" wide
	2x6 railing cap (cut from 2x12s for		**Hardware**	3 ½" deck screws and 1 ¾" deck screws
	the curved section)			Joist hanger nails
Overhead	4x6 posts			Post anchors for anchoring posts to
	2x8s for beams (2 pieces for each)			concrete
	2x6 rafters			T-straps for tying beams to posts
	2x4 top pieces			Joist hangers for 2x8s
Planters	Galvanized liner, made to fit (4x6 over			Angle brackets
	head posts used for part of framing)			Lag screws with washers for
	2x4s for framing			anchoring the ledger
	1x12s for side pieces		**Masonry**	Concrete
	2x8s for top trim			Reinforcing bar
Potting table	2x4s for framing			

ELEVATION

Steps Down
Planter   Bench   Counter
2x8 Top Trim
Lower Deck   Sink Cutout

2x4 Rail   2x6 Cap
4x4 Post
2x2 Balusters
1x10 Fascia
4x6 Posts

POTTING BENCH WITH SINK

Front Perspective   **Side View**

Shelf   Shelf
Countertop
2x8s   1x8s   1x8s

CONSTRUCTION TECHNIQUES

This deck was built 12 feet above the ground, which explains the need for such massive beams and posts. The railing consists of 2x2 balusters and 2x4 rails. Two 1x4s serve as the top rail and support the 2x6 railing cap. To make the curved section of the railing, see page 259. If you plan to build planters as large as the ones shown here, you'll need to reinforce the framing beneath to support their weight. Add joists, or install extra support posts with footings.

Simple Trellis. To provide support for additional living greenery, Marsh erected an elegantly simple trellis and attached it to the house wall. To make the trelliswork, rip pieces of clear cedar one-by to ¾ inch wide. Arrange the pieces in a grid, and then check for squareness. Add short spacers to the back of the trellis to allow room for vines to climb. Drill a pilot hole, and drive a 1 ¾-inch screw into every joint. Attach the trellis to the wall using screws.

TRELLIS DETAIL

1x1s
Spacer

SOAKING AND DINING AREAS WITH SHINGLED SIDING

A small deck with a hot tub already existed, but it didn't provide adequate room for dining and relaxing. The homeowners liked having the tub near the house, but the railing obstructed the view from tub level. Marsh solved this problem by building a new deck area three steps down from the tub and incorporating a glass panel into the railing.

Outside View

Note: Sway bracing and earthquake bracing are not shown.
Verify any similar design with a structural engineer.

SOAKING AND DINING AREAS WITH SHINGLED SIDING, PLAN VIEW

Planter

Decorative Lookout

Bench

Note: Existing Beams and Support for Spa not Shown

Decorative Lookout

2x6 Railing Cap

Existing 10x10 Concrete Tie Beams

Planter with Galvanized Liner

Existing Spa

2x10 Joists 16" O.C.

6x12 Beam

New 18" Pier

New 10"x10" Concrete Tie Beams

6x10 Beam with Decorative Lookout

2x6 Screen Cap

SIDE ELEVATION

Cedar Shingles
2x4
4x4
2x6
22" x 72" Tempered Glass
2x4
2x6
15-lb. Felt
1x6
1x2s
2x4
2x4s 16" O.C.
2x4
½" Plywood
6x6 Posts
6x12 Beam (Chamfered on End)
House
2x10 Joist
2x4 Fascia

MATERIALS USED FOR THIS DECK

Framing	6x6s for posts
(pressure-	6x10s, 6x12s, and 4x10s for beams
treated pine)	2x10 joists
	2x10 ledgers and headers
Decking	2x6s
Fascia	2x4s and 1x6s (See rail detail.)
Railings	4x4 posts
	2x4 bottom and top rails and framing pieces
	2x6 railing caps (one lower and one upper)
	1x6s for vertical fascia pieces
	½" CDX plywood
	15-lb. roofing felt
	Cedar shingles
	½" tempered glass (22" x 72")
	1x2s to hold the glass pane
Planters	Galvanized sheet-metal liners, ordered to fit
	2x4s for framing
	2x6s for top trim
	1x6s or cedar shingles for sides

	1x2s for side trim
Benches	4x4 posts
	2x4 framing pieces
	2x6 seat pieces
Hardware	3 ½" deck screws
	4d nails for shingles
	Joist hanger nails
	Post anchors for anchoring posts to concrete
	T-straps for tying beams to posts
	Joist hangers for 2x10s
	Angled joist hangers for 2x10s
	Angle brackets
	Lag screws with washers for anchoring the ledger
	Lag screws with washers for angled post braces
Masonry	Concrete
	Reinforcing bar

359

STATELY AND SYMMETRICAL

The homeowners wanted a deck that would run along the entire 60-foot length of their house but wouldn't appear monstrous. They also wanted something a bit more formal than the usual deck. To create a stately but not massive look, Marsh designed a curved structure that evokes the shape of a grand piano and used turned and painted balusters in the railing to lighten its effect.

Outside View

Note: Sway bracing and earthquake bracing are not shown. Verify any similar design with a structural engineer.

DESIGN CONSIDERATIONS

Scientists claim that they can quantify beauty in human features: the more symmetrically aligned the eyes, nose, and mouth, the more beautiful (or handsome) the face appears to us. In a deck, however, symmetrical features often mean boring features. But if you start with interesting contours and want to maintain a formal aspect, symmetry may be the best way to go.

The master bedroom, dining and family rooms, and a second bedroom all look out onto the deck. However, the homeowners don't need to look downward to glimpse the treetops and adjacent bay, so Marsh didn't lower the deck as he typically would have.

What the owners now see is a railing with dignity. It features turned balusters that have been painted a classic white, and the railing cap has a round-over detail that you'd expect to see on fine furniture.

Symmetrical Design. The deck has a 16-foot semicircular bulge in its center that feels almost as if it were a ship's prow as you stand looking outward. It provides ample space for a large table and chairs. On both sides, the deck has rectangular sections that each measure about 8 feet wide—large enough for barbecuing, lounging, or dining at a small table.

To further enhance the sense of symmetry, Marsh arranged the diagonal decking boards to meet in the exact center without a divider board. This apparently simple touch requires a lot of meticulous work, but it gives the decking a finished feel like that of an interior floor.

STATELY AND SYMMETRICAL, PLAN VIEW

36" Railing

2x6 Decking

Note: Extra Blocking for
Diagonal Decking Not Shown

4x10 Beams

2x8 Joists 24" O.C.

FRONT ELEVATION

Turned Balusters

2x6 Cap

1x4s

3" Space

1x10 Fascia

4x4 Post

4x10 Beam

2x8 Joist

Corbel

4x6 Post

MATERIALS USED FOR THIS DECK

Framing	4x6 posts	4" deck screws, for the railing
(pressure-	4x10 beams	Joist hanger nails
treated pine)	2x8 joists	Post anchors for anchoring posts to
	2x8 ledgers and headers	concrete
	Douglas Fir corbels for posts	T-straps for tying beams to posts
Decking	2x6s	Joist hangers for 2x8s
Fascia	1x10s, planed as necessary to make	Angled joist hangers for 2x8s
	the curves	Angle brackets
Railings	4x4 posts	Lag screws with washers for
	1x4s for top and bottom rails (planed	anchoring the ledger
	for curved sections)	Carriage bolts for the railing posts
	Turned balusters, painted white	**Masonry** Concrete
	2x10s for curved railing cap sections	Reinforcing bar
	2x6s for straight railing cap sections	
Hardware	3 ½" deck screws	

CONSTRUCTION TECHNIQUES

The sloped site and the deck's elevation called for large posts and beams as well as substantial footings. If your project presents similar challenges, it's best to hire a professional to install the footings and understructure. On a more conventional site, standard structural elements will do. To build the curved fascia and railing cap, see "Sweeping Elegance in a Small Space," page 259, and other of Marsh's decks.

Decking That Meets in the Middle

This feature is trickier to achieve than it appears. If this exact look—diagonally cut boards that butt directly against each other—isn't important to you, then run a divider board down the middle and butt the boards against it. However, this method provides a different look.

Choose dry, stable lumber. Avoid boards with hairline cracks near the ends (known as checking), or plan to cut off these areas, as they will probably enlarge over time. Also, measure all boards for width. They often vary by as much as 1/16 inch, which can cause serious misalignment in this arrangement. Butt together only boards of identical widths.

Plan Ahead. Prepare for the diagonal decking detail at the time you do the framing. Install joists and blocking that will provide ample nailing surfaces for the decking. Try to avoid having to drive nails or screws within 1 1/2 inches of the end of any decking board.

When you install the decking, allow plenty of time to get it right. Begin near the middle of the run rather than at either end. Check your 45-degree cuts carefully for accuracy, and lay out the first boards exactly perpendicular to

each other and at a 45-degree angle to the house. You'll need to make small adjustments as you go in order to keep the butt joints aligned and the gaps between decking boards consistent.

Roundover Detail on the Railing Cap. This profile looks elegant and requires little extra work. Fit your router with a roundover bit, and adjust it to cut only a partial profile. Experiment on scrap lumber until you get the desired look—a 1/8-inch lip at the bottom is a good choice. Once you've cut each railing-cap piece to width and length, rout along both top edges, and then install it.

Curved Railing with Turned Balusters. Choose milled balusters that appeal to you, and give them several coats of exterior white paint. You'll find this much easier than trying to paint them after you've completed the railing.

Once you've installed the railing posts, attach two lengths of 1x4 to their house side, one of them flush with the post tops and the other with its bottom edge about 1/2 inch lower

than the planned bottom of the balusters. For the curved sections, plane the 1x4s until they are just flexible enough to make the curves. Then install the railing cap. To ensure a finished look on the inside of the railing, drill pilot holes, and drive screws through the posts from the outside and into the railing cap and 1x4s.

Attach the balusters, spacing them evenly between the railing posts and butting them up to the railing cap. Next, cut lengths of 1x4 for the other face of the "sandwich" at the bottom. Attach the 1x4s to the posts and balusters.

RAILING DETAIL

2x6 (Curves Cut from 2x12s)

Turned Balusters

1x4s

4x4

PROMENADE WITH CIRCULAR VIEWING AREA

Note: Sway bracing and earthquake bracing are not shown. Verify any similar design with a structural engineer.

DESIGN CONSIDERATIONS

The house has clean, spare lines and floor-to-ceiling glass walls that allow the homeowners to gaze out over the treetops to the bay below. They wanted a deck that would wrap around the house to provide a view from two sides, something the existing deck didn't offer. The existing conventional wooden railing also blocked the limited view it did provide.

The homeowners didn't need a large space, nor were they interested in the usual cooking and dining areas. They did, however, want to link their home more effectively to the outdoors, so Marsh designed a promenade of sorts—wide enough for strolling and placing potted plants with a larger area in the middle for engaging in conversation.

An Eye to the View. With a deck that measures only 8 feet wide in most places, it wouldn't make sense to step the structure downward to improve the view. Each step would eat up at least a foot of usable width.

Instead, Marsh designed a railing that, safe and sturdy though it is, barely seems to exist as you look through it. Made of steel and anodized dark green to blend with the leaves just beyond it, the structure has a contemporary Euro look, but its color and curving contour give it an organic feel. As a complement to this, the glass walls create an unusual relationship between the deck and the house. From certain angles, the decking appears to be an extension of the interior floor rather than a separate space.

Marsh's clients in this case owned a newer home that was set on a severely inclined slope. This factor limited the overall size of the deck, but with the house's modern styling, Marsh felt free to choose almost any shape. The solution he came up with has a pleasantly straightforward look and a distinctive metal railing that doesn't obstruct the view.

Outside View

PROMENADE WITH CIRCULAR VIEWING AREA, PLAN VIEW

10" x 10" Concrete Tie Beam

Railing

1x10 Fascia

2x8 Joists

2x8 Blocking

6x12 Beam

6x8 Flush Bea[m]

2x8 Ledger

Cantilevered Deck Section

10" x 10" Concrete Tie Beam

2x8 Blocking

MATERIALS USED FOR THIS DECK

Framing	6" steel posts	Joist hanger nails
(pressure-	6x12 beams	Post anchors for anchoring posts
treated pine)	6x8 flush beam	to concrete
	2x8 joists	Joist hangers for 2x8s
	2x8 ledgers and headers	Angled joist hangers for 2x8s
Decking	1x6 hardwood	Angle brackets
Fascia	1x10s, planed as necessary to make	Lag screws with washers for anchoring
	the curves	the ledger
Railing (all	2" steel pipe for the rails	Stainless-steel lag screws for attaching
steel	1 ½" steel pipe for the posts	the railing
anodized	¼" steel plates welded to the posts,	**Masonry** Concrete
green and	for attaching to the framing and house	Reinforcing bar
welded	Welded wire mesh made of ¼" steel	
together)	in a 4" square pattern	
Hardware	2" deck screws	

CONSTRUCTION TECHNIQUES

Marsh encountered a formidable challenge in installing the footings for this deck. He sank 18-inch-diameter concrete footings 6 feet into bedrock and tied all footings to each other and to the house with massive steel-reinforced concrete beams. The structural members—6-inch steel posts and 6x12 beams—had to be lifted over the house and into place using a crane. This is definitely a job for a professional.

The techniques used here can be found on some of Marsh's other decks. For instructions on building the curved fascia, for example, see page 259.

Steel Railing

Few homeowners—or even professional carpenters—will have the skills and equipment needed to build a railing like this. The best approach is to construct the framing and then call in a local metalworking company to build the railing to your specifications. This will cost a good deal, but it's the only safe and practical way to get the job done. Note: check with your local building department first. Some codes may specify a smaller-grid steel mesh to prevent small children from climbing the railing.

If you'd prefer to conceal the metal plates and bolt heads, arrange for the fencing company to secure the railing to the inside face of an outside joist at corners. This method may, however, require that you install extra framing pieces.

SIDE ELEVATION

36" Steel Railing
6" Steel Post
Welded Column Cap
1x10 Fascia
6x12 Beam
Turnbuckle Reinforcement
10" x 10" Concrete Tie Beam

RAILING DETAIL

2" Steel Rail
4" Welded Wire Mesh
1½" Steel Post
2x8 Rim Joist
Railing Secured to Joist
Screws into House
Cantilevered Joist

DECKS APPEAL

Rick Parish of Decks Appeal, located near Dallas in Plano, Texas, is one of the few deck builders in the country to have his own showroom. There, you'll see deck samples that show some of his signature design elements, as well as outdoor furniture pieces made to blend well with the decks. By spending all of his time meeting with customers and designing decks, Parish keeps three or more construction crews busy. He starts by listening to the homeowners to get a sense of how they intend to use their deck and how they envision its general contours.

DECKS APPEAL

Plano, Texas

(972) 964-8821

www.decksappeal.com

TECHNIQUES TO USE

Many of Parish's designs are less complicated than they look. He often achieves an appearance of furniture-like detailing by adding simple pieces. However, such detail work requires precise cuts in order to look good. For this purpose, you should consider a quality power miter saw (chop saw) a necessity rather than a luxury.

• Much of the distinctive look of Parish's decks comes from his materials. After carefully selecting dark-colored Con Heart boards that have no loose knots, he chooses the best pieces for the most visible elements of the deck.

• His post design adds elegance without requiring a lot of work. By attaching 2x2s that run up the center of each face of a standard 4x4, he creates a classically fluted column. He also installs banding at the top of each post made of 2x2s and ripped 2x4s, although this detail requires careful cutting and fastening.

• In his designs, Parish avoids butt joints in the decking, which tend to mar its unbroken appearance. This sometimes means dividing a large deck into smaller sections. He's rarely found a good reason to make a deck surface that measures more than 20 feet (the longest standard decking length) in both directions. Though butt-jointed decking can look fine if you prefer a rustic look, avoid it if you want a more finished appearance.

• Not only does Parish recommend regular staining to reduce the punishing effects of sunlight, he also urges customers to avoid damaging their decks with furniture and pots. For instance, by using simple trivets made from 2x2s to hold flowerpots off the deck, they can prevent water stains and scratches, and eventually more serious damage.

• If a deck has gone gray due to neglect, Parish cautions against using a high-pressure washer. These machines, which are sold in home centers and touted as cure-alls for wood surface problems, may actually do more harm than good. On softwoods such as redwood, they can remove the soft part of the grain, leaving a rough surface that can be made smooth again only through heavy sanding. Instead, he recommends a two-step solution: first, spray or sponge on a 50-50 mixture of household bleach and water, which will make the gray disappear almost immediately. Rinse and then brush the deck with a mixture of oxalic acid (wood bleach) and water. This will leave you with a deck that is nearly white. Apply stain, and the wood will look like new.

• Parish designs overhead structures, or pergolas, carefully to provide the desired amount of shade. He runs the top slats, usually 2x2s, in a north-to-south direction so that the sun can shine directly between them only at noon. In the Dallas area, he's found that 2x2s laid 3 inches on center (spaced 1½ inches apart) provide full shade for an hour or two (in the morning on an east-facing deck and in the evening on a west-facing deck). For the rest of the day, the overhead structure will provide filtered shade of varying degree. This much planning may sound complicated, but it will increase the utility of your deck and save work in the long run.

• Parish uses a lot of curves, not only on his decks and railings but sometimes on overhead structures as well. To the homeowner, curves can look daunting, like something better left to a professional. They also cost more in materials; you often need to start with a 2x12 and then waste nearly half of the board. But if you have a professional-grade saber saw and the patience to do things right, you can add impressive-looking curves to your project.

• Parish uses a router fitted with a roundover bit to create the finished look of his decks, usually following up with a sander. If you take some time beforehand to practice your routing on scrap material, you'll find that you can get the near-furniture-quality results you see in his work. Unless you have a lot of experience with a belt sander, however, use this tool with great caution and only with fine-grit sandpaper. It removes wood very quickly and can leave gouges and other blemishes that can't be repaired.

The shade structures, opposite, designed by Parish provide filtered shade for most of the day.

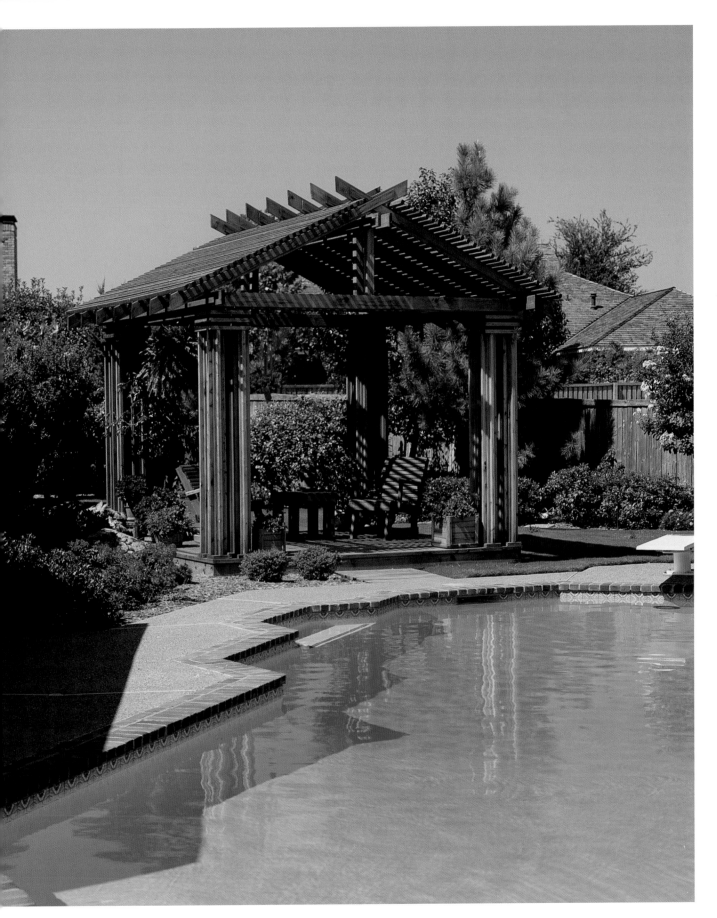

FREESTANDING DECK WITH SPA AND FIRE PIT

Ground View

This deck may be small, but it has lots of flair. Kids and adults can sit around the fire pit and roast marshmallows, then hop into the spa. It almost reminds you of summer camp.

DESIGN CONSIDERATIONS

With decks that sit low above the ground like this one, you don't have to worry about space for parties. When guests show up for the occasional large get-together, they can simply spill over onto the lawn if need be. For the rest of time, this design provides plenty of room for cozy get-togethers—family lounging, barbecuing, and soaking, as well as gathering around the fire.

Parish surrounded the spa with just enough decking so that guests could sit and dangle their legs. (The spa cover, which gets stowed next to the house, doesn't require deck space.) The unit sits three levels up from grade, or about 21 inches. Parish finds that this height makes spa installation easier. (See Construction Techniques, page 295.)

A railing runs around one-half of the spa, more for privacy rather than safety. The balusters are self-spaced; that is, the gaps between them measure the same width (1 ½ inches) as the 2x2 balusters themselves. A "railing" that leads up to the spa actually serves as a towel rack, with two horizontal rails made of rounded 2x2s.

About 5 feet from the spa, a brick fire pit rises about 8 inches above the decking. The pit is not intended for cooking—a conventional grill works better—but it makes an ideal place to gather after supper. With a crackling fire, relaxed conversation naturally takes place. A bench curves halfway around the pit, facing toward the spa.

The first level measures about 12 feet square, allowing enough room for a dining table and cooking area. In one corner, a triangular opening makes a distinctive spot for planting flowers or a small shrub. In fact, angles tend to dominate throughout, giving the deck a pleasantly jumbled look. The assortment of odd angles showcases the spa and fire pit, both of which are octagonal.

FREESTANDING DECK WITH SPA AND FIRE PIT, PLAN VIEW

2x6 Decking

8'

9'6"

2x6 Railing Cap

Spa

2x6 Joists 16" O.C.

12'

22'

8'6"

4'8"

Double 2x6 Flush Beams

Fire Pit

25'

MATERIALS USED FOR THIS DECK

Framing	4x4 posts	**Hardware**	Joist hangers for 2x6s
	Doubled 2x6s for flush beams		Angled joist hangers for 2x6s
	2x6 joists		Angle brackets
Decking	2x6s		Fasteners for joist hangers
Bench	4x4 posts		3" deck screws
	2x6 seat pieces		3" lag screws with washers for
	2x4 framing		bench posts
	2x4 trim for bottom of posts		2 ½" deck screws
Railing	4x4 posts	**Masonry**	Bricks, fire bricks, and mortar for fire pit
	2x4 top and bottom rails		Sand to support spa
	2x2 balusters		Reinforcing bar for fire-pit foundation
	2x6 railing cap		Concrete
Railing/	4x4 posts		Concrete tube forms or lumber for
towel rack	2x2 rails (bars)		building forms
	2x6 railing cap		Solid concrete blocks for footings

CONSTRUCTION TECHNIQUES

A low-to-the-ground deck usually leaves no room for a beam under the joists, so take the time to accurately lay out the many footings that directly support the joists. If local codes allow, dig your footing holes, position the posts, and build the framing before you pour the concrete.

Supporting a Spa with Washed Sand

Parish prefers the technique that follows, but check with your building department before you try it. Local codes may require you to pour a concrete foundation.

After you've completed the framing, but before you lay the decking, dig a hole for the spa. In this case, the top of the 36-inch-deep spa sits 21 inches above grade. The hole should allow about a foot of clearance below the bottom of the spa, so dig the hole approximately 27 inches deep—not a big job.

Tamp the soil at the bottom of the hole; then shovel in and level a foot or so of sand. Set temporary 2x6 blocks on top of the framing to index the future thickness of the decking, and set the spa on top of them, resting its lip directly on the blocks. Shovel sand into the hole until it fully supports the spa.

Now comes the interesting part of the job. Fill the spa halfway with water. Using a garden hose, soak the sand fully to compact it. Add more sand, and then soak it again if necessary. The moisture-compacted sand will form a firm base that will support the spa for decades.

Fire Pit

Unless you have a fair amount of masonry experience, you'd do well to hire a professional mason to build the pit. An octagon poses a serious challenge to the beginner. To start, frame a square hole large enough so that the firebricks will not directly touch the wood. If possible, build the pit before you lay the decking; this work can easily scratch the wood.

At the bottom, excavate a foundation hole if necessary, so the fire pit ends up about 18 inches deep. (The foundation should measure 3 to 4 inches in depth.) Pour a steel-reinforced concrete pad that measures a few inches larger than the pit's diameter. From the foundation, lay firebricks in an octagonal shape to a height of 4 to 6 inches above the decking surface. Cover the firebrick with natural brick, making the total structure about 8 inches higher than the decking.

SIDE ELEVATION

2x6 Cap

2x2s (Edges Rounded)

2x6s

1x6s

2x6

2x2s

2x4s

FIRE PIT DETAIL

Natural Brick

Decking

2x6 Joist

±18"

Firebricks

Reinforcing Bar

Concrete Foundation

CIRCULAR EATING AREA

Here's a bit of whimsy: a round platform, just the right size for a table with chairs, that can be set on top of a deck or patio. The railing is just for looks, while the benches provide a comfortable conversation area.

Ground View

DESIGN CONSIDERATIONS

This little deck offers just enough space for a circular patio table with chairs, plus room for a server to walk around the chairs while people are eating. Whenever you plan an eating area such as this one, with clearly defined borders, first test the dimensions by setting your furniture in place to find out how much room you'll really need.

Although not a safety requirement here, the railing gives the little deck a sense of enclosure. Leaning on it as they look toward the pool, adults can easily keep an eye on the kids—while the railing is there to remind the children that this is adult space.

Parish positioned the benches to the rear of the deck and behind the railing, creating a semi-secluded conversation area. The benches' curved shape makes for good groupings. People are forced to look neither at nor away from each other.

CIRCULAR EATING AREA, PLAN VIEW

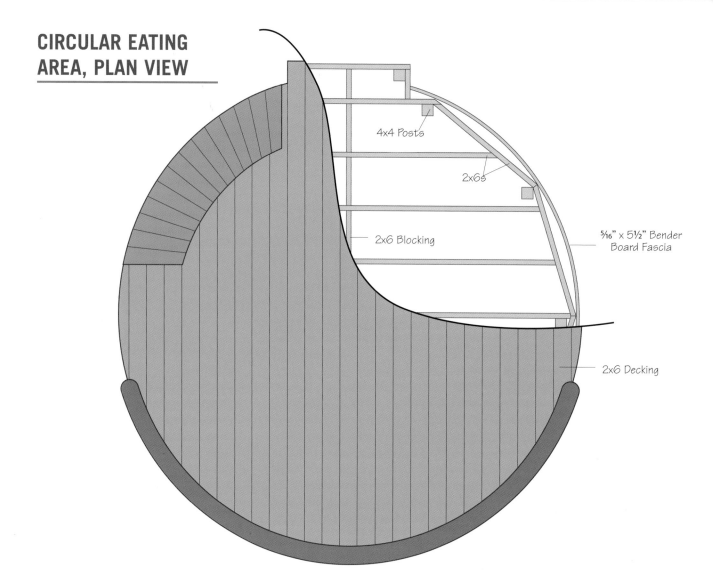

4x4 Posts

2x6s

2x6 Blocking

⁵⁄₁₆" x 5½" Bender Board Fascia

2x6 Decking

MATERIALS USED FOR THIS DECK

Framing	4x4 posts (not needed if you're building on an existing deck or patio)		**Benches**	4x4 posts
	2x6 joists			2x4 framing pieces
Decking	2x6s			⁵⁄₁₆" x 3 ½" bender board, ripped from 2x4s
Fascia	⁵⁄₁₆" x 5 ½" bender board, ripped from 2x6s			2x6s for seat pieces
Railing	4x4 posts		**Hardware**	Joist hangers for 2x6s
	2x4 rails cut out of 2x8s			Angled joist hangers for 2x6s
	2x2 balusters			Fasteners for joist hangers
	2x6 railing cap cut out of 2x12s			3" deck screws
Overhead	4x4s for posts (four for each post)			2 ½" deck screws
	2x8s for beams (two for each beam)			Carriage bolts with washers and nuts for rail posts
	4x6 rafters			
	2x4 top pieces			

CONSTRUCTION TECHNIQUES

If the circular deck is not resting on a solid surface, you'll need to pour numerous footings for such a small space. The impressive benches and railing will both take time to build, but a patient do-it-yourselfer can handle the job without much difficulty.

Building a Low Circular Deck

Start by making an X with three lengths of 2x6: one that spans the length of the deck and two half-long pieces running perpendicular to it that are attached to its center. Check for squareness. Cut the outside pieces. There are ten sides, all of which should measure the same length. Miter-cut the ends of each piece at 18 degrees (leaving you with a 72-degree complementary angle). For a 10-sided frame that measures 10 feet in diameter, cut each piece to 38 inches finished length.

Now, locate the corner points for the framing (10 in all, plus two for the non-circular "landing" section) by measuring from the center of the X and using the outside pieces as guides.

Fasten the pieces together using temporary cleats on top. Measure the diameter across all five pairs of parallel sides, and adjust them so that they come out pretty even. They needn't be perfect. Install posts and footings, if required. If you're building on top of a solid surface, use shims to raise the joists ¼ inch or so to allow the framing to dry out after a rain. Now, fill in the rest of the framing.

Install the posts for the benches, anchoring them securely to the framing. Next, install the decking, allowing it to run wild. Attach a 5-foot 1 ½-inch string and pencil to a nail located at the centerpoint, and mark the decking for a circular cut.

Rails and Top Cap

for a Curved Railing

After you've installed and trimmed the decking, cut lengths of 2x8 and 2x12 for the rails and cap, and arrange them around the perimeter of the decking in the proper locations. Make them a bit longer than needed to start. On each piece, mark for the outside edge by running a pencil along the underside of the board, using the decking as a guide. Cut the boards to shape with a professional-quality saber saw, and then use a compass or scribe tool to mark the inside edge 3 ½ (rails) and 5 ½ inches (cap) in from the outside edge.

Curved Bench

Construct the 2x4 framing as shown in the drawing below, and then attach

the fascia. It will curve in the middle, but it needn't follow the curve that the seat pieces will have.

Cut a number of seat pieces to the dimensions shown, and install them. They will measure a little longer than necessary. Make adjustments as you go, to ensure that you don't end up with a narrow or odd-shaped piece at the end. Make a final cut on both sides with a saber saw; then sand the edges smooth.

SIDE ELEVATION

2x6
4x4
2x4
2x2s
2x4
5⁄16" Bender Board Fascia

BENCH DETAIL

5⁄16" Bender Board Fascia

5½"
3⅜"
±18"
13"
18"
4x4
2x4s
2x2 Trim

TWO LOW LEVELS WITH ANGLES AND AN OVERHEAD

Ground View

Despite their flat yard and the low threshold into their home, these home-owners asked for a deck with at least two levels. To accommodate them, Parish came up with an unusual solution: a deck that rises above the house's floor level, rather than descending from it. Interesting angles, a bench/planter, and an elegant overhead structure make this a soothing place to relax.

DESIGN CONSIDERATIONS

The homeowners wanted to expand the area occupied by an existing rectangular concrete patio—and provide some shade at the same time. For structural reasons, Parish's design follows the shape of the patio, but has dressed up the deck with interesting features that effectively disguise its basic rectangular outline.

Although it has plenty of angles, the deck's perimeter makes use of theme and variation to avoid a jumbled or confused look. For example, the forward section of the upper level, which angles away from the house at 45 degrees, parallels several other lines in the deck. By restating the theme in different ways, Parish avoids a ho-hum symmetrical effect but still ties the whole design together.

The main level offers plenty of room for a table with chairs and a grill, while the upper level provides a pleasant area for conversation, lounging, or just enjoying the foliage. The bench joins two planters that rise slightly above the seat level. With some fairly tall plants, this provides a naturally secluded place to sit and read. The benches form a semicircle of sorts, a shape that promotes conversation during a party.

The overhead structure is supported by "fluted" posts made of 4x4s and 2x2s. Though it requires only a bit of extra work and expense, this detail makes a big difference. An unadorned 4x4 post set in the middle of a deck would look drab and dreary; this variation adds grace and interest. The 2x2 roof pieces run north to south to provide maximum shade and are self-spaced (set 1 ½ inches apart so that the gaps equal the width of the pieces). In a region that gets a lot of sun, the orientation and spacing of these top pieces requires serious planning. (See "Techniques to Use," page 290, for more information on this and on making "fluted" posts.)

TWO LOW LEVELS WITH ANGLES AND AN OVERHEAD, PLAN VIEW

6'   18'6"

2'6"

13'6"

9'

14'

2x6s

2x6 Headers

1x6 Fascia

Planter

Bench

SIDE ELEVATION

2x2s

2x6

2 2x8s   4x4 Post with
2x2 Trim

2x4   1x6s

2x6s

MATERIALS USED FOR THIS DECK

Framing	2x6 joists laid on a patio surface Shims	**Planters**	Pressure-treated 2x4s, for bottom plates and framing pieces
Decking	2x6s		Redwood 2x4s for top trim
Fascia	1x6s		Tongue-and-groove redwood 1x6s,
Overhead	4x4s and 2x2s for posts		clear all-heart, for sides
	2x8s for beams		Silicone caulk
	2x6 rafters		Pea gravel for bottom
	2x2 top and bottom trim pieces	**Hardware**	Joist hangers for 2x6s
Benches	4x4 posts		Anchors to attach overhead to roof
	2x4 framing pieces		Fasteners for joist hangers
	2x6 seat pieces		2 ½" and 3" deck screws
	2x2 trim at bottom of posts		

CONSTRUCTION TECHNIQUES

If you don't have a patio surface on which to lay the joists, use standard framing techniques. On a deck this low, which doesn't allow room for a beam under the joists, you'll need to tie the joists to flush beams using joist hangers. For the overhead, figure out ahead of time exactly how you'll tie the rafters to the roof or eave.

Framing Over a Patio Surface. In Dallas, where frost heave is not a concern, Parish may simply lay the framing on top of an existing patio. If your area is subject to frost, the local building department will probably require that you dig footings that extend below the frost line. As an alternative, you may be able to build a floating deck that rises and falls a bit as the seasons change. *In that case, do not attach the framing to the house with a ledger board.* However, if you omit the ledger but still attach the overhead to the house, you run a risk of damaging the roof.

As long as you use 2x6 or larger joists, you needn't attach them to the concrete; just set them in place. If the threshold to the house sits so low that you're forced to use 2x4s or 2x2s, you may need to anchor them.

Orient the joists so that rainwater will flow easily beneath the deck. Most patios are sloped slightly for drainage, so this usually means setting the joists perpendicular to the house. As long as the slope is not severe, you may prefer simply to lay the joists on top and allow the deck slope as well. If you'd rather level the deck, build the framing and then use shims.

Overhead with Fluted Posts. Secure the posts to the deck framing using bolts. Add the 2x2 wraparound trim at the bottom (after decking) and near the top of the post; then position the members for the beams to rest on. Plumb the posts, temporarily brace them, and then add the beams. To add the fluting, attach a centered 2x2 to each face of all 4x4s.

Two rafters on each side measure 12 inches shorter than the middle rafters. When installing the top pieces, allow the shorter, outermost pieces to run wild. Then, make chalk-line marks and trim them to length.

The Planters. Parish's planters sit directly on top of the decking, though he provides drainage by adding a generous layer of pea gravel at the bottom so that the decking can dry out. If your area stays wet for long periods, however, you may want to use another design.

Attach a frame of pressure-treated 2x4s to the deck, laid flat, and seal it with silicone caulk. Build a second frame as shown, using the same material. Clad the outside with clear, all-heart 1x6 tongue-and-groove redwood. For this application, any knots will cause problems. Like the sides of a hot tub, the redwood will expand and seal when it absorbs moisture. Cover the top with a cap of 2x4 redwood.

For drainage, pour in a layer of 6 or more inches of pea gravel. Add light soil that contains plenty of peat moss or other organic matter.

OVERHEAD DETAIL

2x2s
2x6s
2 2x8s
2x2 Trim
"Fluted" Post
2x2 Trim

POST, PLAN VIEW

2x2
4x4

PLANTER DETAIL

2x4 Cap
2x4s
1x6s
Treated 2x4s

RESOURCE GUIDE

This list of manufacturers and associations is meant to be a general guide to additional industry and product-related sources. It is not intended as a listing of products and manufacturers represented by the photographs in this book.

Advanced Concrete Enhancement

11070 Fleetwood St., Ste. F
Sun Valley, CA 91352
818-504-0424
Manufactures decorative concrete barbecues, outdoor kitchen sinks, countertops, surrounds, and flooring.

Alcoa Home Exteriors

201 Isabella St., Ste. 500
Pittsburgh, PA 15212-5858
412-315-2900
www.alcoa.com
Manufactures aluminum and synthetic building materials, including deck products under the Oasis brand.

Alumatec Industries

529 Orange Ave.
Daytona, FL 32114
386-255-1566
Manufactures and installs a complete line of aluminum, stainless-steel, and brass railings.

Andersen Corporation

100 Fourth Ave. N.
Bayport, MN 55003-1096
800-426-4261
www.andersenwindows.com
Offers a full line of patio doors and windows.

APA – The Engineered Wood Association

7011 South 19th St.
Tacoma, WA 98466
253-565-6600
www.apawood.org
A nonprofit trade association that produces a variety of engineered-wood products.

Atlantis Outdoor Kitchens

3304 Aerial Way Dr.
Roanoke, VA 24018
877-223-4537
www.outdoorkitchensbyatlantis.com
Manufactures durable, polymer outdoor cabinetry in a variety of colors and designs.

AZEK Building Products

801 E Corey St.
Scranton, PA 18505
877-275-2935
www.azek.com
Makes synthetic trim products, including balustrades, moldings, and lattice skirting.

Baldwin Lawn Furniture

440 Middlefield St.
Middletown, CT 06457
800-344-5103
www.baldwinfurniture.com
Builds outdoor furniture, planters, and pergolas.

Blue Rhino

5650 University Pkwy., Ste. 400
Winston-Salem, NC 27105
800-762-1142
www.bluerhino.com
Offers a full line of grills, heaters, and other outdoor appliances, plus a propane tank exchange program.

CableRail/Feeney Architectural Products

2603 Union St.
Oakland, CA 94607
800-888-2418
www.feeneyinc.com
Manufactures a line of standard and custom cable stainless-steel cable assemblies.

California Redwood Association

405 Enfrente Dr., Ste. 200
Novato, CA 94949-7206
888-225-7339
www.calredwood.org
Offers technical information about the use of redwood for decks and other structures.

Cascades

404 Marie-Victorin Blvd.
Kingsey Falls, QC, Canada J0A 1B0
819-363-5100
www.cascades.com
A packaging product leader that also makes decking from recycled plastic under the Perma-deck brand.

Classic Garden Design

1 Katydid Ln.
Weston, CT 06883
203-226-2886
www.classicgardendesign.com
Designs and installs residential patios, perennial gardens, pergolas, walks, fences, and outdoor kitchens.

Consumer Product Safety Commission (CPSC)

4330 East-West Hwy.
Bethesda, MD 20814
800-638-2772
www.cpsc.gov
Organization charged with protecting the public from unreasonable risks of serious injury or death from more than 15,000 types of consumer products.

Coolaroo/GALE Pacific
285 W. Central Pkwy., Ste. 1704
Altamonte Springs, Florida, 32714
407-772-7900
www.coolaroousa.com
Manufactures shade sails, umbrellas, and other shade devices that feature knitted outdoor fabric.

Correct Building Products
8 Morin St.
Biddeford, ME 04005
207-284-5600
www.correctdeck.com
Maker of CorrectDeck, a composite decking material.

Dacor
14425 Clark Ave.
City of Industry, CA 91745
800-793-0093
www.dacor.com
Designs and manufactures a full line of outdoor grills, built-in grills, grill carts, warming ovens, and side burners.

Deck Images
12590 127th St. S.
Hastings, MN 55033
651-437-5356
www.deckimages.com
Manufactures powder-coated aluminum and glass railing systems for residential and commercial markets.

Deckmaster
205 Mason Cir.
Concord, CA 94520
800-869-1375
www.deckmaster.com
Makes bracket-style hidden deck fasteners.

Deckorators
50 Crestwood Executive Center, Ste. 308
Crestwood, MO 63126
800-556-8449
www.deckorators.com
Manufactures a wide range of aluminum balustrades and glass railings in many colors and designs.

DekBrands
650 25th Ave. SE
Minneapolis, MN 55414
800-664-2705
www.deckplans.com
Produces easy-to-do deck systems, including the award winning Floating Foundation Deck System.

DESA
2701 Industrial Dr.
Bowling Green, KY 42101
866-672-6040
www.desatech.com
Maker of security lights with motion detectors and deck heaters, including umbrella stands with built-in heaters.

Dry-B-Lo
4108 Hamilton Mill Rd.
Buford, GA 30519
770-521-5404
www.dry-b-lo.com
Manufactures aluminum deck drainage systems that keep the space below decks dry.

EB-TY Hidden Deck-Fastening Systems
P.O. Box 5389
North Branch, NJ 08876
800-438-3289
www.ebty.com
Makes biscuit-style hidden deck fasteners.

Empyrean International
930 Main St.
Acton, MA 01720
800-727-3325
www.empyreanapf.com
Custom-designed homes that often feature decks. Brands include Deck House, Acorn, and The Dwell Homes by Empyrean.

Forest Stewardship Council-U.S.
708 First St. N, Ste. 235
Minneapolis, MN 55401
612-353-4511
www.fscus.org
A nonprofit organization devoted to encouraging the responsible management of the world's forests.

Gaco Western
200 W Mercer St., Ste. 202
Seattle, WA 98119
866-422-6489
www.gaco.com
Manufactures a high-quality acrylic polymer waterproof surface protection for plywood or plank decks.

Hadco Lighting
100 Craftway Dr.
Littlestown, PA 17340
717-359-7131
www.lightinganddecormag.com
Offers a large variety of outdoor lighting designed for decks, including post, step, path, and area lights.

Hearth & Home Technologies
7571 215th St. W
Lakeville, MN 55044
952-985-6000
www.hearthnhome.com
Offers a complete line of gas, electric, and wood-burning heating products.

Hooks and Lattice

6056 Corte Del Cedro
Carlsbad, CA 92011
800-896-0978
www.hooksandlattice.com
All styles of window boxes designed for every application, including deck railings.

Jacuzzi

13925 City Center Dr., Ste. 200
Chino, CA 91709
909-606-1416
www.jacuzzi.com
Manufactures a full line of hot tubs and deck spas.

LockDry

Nexan Building Products, Inc.
1213 26th St. SW
Cullman, AL 35055
888-739-6172
www.lockdry.com
Patented aluminum deck and railing systems with built-in continuous gutters.

Marvin Windows and Doors

P.O. Box 100
Warroad, MN 56763
888-537-7828
www.marvin.com
Makers of windows and doors, including sliders and French doors.

NanaWall Systems

100 Meadowbrook Dr., Ste. 250
Corte Madera, CA 94925
888-411-6262
www.nanawall.com
Manufactures folding wall systems of easy-to-open glass panels.

National Fenestration Rating Council (NFRC)

6305 Ivy Ln., Ste. 140
Greenbelt, MD 20770
301-589-1776
www.nfrc.org
A nonprofit organization that administers the only uniform, independent rating and labeling system for the energy performance of patio doors and other products.

Pella Corporation

102 Main St.
Pella, IA 50219
877-473-5527
www.pella.com
Produces energy-efficient patio doors and windows.

Progress Lighting

P.O. Box 6701
Greenville, South Carolina 29606
864-678-1000
www.progresslighting.com
Makes wall lanterns that have motion detectors built into the mounting plate or the lantern itself, as well as deck and landscape lights.

Punch! Software

Navarre Digital Services, Inc.
9700 W 76th St., Ste. 116
Eden Prairie, MN 55344
800-395-0277
www.punchsoftware.com
Software company specializing in home and landscaping design programs.

Royal Crown Limited

10 Roybridge Gate, Ste. 201
Vaughan, ON, Canada L4H 3M8
800-232-5690
www.royalcrownltd.com
Produces vinyl deck planks and railing products under the Triple Crown Fence, Brock Deck Systems, Brock Deck, and Deck Lok Systems brands.

Shade Sails

2216 Padre Blvd., Ste. B #77
South Padre Island, TX 78597
956-772-4711
www.shadesails.com
Imports tensioned, UV-treated fabric canopies.

ShadeScapes Americas

122 E Bridge St.
Hotchkiss, CO 81419
888-217-4446
www.shadescapesamericas.com
Manufactures side- and center-post shade umbrellas.

Southern Pine Council

6660 Riverside Dr., Ste. 212
Metairie, LA 70003
504-443-4464
www.southernpine.com
A trade association that offers information on deck building with treated lumber.

Starborn Industries
45 Mayfield Ave.
Edison, NJ 08837
800-596-7747
www.starbornindustries.com
Manufactures stainless-steel deck fastening systems, including Headcote and DeckFast brand screws.

Summer Classics
3140 Pelham Pkwy.
Pelham, AL 35124
888-868-4267
www.summerclassics.com
Manufactures deck and garden furnishings in wrought aluminum, wrought iron, and woven resin.

Summerwood Products
735 Progress Ave.
Toronto, ON, Canada M1H 2W7
800-663-5042
www.summerwood.com
Offers prefab customized kits for outdoor structures such as gazebos, pool cabanas, and spa enclosures.

Sundance Spas
13925 City Center Dr., Ste. 200
Chino Hills, CA 91709
800-883-7727
www.sundancespas.com
The largest manufacturer of acrylic spas.

Sustainable Forestry Initiative
2121 K St. NW, Ste. 750
Washington, DC 20037
202-596-3450
www.sfiprogram.org
A comprehensive forestry management program developed by the American Forest & Paper Association.

Tiger Claw
400 Middle St., Ste. J
Bristol, CT 06010-8405
800-928-4437
www.deckfastener.com
Manufactures products for the construction industry, including hidden deck fasteners.

Timber Holdings
451 S River Rd.
Bedford, NH 03110
888-932-9663
www.ironwoods.com
Supplies the Iron Wood brand of ipé hardwood lumber. Check the Website to locate a lumber yard near you.

TimberTech
894 Prairie Rd.
Wilmington, OH 45177
800-307-7780
www.timbertech.com
Manufacturers composite decking and railing systems, fascia boards, and specialty trim.

Trex
160 Exeter Dr.
Winchester, VA 22603
800-289-8739
www.trex.com
Specializes in composite decking materials.

GLOSSARY

Actual Dimension: The exact measurement of a piece of lumber after it has been milled, generally ½ inch less each way than the advertised size. For example, a typical 2x4's actual dimension is 1½ x 3½ inches.

Architectural Scale Ruler: A three-sided ruler that enables you to convert large dimensions to a small scale in a drawing, including ⅛-, ¼-, and ½-inch scale.

Balusters: The vertical pieces, generally made of 2x2s, that fill in spaces between rail posts and provide a fence-like structure.

Beam: The term for any large framing member of four-by or doubled two-by material.

Breadboard Edge: A long strip of wood, typically 1x2 or larger, fastened along the edge of a deck to cover the end grain of decking boards.

Bridging: Usually short, solid blocks of lumber made of joist material that are cut to fit snugly between the joists to prevent twisting.

Building Codes: National and local rules regulating building practices. Generally, codes encompass structural, electrical, plumbing, and mechanical remodeling and new construction. Code compliance is checked by on-site inspections.

Building Permit: An authorization to build or renovate according to plans approved by the local building department. Generally, any job that includes a footing or foundation or that involves any structural work or alterations requires a permit.

Cantilever: The outer part of a deck floor frame that extends beyond the main beam, floating without additional support.

Carriage: A cut stringer with a sawtooth shape on its top edge that runs at midspan on wide stairs.

Countersink: A shallow hole drilled to house the head of a lag screw or bolt. The hole diameter is generally the size of the washer used with the fastener.

Curing: The slow, ongoing chemical action that hardens concrete.

Dado: A channel cut across the grain of a piece of wood to house the end of another component in a joint.

Dipping: A treatment in which wood is immersed in a bath of preservative for several minutes, then allowed to air-dry.

Fascia: A facing board (generally one-by material) that covers the exposed ends or sides of deck framing.

Footing: A masonry base, usually concrete, that supports a post, beam, or steps.

Frost Line: The maximum depth at which soil freezes, as specified by local building departments, which require footings below the line to prevent heaving.

Grade: Ground level. At-grade means at or on the natural ground level.

Header Joist: The outermost joist, also called a belt, set at right angles to and across the ends of the on-center joists that support the decking.

Joist: Horizontal structural member, usually two-by lumber, commonly set 16 inches on center to support deck boards.

Joist Hanger: A U-shaped metal connector that joins a joist, generally at right angles, to another board, such as a ledger. Similar hardware is available for other structural joints.

Kickback: The lurching, backward action of a power saw when the blade binds in a cut.

Lattice: A cross-pattern structure generally used for skirting that is made of wood, metal, or plastic.

Ledger: A horizontal board attached to the side of a house (bolted into the framing) that supports one end of the deck joists.

Nominal Dimension: The identifying size of stock lumber, such as 2x4 and 2x6, even though the boards are a half inch smaller each way.

On Center: A point of reference for measuring framing that is installed in a modular layout. The spacing, typically 16 inches, is figured from the center of one framing member to the center of the next; abbreviated o.c.

Penny: The colloquial measure of nail length, generally abbreviated with the letter d, as in 10d (ten penny). (2d, 1 in.; 3d, 1¼ in.; 4d, 1½ in.; 5d, 1¾ in.; 6d, 2 in.; 7d, 2¼ in.; 8d, 2½ in.; 9d, 2¾ in.; 10d, 3 in.; 12d, 3¼ in.; 16d, 3½ in.; 20d, 4 in.; 30d, 4½ in.; 50d, 5½ in.; 60d, 6 in.)

Pier: A masonry support, similar to a footing, generally made of concrete poured into a form that extends from below the frost line to a few inches aboveground.

Plan Drawing: A drawing that shows an overhead view of the deck and specifies the locations and sizes of components.

Plumb: Vertically straight in relation to a horizontally level surface.

Plunge Cut: A cut with a circular saw that starts in from the edge of a board

Post: A vertical component, usually a 4x4, that can support beams, joists, and railings.

Post Anchor: A metal fastener that secures a post to a concrete pier and inhibits decay by holding the post a bit above the concrete.

Posthole Digger: A clamshell-shaped tool used to dig holes for posts.

Power Auger: A tool (generally rented) powered by a gasoline engine that excavates post holes with a large auger screw.

Rabbet: A ledge-shaped recess cut along one edge of a board.

Rail: A horizontal component placed between or on a row of posts.

Rip Cut: A cut made with the grain on a piece of wood.

Riser: A vertical board (set on edge) that closes off the open space between treads.

Site Plan: A drawing that shows your project at a scale small enough to include the house, yard, and nearby property lines. To obtain a permit, a site plan is typically required, along with drawings that show construction details.

Skirting: Material that covers or screens the space between the edge of the deck and the ground, generally made of narrow slats, such as 1x2s, or lattice.

Span: The distance on a horizontal component, such as a joist, between supports. Span limits for all types and sizes of lumber are controlled by building codes.

Stringer: A wide, angled board that supports stair treads and risers. Cut or housed stringers run on the outside edges of stairs.

Synthetic Decking: Any engineered decking material made from plastics and/or recycled wood products.

Toenailing: Joining two boards together by nailing at an angle through the edge of one board into the face of another.

Top Cap: A horizontal piece of lumber laid flat across the tops of posts or top rails.

Tread: A horizontal stair board (generally several spaced boards in deck construction), laid flat on stringers.

Treated Lumber: Wood that has had preservative forced into it under pressure to make it decay resistant. In the past, arsenic was used to treat wood. Today, alkaline copper compounds are the primary treatment chemicals.

Metric Equivalents

Length

1 inch	25.4mm
1 foot	0.3048m
1 yard	0.9144m
1 mile	1.61km

Area

1 square inch	645mm²
1 square foot	0.0929m²
1 square yard	0.8361m²
1 acre	4046.86m²
1 square mile	2.59km²

Volume

1 cubic inch	16.3870cm³
1 cubic foot	0.03m³
1 cubic yard	0.77m³

Common Lumber Equivalents

Sizes: Metric cross sections are so close to their U.S. sizes, as noted below, that for most purposes they may be considered equivalents.

Dimensional lumber	1 x 2	19 x 38mm
	1 x 4	19 x 89mm
	2 x 2	38 x 38mm
	2 x 4	38 x 89mm
	2 x 6	38 x 140mm
	2 x 8	38 x 184mm
	2 x 10	38 x 235mm
	2 x 12	38 x 286mm
Sheet sizes	4 x 8 ft.	1200 x 2400mm
	4 x 10 ft.	1200 x 3000mm
Sheet thicknesses	¼ in.	6mm
	⅜ in.	9mm
	½ in.	12mm
	¾ in.	19mm
Stud / joist spacing	16 in. o.c.	400mm o.c.
	24 in. o.c.	600mm o.c.

Capacity

1 fluid ounce	29.57mL
1 pint	473.18mL
1 quart	0.95L
1 gallon	3.79L

Weight

1 ounce	28.35g
1 pound	0.45kg

Temperature

Fahrenheit = Celsius x 1.8 + 32
Celsius = Fahrenheit - 32 x 5/9

Nail Size and Length

Penny Size	Nail Length
2d	1"
3d	1¼"
4d	1½"
5d	1¾"
6d	2"
7d	2¼"
8d	2½"
9d	2¾"
10d	3"
12d	3¼"
16d	3½"

INDEX

INDEX

PHOTO CREDITS

Illustrations by: Vincent Alessi, Clarke Barre, Ron Carboni, Craig Franklin, Michael Gellatly, Kathleen Rushton and Paul M. Schumm

All photography by John Parsekian/CH, unless noted otherwise.

Front cover: Todd Caverly, design: Peter Bethanis & Associates
Back cover: *top* Brian Vanden Brink, architect: Stephen Blatt; background Artazum/Shutterstock
page 1: Lertsakwiman/Shutterstock **page 2:** John Parsekian, design/builder: Bob Kiefer **page 3:** Irina Mos/Shutterstock **page 7:** Jay Graham **page 9:** Rick Parish **page 10:** Tony Giammarino/Giammarino & Dworkin, design: Larry Gooss **pages 12–13 :** Tony Giammarino/Giammarino & Dworkin, design: Larry Gooss **page 14:** *top* Brad Simmons; center Tria Giovan; *bottom* Brian Vanden Brink, architect: Pete Bethanis **page 15:** Tony Giammarino/Giammarino & Dworkin, design: Vicki O'Neal **pages 16–17:** *top left* Brian Vanden Brink; *top right* Brian Vanden Brink, architect: Dominic Mercadante; *bottom right* Jessie Walker; *bottom left* Michael S. Thompson **page 18:** Brian Vanden Brink, design: Weatherend Estate Furniture **page 19:** *top* Tria Giovan; *bottom* carolynbates. com **page 20:** carolynbates.com **page 21:** Tria Giovan **page 22:** Brian Vanden Brink, architect: Pete Bethanis **page 25:** Brian Vanden Brink, architect: Stephen Blatt **page 26:** courtesy of California Redwood Association **pages 28–29:** *left* Mark Lohman; center Michael S. Thompson; *top right* Brad Simmons; *bottom right* John Glover **page 30:** Randall Perry **page 31:** *top* Ron Sutherland/ Garden Picture Library; *bottom* Jessie Walker **page 32:** Jessie Walker **page 33:** *top* Brad Simmons; *bottom* courtesy of California Redwood Association **page 34:** Tria Giovan **page 35:** *top* Ron Sutherland/Garden Picture Library; *bottom* Brad Simmons **page 39:** Mark Lohman **page 51:** Todd Caverly, design: Peter Bethanis & Associates **page 53:** Brian Vanden Brink **page 54:** Jessie Walker **page 55:** all courtesy of California Redwood Association **page 56:** carolynbates.com **pages 60, 62:** David Schiff **page 67:** Tony Giammarino/Giammarino & Dworkin **page 69:** *top* Jessie Walker **pages 71:** David Schiff **page 72:** Maria O'Hara/Garden Picture Library **page 75:** *top* Brad Simmons **page 77:** *top* Mark Lohman **page 85:** Tony Giammarino/Giammarino & Dworkin, design: Arthur Ritter **page 86:** Derek Fell **page 92:** *top right* Jessie Walker **page 93:** carolynbates.com **page 101:** Tony Giammarino/ Giammarino & Dworkin, design: Cheryl Palmore **page 102:** Brad Simmons **page 108:** Randall Perry **page 113:** *left top and bottom* David Schiff **page 119:** courtesy of Arch Wood Protection **page 127:** *bottom* Jessie Walker **page 128:** Jessie Walker **page 132:** Brad Simmons **page 134:** *top* Tony Giammarino/Giammarino & Dworkin, design: Arthur Ritter **pages 136–137:** David Schiff **page 145:** Mark Samu, architect: Andy Letkovsky **page 147:** Mark Samu **page 148:** Jessie Walker **page 151:** Tony Giammarino/Giammarino & Dworkin, design: Vicki O'Neal **page 154:** carolynbates.com **pages 157, 161:** David Schiff **page 164:** *top left* courtesy of TimberTech; *right* and *bottom left* David Schiff **pages 165, 166** all David Schiff **page 171:** Tony Giammarino/Giammarino & Dworkin, design: Larry Gooss **page 175:** David Schiff **page 186:** *top left* Randall Perry **page 188:** Brian Vanden Brink **page 190:** David Schiff **page 191:** Brian Vanden Brink **page 193, 201–212** all David Schiff **pages 214–215:** *top* middle Steve Budman; *top right* Steve Cory; *bottom right* Flat Rock Photography; *bottom* middle Dan Sellars, courtesy of California Redwood Association; *bottom left* Jay Graham **pages 246:** *top* Trex Company; middle and *bottom* Steve Cory **pages 246–251** Steve Cory **page 254** *left* Trex Company; *right* Kim Katwijk **page 255** Trex Company **pages 256–257, 260–261** Steve Cory **pages 262–265:** all Steve Budman **pages 308–313, 316–319, 321–325, 327–331, 333–335:** all Flat Rock Photography **pages 336–339:** all Jay Graham **page 370:** *top* & center Rick Parish; Dan Sellers, courtesy of California Redwood Association **page 371:** Dan Sellers, courtesy of California Redwood Association **page 373:** Greg Hursley, courtesy of California Redwood Association

Have a home improvement, decorating, or gardening project? Look for these and other fine Creative Homeowner books wherever books are sold.

The complete manual for plumbing projects. Over 750 color photos and illustrations. 304 pp.; 8¹/₂" x 10⁷/₈"

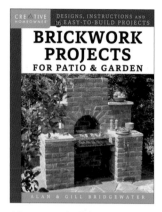

16 easy-to-build projects. 285 color photos and illustrations. 160 pp.; 8" x 10"

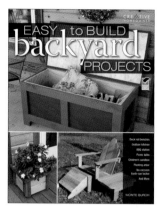

18 simple projects you can build Step by step instructions. 160 pp.; 8¹/₂" x 10⁷/₈"

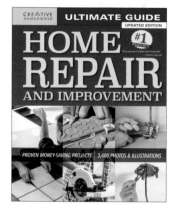

The ultimate home-improvement reference manual. Over 300 step-by-step projects. 608 pp.; 9" x 10⁷/₈"

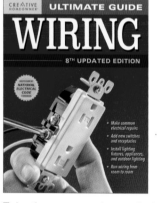

Take the guesswork out of wiring projects. Over 950 color photos and illos. 304 pp.; 8¹/₂" x 10⁷/₈"

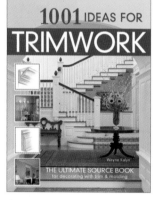

Complete source book for molding trim. 1,000+ color photos and illos. 256 pp.; 8¹/₂" x 10⁷/₈"

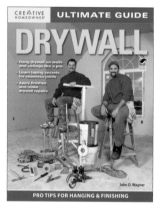

A complete guide, covering all aspects of drywall. Over 450 color photos. 176 pp.; 8¹/₂" x 10⁷/₈"

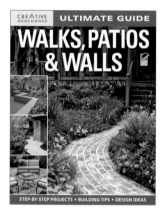

Build landscape structures from concrete, brick, stone. 545 photos and illos. 240 pp.; 8¹/₂" x 10⁷/₈"

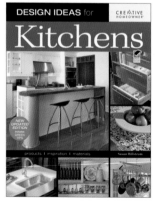

Inspiration for creating an attractive, up-to-date kitchen. Over 500 color photos. 224 pp.; 8¹/₂" x 10⁷/₈"

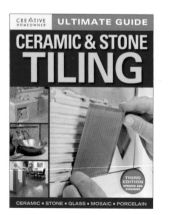

Latest trends in ceramic, stone, porcelain, glass, and mosaic tiles. 650 color photos and illustrations. 240 pp.; 8¹/₂" x 10⁷/₈"

The quick and easy way to grow fruit and vegetables. Over 300 color photos and illos. 384 pp.; 8¹/₂" x 10⁷/₈"

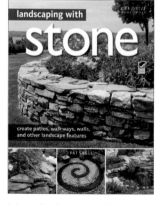

Ideas for incorporating stone into the landscape. Over 335 color photos. 224 pp.; 8¹/₂" x 10⁷/₈"

For more information and to order direct, visit our Web site at **www.creativehomeowner.com**